WHI Bible Translation SHOULD I USE?

WHICH

Bible

Translation

SHOULD I USE?

A Comparison of 4 Major Recent Versions

Andreas J. Köstenberger and David A. Croteau, Editors

FOREWORD BY JOE STOWELL

B&H
ACADEMIC
NASHVILLE, TENNESSEE

Which Bible Translation Should I Use?
Copyright © 2012 by Andreas Köstenberger and David Croteau

All rights reserved.

ISBN: 978-1-4336-7646-8

Published by B&H Publishing Group
Nashville, Tennessee

Dewey Decimal Classification: 220.5
Subject Heading: BIBLE—VERSIONS\BIBLE—HISTORY

Scripture quotations marked ESV are from The Holy Bible, English Standard Version, copyright © 2001, 2007, 2011 by Crossway Bibles, a division of Good News Publishers. Used by permission. All rights reserved.

Scripture quotations marked HCSB are from the Holman Christian Standard Bible ® Copyright © 1999, 2000, 2002, 2003, 2009 by Holman Bible Publishers. Used by permission.

Scripture quotations designated (NIV) are from THE HOLY BIBLE: NEW INTERNATIONAL VERSION®. NIV®. Copyright © 1973, 1978, 1984, 2011 by Biblica. All rights reserved worldwide.

Scripture quotations marked NLT are taken from the Holy Bible, New Living Translation, copyright © 1996, 2004, 2007. Used by permission of Tyndale House Publishers, Inc., Wheaton, Illinois 60189. All rights reserved.

Page 205 is an extension of the copyright page.

Printed in the United States of America

1 2 3 4 5 6 7 8 9 10 11 12 • 17 16 15 14 13 12
VP

Contents

Abbreviations for Bible Versions

KJV 1611	King James Version
ERV 1885	English Revised Version
ASV 1901	American Standard Version
RSV 1953; 1971	Revised Standard Version
AB 1965; 1987	Amplified Bible
NASB 1971; 1995	New American Standard Bible
LV 1971	Living Bible
NEB 1970; 1989	New English Bible
TEV 1976; 1992	Today's English Version (also Good News Bible)
NIV 1978; 1984; 2011	New International Version
NKJV 1982	New King James Version
NRSV 1989	New Revised Standard Version
NLT 1996; 2004; 2007	New Living Translation
NET 2001; 2003; 2005	New English Translation/NET Bible
ESV 2001; 2007; 2011	English Standard Version
HCSB 2003; 2009	Holman Christian Standard Bible
TNIV 2005	Today's New International Version

Foreword

Translation is a tricky business, particularly when it comes to translating ancient texts in varying languages in order to make them relevant to the culture and at the same time true to the text. No one has been more challenged in this task than Wycliffe Bible Translators who have gone throughout the world in order to translate God's Word for tribes that originally had no written language. It is staggering to think of first creating a written language that is true to the verbal environment and then subsequently tackling the task of translating the Bible into that illiterate context. Often the challenges are more than just the pursuit of a good translation. One of my friends went to Papua, New Guinea, as a translator. She met daily with the village chief to learn the language as the first step toward getting it into written form. The village chief sat before her in his native garb, which was nothing at all. Finally, she gave him a pair of Bermuda shorts with a belt and asked him to please come back the next day with them on. He showed up the next day wearing the belt but no shorts!

For scholars who sit in cloistered rooms with sophisticated resources and gather in committees to hammer out exact meanings of words and phrases, the task is somewhat less complicated but nonetheless still daunting. Language is like beauty; its meaning is in the eye of the beholder. And one element that adds to the complexity is the controversy that inevitably swirls around the agendas and personal perspectives of the constituencies who are the recipients of the finished work. Unfortunately, controversy leads to confusion for many Christians and can, in fact, undercut confidence in God's Word as the divinely inspired source of wisdom and knowledge for all of life and practice. Their questions may range from, Which Bible should I use? to Which Bible should I trust?

The book you are about to read will be a great help in answering these questions. The four sections of the book discuss four major translations: the English Standard Version, the New International Version, the Holman Christian Standard Bible, and the New Living Bible. In these pages you will discover the differing philosophies of translating, yet the unifying passion and determination of each of these translations is to remain true to God's Word.

To set the stage, permit me personally to reminisce and give you a sense of history that in the end should strengthen and support your ongoing confidence in God's work in preserving his Word. The Bible has been an integral part of my life since I can remember. I recall singing songs in Sunday school that taught me at an early age to revere Scripture. We would sing, "The B-I-B-L-E, yes that's the book for me, I stand alone on the Word of God, the B-I-B-L-E!" Memorizing extended passages would be rewarded with scholarships to summer camps. "Sword drills" taught us to find passages quickly, and if we won the contest, we would get stars on a chart.

Not only was the Bible at the center of my early childhood development, but I was also taught to revere the book highly. When I asked my dad why we had a pulpit in the center of the platform instead of on each side with an altar in the middle, he informed me that in our church the Word of God was central. I was taught never to stack another book on top of the Bible but always to have the Bible on top. I would soon realize that I wasn't the only one who cared about the Bible's being held in high esteem. On an early trip into the former Soviet Union, I turned the cover of my Bible back under the rest of the Bible as I held it in one hand while preaching, only to discover later that treating the Bible like this was a great offense to the Russian believers to whom I was preaching. A friend from Eastern Europe who was visiting the U.S. was aghast when he saw someone set the Bible on the bathroom floor while using the facility.

The translation we used was also important. Back in those days, the predominant text for my kind of Christian was the King James Version. The Revised Standard Version was the text mainstream Protestant liberals used. The Douay Version was the translation for the Roman Catholics. And if you were really a solid Protestant evangelical back in those days, you carried a Scofield Reference Bible, which had extensive notes in the King James text to help you understand the concepts in the text more clearly from a dispensational point of view.

But then things started to change. While the New American Standard Bible had been on the scene for some time, the Good News Bible, the Amplified Bible, and the J. B. Phillips paraphrase of sections of the New Testament were the first of several entries into an era of new translations. But nothing upset the apple cart of traditionalists more than Ken Taylor's paraphrase, The Living Bible. The rub was that it was not a literal translation but a paraphrase that he had written to help his children understand Scripture more readily. He shopped it with publishers only to find that no publisher wanted to take the high risk of publishing such a controversial concept as a major paraphrase of Scripture. So he opened his own publishing house, now called Tyndale Publishers. The Living Bible was a smashing success (much to the dismay of all the publishers who had turned it down). But with that success came bucket-loads of controversy. Articles, sermons, pamphlets, and books targeted Taylor's popular edition of the Bible. The translations war was officially underway. The King James Only movement soon emerged in defense of the KJV claiming that their Bible was the only true word from God that could be trusted. Opponents joked that their mantra was, "If the King James was good enough for Paul, then it is good enough for me."

But this was only the beginning. Soon the New International Version appeared on the scene. Its intent was to provide a translation that was more readable than the American Standard Version (1901) and more linguistically relevant than the King James Version (1611). Again the smell of smoke was in the air as opponents pointed out passages that in their mind undermined the best intentions of the text. To make matters more complicated, several years later the NIV was reintroduced as Today's New International Version, partially in an attempt to make the gender references in its text more acceptable in a gender-sensitive world. At this point all bets were off, as Bibliophiles took up sides in heated exchanges with barbed accusations. Just in the nick of time, the English Standard Version appeared, which provided a safe landing place for those who did not want to go back to the days of the KJV but yet felt a sense of discomfort with the TNIV.

Dustups over translations are not a new phenomenon. In the sixteenth and early seventeenth centuries, the Geneva Bible was held up as the accepted text. In its notes were references that undermined the divine right of kings. Needless to say, that bothered sovereigns who claimed they ruled by divine right. So King James I of England commissioned a Bible that would be more readable to the common man and eliminate the bent against seated rulers. The pilgrims would not be swayed by this newfangled approach to Scripture and carried the Geneva Bible to the new lands of America as an act of loyalty to the "true text" and, in a sense, as an act of protest against what they assumed was a politically motivated KJV.

Not to be deterred in our generation, the proliferation of preferences in terms of Bible choices continues. There is now a New King James Version for KJV fans. The Living Bible has been updated and more literally translated and is now published as the New Living Translation. The Holman Christian Standard Bible is now available, and a new edition of the NIV has just recently hit the market. So what is a Christian to do and think in regard to the authority and accuracy of God's Word in the face of such a crowded and sometimes contentious field of choices?

When all the smoke clears and the often-blemished history of swirling controversies about Bible translations moves forward, it gives me great confidence to note that God's Word still prevails in all of its wisdom and transforming power. Throughout 20 centuries of translation work, God's Word is still a lamp to our feet and a light to our path in an increasingly dark and foreboding world. It is still that two-edged sword cutting deep into the motives of our hearts, a seed that when received and nurtured bears good fruit, a mirror in which we behold ourselves as we really are and a rock upon which we can securely plant the foundations of our lives. It remains profitable for teaching, for reproof, for correction, and, for training in righteousness so that we can become competent and equipped for every good work. We revel in the depth and wisdom of the knowledge of God that we discover in its pages. And, as the psalmist promised, it endures to every generation. So, while there will never be a perfect translation, in the hand of God, our best efforts will continue to provide a sovereignly preserved Word from our Father in heaven to bless and direct fallen people like us as we live on earth.

Joe Stowell
President, Cornerstone University,
Grand Rapids, Michigan

To the Reader

We are so glad you picked up a copy of this book. Which Bible translation should I use? is one of the questions we get asked most often by our students and people in the churches. It is an exceedingly important question and yet one that is not easy to answer in one or two sentences. Whether you and I realize it or not, translating the Bible from the original Greek and Hebrew into contemporary English is a complex and delicate undertaking. In many ways we are spoiled by the unseen, hard labors of translators in our day and in ages past. We can just walk into any LifeWay or other Christian bookstore, or go online and order any number of Bibles or study Bibles in various translations, many of them excellent.

But how do Bible translations come into being? And how do translators make their decisions on how to translate a particular passage in Scripture? Which Bible translation *should* you use? Two points immediately come to mind. First, Bible translation, by and large, is done by committees rather than individuals working alone and in isolation. For this reason the Bibles you and I have reflect the majority consensus of a given translation committee. The process in arriving at such a consensus may well involve negotiation or compromise (which, in this context, is not necessarily a bad thing). This is a commendable way to proceed in that committees tap into the collective wisdom of a group of Bible scholars to weigh translation options from every conceivable angle.

Then, once the work of the scholars on the committee is done, and sometimes while their work is still ongoing, the English stylists get to work. They ensure that a translation does not merely reflect our best knowledge of the meaning of a given word in the original Greek or Hebrew but that it is rendered in readable, idiomatic English. In this sense it is actually the English stylists, not the Greek or Hebrew scholars, who have the last word! That said, Bible translation is a team effort with a considerable number of individuals making their contribution based on their respective areas of expertise.

The second point you may want to keep in mind as you make your way through this volume is that behind the various ways in which a given translation renders a certain passage is a translation philosophy. By this I mean the larger underlying principles and convictions that serve as the overall framework for a particular Bible translation. In essence the spectrum here ranges from literal, word-for-word translations (formal equivalence) to free, idiomatic thought-for-thought renderings (functional equivalence, also sometimes called dynamic equivalence). In between are translations that aim for a combination of literal accuracy and idiomatic readability. One translation, the HCSB, even coined their own phrase to describe this aim in translation: "optimal equivalence."

Another aspect of Bible translation philosophy is the way a committee decides to handle gender issues. Several titles have been given to describe this translation issue: gender-inclusive, gender-neutral, and gender-sensitive. All three terms are different ways in which versions approach the issues of the gender communicated by certain words in Bible translation. A dialogue is occurring over whether certain words and phrases in Hebrew and Greek were originally referring to one specific gender or are generic and universal. For example, when Jesus said, "I will make you fishers of men" (Matt 4:19b ESV), did the word for "men" refer to only males or both males and females? Some translations replace the word "men" with "people" (NIV, NLT, HCSB); others retain the expression in the understanding that readers today will readily discern that the term refers to people in general. Another example comes from the phrase "son of man" in Hebrews 2:6. This phrase is a citation of Psalm 8:4 and could refer to a specific "son of man" (ESV and HCSB) or to "human beings" in general (TNIV). While all four translations agree that some words or phrases are gender neutral, the application of this in translation practice is hotly debated. Part of the debate is over the English language itself and whether English has changed in its use of certain words. The word *man* has been used in English to refer to "humanity in general" for many years, but some, perhaps even many, believe this use is fading in English. Another example is the use of the generic pronouns *he, him,* and *his*. Are these still used to refer to people without reference to gender, or do they communicate maleness? These issues and questions will be addressed in the following chapters.

So, then, which Bible translation should you and I use? In the following pages, we will try to give you what you might call a "buyer's guide" to some of the best and most recent English translations on the market today. First, you can read a succinct introduction on the history of translating the Bible into English over the centuries. This will help set the stage for the rest of the volume in which four leading experts discuss four major recent English Bible versions: the ESV, the NIV, the HCSB, and the NLT. Each of the essays will begin by laying out some of the guiding principles of the particular translation before discussing 16 specific passages that will serve as a basis for comparison of the distinctive natures of these four translations.

Three of the contributions in this volume (Grudem, Moo, and Clendenen) were originally presented as part of the Fall 2011 Liberty University Biblical Studies Symposium on Bible translation. You will notice QR codes inserted at various points throughout these chapters. By scanning the code with your mobile device, you can view a video clip of that contributor addressing the biblical passage under discussion. If you do not have a mobile device, the videos clips are also available at http://www. bhpublishinggroup.com/translation. The full-length video presentations from the symposium are available from Liberty University at http://www. liberty.edu/academics/religion/index.cfm?PID=24987.

Once you have read the four chapters, you will be well on your way to making an informed decision as you formulate your answer to the question, Which Bible translation should I use?[1]

---

[1] While some versions (e.g., the New American Standard Bible) italicize words in the text of the translation, the four translations discussed in this volume do not. So any italicized words in Bible quotations in the chapters that follow reflect the contributors' emphases.

A Short History of Bible Translation

Andreas J. Köstenberger and David A. Croteau

You may be overwhelmed by the options of Bible translations available in the English language and by the various controversies regarding many popular versions. You may wonder how to evaluate which translation is best for you. In this book we will focus on a few major contemporary translations. Before addressing these modern-day translations, however, it will be helpful to understand the background to this dialogue. We will give a brief history and compare certain translations to observe how they deal with particular words, phrases, and sentences in order to give you an idea about how translations differ. We hope tracing these differences through history will give you a more informed perspective regarding the translation differences dealt with in the remainder of this book.

The Earliest Translations of the Old Testament into Non-English Languages

The translation of the Bible from its original languages into other languages began before the Bible was completely written. The Old Testament was translated from Hebrew into Greek and was probably completed about 100 to 200 years before Jesus was born. This became known as the *Septuagint*, abbreviated as LXX in the footnotes of many translations. The Septuagint was not the product of a translation committee that had a specific translation philosophy it followed closely.[1] Then what is it? While the Septuagint is at times fairly literal in its translation, it is hardly a word-for-word translation from the Hebrew. Many people are surprised to learn that there was not a single version considered "the official" Septuagint. In fact, it is probably best to refer to "Septuagints," since there are many variations between manuscripts.

Before the New Testament was written, the Hebrew Old Testament had been translated into Aramaic, the primary language of Israel (and other areas toward the east). When an Old Testament passage was read out loud in a synagogue, it was read in the Hebrew language. Then a leader of the synagogue would translate or paraphrase the Hebrew text into Aramaic. Eventually, these translations began to be written down. These Aramaic translations, known as the *Targumim*, began to be recorded around the same time as the Septuagint. The Targumim were not literal, word-for-word translations. Instead, many times the translators would import their interpretation of the passage into their translation. The Targumim were used in Jewish worship and preaching from before the time of Jesus for the next 1,000 years. It was several centuries before there was a standard Aramaic text.

The Earliest Translations of the Entire Bible into Non-English Languages

The early church translated the entire Bible from Hebrew and Greek into Latin. Because Christianity was not centralized in its early years, many versions were produced and were being used throughout the churches. Pope Damasus (late 4th century AD) commissioned Jerome to edit existing translations of the Bible in Latin so the church could have a standard Latin version. This translation project by Jerome became known as the *Vulgate*. It became so widely accepted that the older Latin translations[2] have become very rare. The translation of the Vulgate by Jerome differs from most other translations from this time period because the translation was accomplished by a scholar who knew Hebrew and Greek; most translations were not connected to any specific person.

Syriac translations of the Bible probably began in the second century AD, but in the fifth century a Syriac translation called the Peshitta replaced all previous versions. The Old Testament was translated from the Hebrew

---

[1] This has been the approach of many translations since the Geneva Bible (1560).
[2] Known as the "Old Latin."

and the New Testament from the Greek. *Coptic* versions of the Bible were in existence by the third and fourth centuries, and these translations were based on the Septuagint Old Testament and Greek New Testament manuscripts. Many other translations were made of the Bible, but they were translated from these previous translations and not from the Hebrew and/ or Greek texts. The translations in this category include the *Georgian*, *Armenian*, *Gothic*, and *Ethiopic* versions. These translations were not purely academic exercises but were attempts at making the Scriptures accessible to followers of God who did not know the original languages.

The Bible in English

The Earliest Known English Translations

For many centuries the Bible of English-speaking Christians was the Latin Vulgate. Some parts of Scripture were probably translated into Old English in the seventh and eighth centuries, but they do not exist today. The earliest translations still preserved are contained between the lines of text on Latin manuscripts. One of the earliest of these manuscripts dates to the tenth century. The Wessex Gospels is the first translation of the Gospels preserved in Old English.[3]

John Wycliffe, driven by his belief in the supreme authority of the Bible, began an ambitious translation project in the fourteenth century. Some scholars have referred to Wycliffe as "The Morning Star of the Reformation." The Gospels (and possibly the entire New Testament) were translated by Wycliffe himself. However, it was probably his associates who completed the translation of the Old Testament. The translation was based on the Latin Vulgate and was woodenly literal to the point of sometimes being almost impossible to understand.[4] Wycliffe died of a stroke, and about six months after his death, his body was exhumed and burned to ashes for being declared a heretic.[5] His books were ordered to be destroyed, and it was illegal for any layperson to have a copy of the Bible

---

[3] Aelfric was a main contributor to a translation of Genesis through Judges that occurred about the same time as the Wessex Gospels.

[4] The structure of a sentence in Hebrew or Greek can be radically different from English sentence structure. While English typically begins with a subject followed by a verb and then an object, Greek (for example) could change the word order to object, subject, and then verb. Keeping the words in the same order as the original language does not always communicate what the original text was trying to say.

[5] His views on predestination, authority, wealth and possessions, the Lord's Supper, and the papacy were among the charges.

translated by Wycliffe. Anyone found in possession of a Wycliffe Bible was considered a heretic.

Wycliffe's translation was revised shortly after its completion, and this revision, probably accomplished by John Purvey, translated the Scriptures much more clearly. Purvey states his translation philosophy in the preface to this revision:

> First, it is to be known that the best translating out of the Latin into English is to translate after the sentence and not only after the words, so that the sentence be as open, or opener, in English as in Latin, and go not far from the letter; and if the letter may not be followed in the translating, let the sentence ever be whole and open, for the words ought to serve to the intent and sentence, or else the words be superfluous or false.[6]

F. F. Bruce concludes concerning Purvey's translation philosophy that the translator should "not depart from the letter of the original more than is necessary to convey the true and plain sense."[7] Even though any use of an English Bible was forbidden by the authorities, the Lollards (followers of Wycliffe)[8] continued to circulate the revised translation widely. It became the main English Bible in the fifteenth century.

A couple of selections from Wycliffe's translation might help us understand this translation better. In Matthew 5:9, Wycliffe's translation uses the phrase "God's children,"[9] rather than "sons of God," which is a more literal translation from the Greek. Interestingly, in Ephesians 2:3, the phrase "children of wrath" has been translated as "sons of wrath."[10] Rather than translating John 3:16 with the common "whoever believes" or "everyone who believes," Wycliffe's translation has "each man that believeth."[11] The adverb translated with "so" by Wycliffe could refer to the extent of God's love for the world (which appears to have been Wycliffe's own interpretation) or the way in which he demonstrated his love. Another controversial word in this verse is the Greek word *monogenēs*, which Wycliffe translated as "only begotten."[12] He struggled with translating some technical words from the Greek. This can be seen

---

[6] F. F. Bruce, *History of the Bible in English* (New York: Oxford University Press, 1978), 19–20.
[7] Ibid., 20.
[8] So named by Pope Gregory XI.
[9] Lit., "Goddis children."
[10] Lit., "the sones of wraththe."
[11] Lit., "ech man that bileueth."
[12] Lit., "oon bigetun."

in Luke 17:3 where he said that if your brother does "penance,"[13] forgive him, rather than using "repent" as most translations do today. However, in Matthew 27:3, Wycliffe said that Judas "repented."[14] He also has an interesting translation of 1 Timothy 2:12, saying that the woman should not teach "neither to have lordship on the husband."[15]

In this brief selection, one can see that Wycliffe was not overly rigid in his use of gender, translating a word many scholars would consider gender specific, "sons," as "children," and a word many scholars would consider a gender-neutral word, "children," as "sons." The translation does not shy away from masculine references, as would be expected. He understood the verb *authentein* in 1 Timothy 2:12 as "having lordship" and saw it exclusively in the relationship of a wife to her husband. Finally, just reading a few verses leads to the conclusion that Wycliffe retained the word order of the Greek (and sometimes Latin) even when the English rendering hardly made any sense.

Translations in the Sixteenth Century

According to R. T. France, two factors separate sixteenth-century translations from the previous ones: (1) the rediscovery of Hebrew and Greek by European scholarship, and (2) the printing press.[16] The Hebrew Bible was first printed on a printing press in 1488 and the Greek New Testament in 1516. This new setting created an opportunity for someone to undertake translating the Scriptures into English from the original languages more precisely than had been accomplished previously. A leading figure of the Protestant Reformation in England took up this task.

William Tyndale (1494–1536), influenced by both Erasmus and Luther, translated much of the Bible into English for laypeople. In 1526, he completed translating the New Testament, but in England at that time it was forbidden to translate the Bible into English. For this reason it was printed in Worms, Germany (the location of Luther's Diet of Worms a few

---

[13] Lit., "do penaunce."

[14] Lit., "he repentide." The Greek word in Luke 17:3 means "to change one's way of life as the result of a complete change of thought and attitude with regard to sin and righteousness" (Johannes P. Louw and Eugene A. Nida, eds., *Greek-English Lexicon of the New Testament Based on Semantic Domains*, 2 vols. [New York: United Bible Societies, 1988, 1989], 41.52). The Greek word in Matt 27:3 means "to feel regret as the result of what one has done" (ibid., 25.270).

[15] Lit., "nether to haue lordschip on the hosebonde."

[16] Dick France, "The Bible in English: An Overview," in *The Challenge of Bible Translation: Communicating God's Word to the World*, ed. Glen G. Scorgie, Mark L. Strauss, and Steven M. Voth (Grand Rapids: Zondervan, 2003), 181.

years earlier). Tyndale had it smuggled into England because of his commitment to get God's Word into the hands of the laity.

Tyndale was heavily influenced by Martin Luther's translation into German. Four years before Tyndale completed his translation, Luther finished the German New Testament. Several of Tyndale's translations have been traced to Luther, including "mercy seat," "twinkling of an eye," "let there be light," and "the spirit is willing, but the flesh is weak."[17] Luther's Bible (completed in 1534) remains one of his greatest achievements. It had a lasting impact on Christianity in Germany and the German language itself.

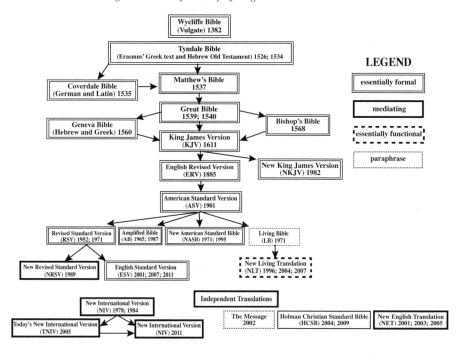

Figure 1: A Brief History of English Bible Translation

Tyndale's New Testament was based on Erasmus's 1522 Greek New Testament. This translation became the basis for nearly all English translations for centuries. While Tyndale translated the Pentateuch and other Old Testament books, he continued to revise his New Testament translation.

---

[17] See Douglas J. Moo, *The Epistle to the Romans* (Grand Rapids: Eerdmans, 1996), 232, n. 62, for the first example.

The 1534 edition of the New Testament became the standard Tyndale edition. Tyndale was tried and found guilty of heresy; his views on justification by faith, adult baptism, and prayer to the saints. He was strangled and burned at the stake. His last words were "Lord! Open the king of England's eyes."[18] God answered that prayer! Four years after Tyndale's death, the same king who condemned him, Henry VIII, commanded four translations to be published in England.

Tyndale followed Wycliffe in translating Matthew 5:9 with "children of God,"[19] but did not follow him in Ephesians 2:3, preferring "children of wrath." Tyndale made an interesting adjustment in John 3:16, concluding that "none that believe in him should perish."[20] Tyndale also believed the adverb should be translated as "so," indicating the extent of God's love. However, he translated *monogenēs* simply as "only." Tyndale made a significant, enduring, and controversial change in translating the Greek words previously rendered "do penance" as "repent" and "repentance," as in Luke 17:3. The phrase "do penance" seems to be referring specifically to the Catholic doctrine of penance, and Tyndale wanted to be faithful to the original text while not affirming a practice with which he disagreed. Most translations have continued to use the word "repent" since Tyndale. He also kept "repented" from Wycliffe's translation in Matthew 27:3. In 1 Timothy 2:12, Tyndale differed from Wycliffe in two key ways. First, he translated the verb *authentein* as "have authority"[21] rather than "have lordship." Second, he saw the verse in relationship to men and women in general, in contrast to Wycliffe's translation of it as being between a husband and wife. In another effort to avoid associations with Catholicism, Tyndale translated *ekklēsia* with the English word "congregation" (see Matt 16:18; Acts 5:11) rather than the common "church," as Wycliffe had done.

Tyndale's literary ability is obvious on nearly every page. Compare his translation to that of Wycliffe's overly literal and awkward translation, and his brilliance becomes obvious. He truly wanted English Christians to understand Scripture and translated the text with this in mind. He does not embrace much in terms of gender-neutral translations, but his translation of Matthew 5:9 demonstrates that this translation concept was not off-limits for him. While still maintaining an essentially literal translation

---

[18] John Foxe, *Foxe's Book of Martyrs*, rev. ed., ed. Harold J. Chadwick (Gainseville, FL: Bridge-Logos, 2001), 133.

[19] Lit., "children of God."

[20] Lit., "none that beleve in him shuld perisshe."

[21] Lit., "have auctoricie."

philosophy, Tyndale produced an English translation of the Bible that was eminently more understandable than any before it.

Miles Coverdale's Bible in 1535 was the first complete Bible printed in English. Coverdale was a friend of Tyndale's, and he made no claim to have translated from Hebrew or Greek. Instead, he essentially revised Tyndale's translation, utilizing Luther's translation as an aid. Two years later, in 1537, Thomas Matthew's Bible was published. It was the first English Bible published with official approval by the king of England. It was compiled and edited by John Rogers (writing under a false name), who was also a friend of Tyndale's. Matthew's Bible was the Tyndale Bible in the parts that Tyndale completed, with the remainder taken from Coverdale.

Now that the king had officially approved of a translation, the way was paved for an authorized translation. Coverdale was given the task of revising Matthew's Bible, and the result was the Great Bible (1539). It was the official Bible of England for approximately 20 years. The Great Bible's main weakness was that much of the Old Testament translation was not based on the Hebrew text but on the Latin Vulgate and even some German translations.

Some significant developments occurred with the next important translation: the Geneva Bible (1560). First, this translation was completed by a group of scholars, not one man. Second, the entire Old Testament was translated from the Hebrew text. Third, it contained introductions to the books of the Bible, maps, cross-references, and indexes. Some scholars have called it the first study Bible. Since it was produced and printed in Geneva, the notes were heavily Calvinistic. It was the first English Bible translation to use both chapters and verse numbers.[22] The Geneva Bible quickly replaced the Great Bible and became the Bible of William Shakespeare, John Bunyan, and John Knox.[23]

The King James Bible

King James I of England did not appreciate the Geneva Bible because he thought the notes that accompanied the translation were too partial toward Calvinistic thinking. Therefore, he assembled a diverse group of the best scholars to form a translation committee in 1604, nearly 50 scholars in all.

---

[22] It used the verse numbers given by Robert Estienne (Stephanus).

[23] Some other translations completed in the sixteenth and early seventeenth centuries include the Taverner's Bible (1539), Edmund Becke's Bible (1549), The Bishop's Bible (1568), and the Rheims-Douay Bible (1582–1610; a Roman Catholic translation).

Rules and procedures were formed, and translation began in 1607. It was published in 1611.

A wonderful 11-page preface preceded the translation. Unfortunately, most modern printings of the King James Bible do not include this preface.[24] A reading of the preface makes clear the justification for Bible translation; that the King James Bible was a revision (not a fresh translation); and several other points of view of the translators that could correct some thoughts about the King James Bible if known today. For example, while the translators did not include study notes as in the Geneva Bible, they did include marginal notes. Some of their adversaries thought it inappropriate to include alternate translations of the verse in the margin (like footnotes today), even when the original was less than clear, so the translators responded:

> It hath pleased God in his divine providence, here and there to scatter words and sentences of that difficulty and doubtfulness, not in doctrinal points that concern salvation, (for in such it hath been vouched that the Scriptures are plain) but in matters of less moment, that fearfulness would better beseem us than confidence.

They continued by explaining that many words in Scripture occur only once. For example, they mention certain birds, beasts, and stones, which even the Hebrews had difficulty translating. Another key point was that they argued for a degree of flexibility in translating one Hebrew or Greek word with several English words: "We have not tied ourselves to an uniformity of phrasing." They found it impossible to find one English word that could articulate all the meanings of a Hebrew or Greek word. Finally, they reference Augustine in a way that modern students of the Bible should take to heart: "Therefore, as S. Augustine saith, that variety of Translations is profitable for the finding out of the sense of the Scriptures . . . so diversity of signification and sense in the margin, where the text is not so clear, must needs do good, yea, is necessary, as we are persuaded." Here they commend the use of a variety of translations and alternate readings in the margins of a translation.

The King James Bible (KJV) is an excellent work of scholarship. The translation quickly became the common English translation used in England and, practically speaking, was really the only English translation

---

[24] It can be found at http://www.ccel.org/bible/kjv/preface/pref1.htm.

in significant use between the mid-seventeenth century and 1881. The main deficiency of the KJV has nothing to do with the translators themselves. The Greek and Hebrew texts they used were inferior to the texts available to scholars today. For the New Testament Greek text, they used Stephanus's 1550 text (unfortunately known as the "Received Text" or "Textus Receptus"). Stephanus's text was based on later copies of Greek texts that had revisions and expansions from the originals. A few times (e.g., 1 John 5:7) no Greek text was available, and the Vulgate was translated back into Greek. The text of the KJV was edited several times, including 1629, 1638, 1762, and 1769. Nearly all of the changes related to printing errors, a change in typeface, the standardization of spelling, and some minor phrase changes.

The influence of Tyndale's translation on the KJV can hardly be overstated. It is estimated that more than 75 percent of the KJV can be traced to Tyndale.[25] Therefore, many of the features discussed above with Tyndale's translation apply to the KJV as well. In Matthew 5:9, the King James followed Tyndale with the phrase "children of God." In Luke 17:3 and Matthew 27:3, the King James followed Tyndale by including the word "repent." In John 3:16, the King James offered "whosoever believeth in him," which was different from Tyndale and Wycliffe but followed Coverdale and the Geneva Bible.[26] The KJV translated the adverb as "so," referring to the extent that God loved the world.[27] It translated *monogenēs* with "only begotten," following Wycliffe, the Bishop's Bible, and Geneva.[28] The King James, against Tyndale (but with Wycliffe), translated *ekklēsia* with the English word "church," not "congregation." Finally, in 1 Timothy 2:12, the KJV sided with the Geneva Bible in that *authentein* is understood as a reference to "usurping authority" and in relationship to "the man," not a woman's husband.

The King James has about three places where it appears to favor gender-neutral readings (the phrase "children of God"),[29] but it remains steadfast against that translation philosophy on the whole. It heavily depended upon previous versions, including Wycliffe's, Tyndale's, Coverdale's, and the Geneva Bible.

---

[25] Some estimates say the KJV follows the Geneva Bible nearly 90 percent of the time.
[26] Coverdale had "who so euer beleueth in hi," and the Geneva had "whosoeuer beleeueth in him."
[27] As did Coverdale, Geneva, and the Bishop's Bible.
[28] Contrary to Coverdale and Tyndale.
[29] Besides Matt 5:9, see Luke 20:36 and Gal 3:26.

Nineteenth- and Early Twentieth-Century Translations

While the KJV was not the only translation available, it reigned supreme among English translations. However, the English Revised Version (ERV) committee completed the New Testament in 1881 and the Old Testament in 1885. It retained a strict translation philosophy. American representatives served on the ERV committee, but they had a significantly weaker voice in the decisions compared to the scholars in England. Once the ERV was completed, the American committee continued working to produce a translation for the United States. The American Standard Version (ASV) was completed in 1901. This latter committee was not as conservative in its translation philosophy.

The ASV's translations are similar to translations that are essentially literal today. One notable exception is the use of "Jehovah" instead of "the LORD." Matthew 5:9 is translated as "sons of God," and John 3:16 contains "whosoever believeth." The adverb in John 3:16 is translated "so," and Jesus is called God's "only begotten" Son. Luke 17:3 uses the verb "repent," as does Matthew 27:3. The key verb in 1 Timothy 2:12 is translated as "to have dominion over," and the object is "a man." The ASV, and most major translations that followed it, retained the translation of "church" for the Greek word *ekklēsia*.

Revisions of the American Standard Version

The first major revision of the ASV was the Revised Standard Version (RSV) of 1952. This translation committee was attempting to revise the ASV so it would be more readable and less literalistic. The committee received harsh criticism, including accusations the translators wanted to undermine the deity of Christ. An example of a controversial translation is in Isaiah 7:14: "Behold, a young woman shall conceive and bear a son." Translations have typically rendered the Hebrew word *almah* as "virgin." The RSV also agreed with Tyndale by stating that Jesus was God's "only" Son in John 3:16.

Two major versions have spawned from the RSV. The first was the New Revised Standard Version (NRSV) in 1989. This committee was charged to update the language (ridding the translation of King James archaic language), achieve greater accuracy and clarity, and "eliminate masculine-oriented language concerning people."[30] The "thous" were eliminated,

---

[30] Bruce M. Metzger, *The Bible in Translation: Ancient and English Versions* (Grand Rapids: Baker, 2001), 156.

and gender-inclusive language was used more comprehensively than ever before. The NRSV retained "young woman" in Isaiah 7:14. It returned to "children of God" in Matthew 5:9 and used the verb "repent" in both Luke 17:3 and Matthew 27:3. The adverb in John 3:16 is translated to refer to the extent of God's love ("so"), and Jesus is called God's "only" Son. In 1 Timothy 2:12, the NRSV says that a woman is neither to teach nor "to have authority over a man." A final interesting translation is Matthew 4:19, where Jesus says, "I will make you fish for people," rather than "fishers of men."

The second major version from the RSV is the English Standard Version (ESV) of 2001. The ESV committee sought to alleviate some objections from conservative Protestants over certain verses in the RSV. The committee was also concerned with recent "thought for thought" translations. While the ESV was much more restrained in its use of gender-neutral language than other contemporary versions, it still employed more gender-neutral phrases than its predecessor, the RSV. It does retain "sons of God" in Matthew 5:9. However, it does not have "repent" in Matthew 27:3 describing Judas but says that he "changed his mind." In John 3:16, the ESV agreed with the NRSV in translating the adverb and the word *monogenēs*. However, the ESV also included a footnote giving an alternate translation: "For this is how God loved the world." Finally, the ESV includes a footnote at the end of John 3:15 stating that "[s]ome interpreters hold that the quotation ends at verse 15." The ESV has quickly grown in popularity and is now among the top five Bible translations sold today.

The Amplified Bible is also a revision of the ASV. This is truly one of the most unique English translations. The translators used a series of punctuation marks to inform readers of different aspects of the translation. For example, when a phrase is in brackets, it indicates that the words within the brackets are not explicitly contained in the original texts. A few examples should clarify what this translation is like.

Matthew 5:9 reads, "Blessed (enjoying enviable happiness, spiritually prosperous—with life-joy and satisfaction in God's favor and salvation, regardless of their outward conditions) are the makers and maintainers of peace, for they shall be called the sons of God!" The word "blessed" is defined by the translators by the terms in parentheses. Luke 17:3 says, "Pay attention and always be on your guard [looking out for one another]. If your brother sins (misses the mark), solemnly tell him so and reprove him, and if he repents (feels sorry for having sinned), forgive him." The translators define repent as "feels sorry for having sinned."[31] In John 3:16, the phrase "believes in" is followed in parentheses by "trusts in, clings to, relies on." Regarding the adverb, this translation unmistakably favors the extent understanding: "For God so greatly loved and dearly prized the world." For the controversial word *monogenēs*, it includes "only begotten" followed by a parentheses with the word "unique." Finally, 1 Timothy 2:12 concludes with the phrase "in religious assemblies" in brackets. According to Fee and Strauss, one of the main weaknesses of the Amplified Bible "is that readers may simply pick whichever meaning they like instead of discerning the single correct meaning that fits the context."[32] At other times the readers could conclude incorrectly that all the possible meanings of a word are applicable to any one particular use of the word.[33]

Another major revision from the ASV is the New American Standard Bible (NASB), which first appeared in 1971 and was updated in 1995. The NASB is a translation by conservative evangelicals desiring to use an essentially literal translation philosophy. The translators were willing to sacrifice English style in order to retain a literal translation. Several interesting approaches to Bible translation were adopted by the 58 translators. First, they used "Thy," "Thou," and "Thee," but only when used in prayer to God. This was eliminated in the updated edition. Second, they capitalized all pronouns referring to deity. Third, when the New Testament quotes the Old Testament, the quotation is put in small capital letters.

The NASB retains "sons of God" in Matthew 5:9. It uses "repents" in Luke 17:3 but correctly translates the verb in Matthew 27:3 as "felt remorse." It understands John 3:16 as referring to the extent of God's love for the world. While Jesus is described as God's "only begotten" Son in the text, a footnote adds that the word could mean "*unique*, only one of His kind." The verse is left in quotations without any footnote stating that the quote might end at verse 15. The NASB was one of the first translations

---

[31] Note footnote 15 above.

[32] Gordon D. Fee and Mark L. Strauss, *How to Choose a Translation for All Its Worth: A Guide to Understanding and Using Bible Versions* (Grand Rapids: Zondervan, 2007), 149. See also the comment by Gordon D. Fee and Douglas Stuart, who say that the Amplified Bible "has had a run of popularity far beyond its worth. It is far better to use several translations, note where they differ, and then check out those differences in another source, than to be led to believe that a word can mean one of several things in any given sentence, with the reader left to choose whatever best strikes his or her fancy" (Gordon D. Fee and Douglas Stuart, *How to Read the Bible for All Its Worth* [Grand Rapids: Zondervan, 1993], 43).

[33] It is a word study fallacy to read a word's entire range of meaning into one specific usage. This is called the "illegitimate totality transfer" fallacy (cf. D. A. Carson, *Exegetical Fallacies*, 2nd ed. [Grand Rapids, MI: Baker Academic, 1996], 60).

to adopt "to exercise authority" in 1 Timothy 2:12.[34] One example of an awkward rendering in the NASB is Joshua 15:18: "So she alighted from the donkey." The use of archaic vocabulary, in this instance carried over from the ASV, may make this translation difficult for some modern readers to understand.[35]

On the opposite side of the translation spectrum (see fig. 1) from the NASB is the Living Bible. Also revised from the ASV, the Living Bible was the work of Kenneth Taylor. Taylor was frustrated in his family devotions because his children did not understand the Bible passage they were reading (either the KJV or RSV). So he started paraphrasing the passage, giving the basic thought of the passage, and then his children were able to answer his questions. He realized that he should write out these paraphrases before the devotion rather than doing them on the spot. Thus the Living Bible was born. In earlier editions[36] it was well received by organizations such as Youth for Christ and Young Life, as well as by Billy Graham. It was the best-selling book in America in 1972 and 1973. Taylor started Tyndale House Publishers in 1962 in order to publish his paraphrase.[37]

The Living Bible is not a translation but a paraphrase. It is loosely tied to the ASV, with Taylor summarizing the main thought of the passage. It retains "sons of God" in Matthew 5:9, stating that they are "happy," instead of "blessed." Instead of using the word "repent" in Luke 17:3, it says to "forgive him if he is sorry." Judas is said to have "changed his mind" in Matthew 27:3. Women are never to "lord it over" men in 1 Timothy 2:12. A final example comes from Acts 13:48. While most translations say that those who were "appointed" (NASB) or "ordained" (KJV) for eternal life believed, the Living Bible says, "and as many as wanted eternal life, believed."

In 1989, Tyndale House Publishers decided to revise the Living Bible. The revision turned into a new translation. With the help of about 90 scholars, the New Living Translation (NLT) was published in 1996. A second edition was published in 2004, and a minor update occurred in 2007. In July 2008, the NLT was number one on the Christian Booksellers Association list among Bible translations, temporarily unseating the New International Version from the top spot where it had remained for more

---

[34] The Darby Bible (1884) uses "to exercise authority."

[35] The use of "alighted" can be traced back to the Bishop's Bible (1568).

[36] Called *Living Letters*.

[37] The name is in honor of William Tyndale and the translation he completed in 1526. Interestingly, Taylor was working at Moody Press when he did this.

than two decades.[38] The second edition moved further away from a paraphrase and more solidly into the category of functional equivalence in its translation philosophy.

The NLT translates Matthew 5:9 with the phrase "children of God," as Wycliffe, Tyndale, and the KJV did. Though the word "repentance" is rare in the NLT, it is used in Luke 17:3.[39] Judas is "filled with remorse" in Matthew 27:3. John 3:16 is retained in quotation marks (without any accompanying footnote). The adverb is translated as "so much," and Jesus is described as God's "one and only" Son. And women are not to "have authority" over men in 1 Timothy 2:12.

Independent Translations

An independent translation refers to a translation that was not a revision of a previous translation. Instead, the translators went back to the Hebrew and Greek texts without reference to an existing translation. The first translation we will discuss in this category is the translation that has successfully replaced the KJV as the standard translation in use in American churches: the New International Version (NIV).

The NIV project began as two separate committees, one appointed by the Synod of the Christian Reformed Church in 1956 and one by the National Association of Evangelicals in 1957, which combined into a joint committee. They began translating the Gospel of John in 1968 and published it in 1969. The New Testament was completed in 1973, and the entire Bible was published in 1978. There was a minor update in 1984. The approximately 100 scholars held to a high view of Scripture and were committed to the authority and infallibility of the Bible.

Controversy arose when plans for a 1997 revision in the United States were revealed.[40] The translation committee was going to use "inclusive language," meaning that many masculine pronouns would be replaced with gender-neutral ones. *WORLD* magazine published a story on March 29, 1997, titled, "The Stealth Bible: The popular New International Version Bible is quietly going 'gender-neutral.'"[41] Both Zondervan and the translation com-

---

[38] See http://www.nltblog.com/index.php/2008/08/nlt-1-on-july-cba-bestseller-list.

[39] It only occurs six times in the New Testament of the NLT, while it occurs 22 times in the NASB New Testament.

[40] The NIVI (New International Version: Inclusive Language Edition) was published in the UK by Hodder & Stoughton in 1995. In the preface to the inclusive-language NIV, the Committee on Bible Translation noted "that it was often appropriate to mute the patriarchalism of the culture of the biblical writers through gender-inclusive language when this could be done without compromising the message of the Spirit."

[41] See http://www.worldmag.com/articles/418.

mittee responded and accused *WORLD* of misrepresenting the facts. The outcome of the controversy was that the planned revision was cancelled.

However, while the 1984 NIV was not going to change, the translators and Zondervan did produce a new translation in 2005: Today's New International Version (TNIV). Keith Danby, president and chief executive officer of Biblica (a Bible translation organization), said that they "erred in presenting past updates, failed to convince people revisions were needed and 'underestimated' readers' loyalty to the 1984 NIV."[42] The TNIV never really caught on with readers. Therefore, admitting it was a mistake to "freeze" the NIV to its 1984 edition,[43] both the TNIV and the 1984 version will no longer be published in favor of the updated NIV 2011.[44]

The NIV 2011 has changed the NIV 1984's "sons of God" to "children of God" in Matthew 5:9. While it retains the word "repent" in Luke 17:3, it says, "They repent . . . forgive them," rather than the NIV 1984's "He repents . . . forgive him." In Matthew 27:3, both say that Judas was "seized with remorse." John 3:16 was in quotation marks in the NIV 1984 but not in the updated NIV. The adverb is translated the same in both translations as a reference to the extent of God's love. Both translations also refer to Jesus as God's "one and only" Son. The NIV 1984 said that women were not "to have authority" over a man in 1 Timothy 2:12. The first edition of the TNIV repeated that, but a second edition changed it to "assume authority." The NIV now reads "assume authority."

A second major independent work was not accomplished by a committee but by one man: Eugene Peterson. *The Message*, completed in 2002, is a paraphrase of the Bible. The goal of this paraphrase is for the contemporary reader to encounter the text with the style and idiom of contemporary English. Speaking about his own project, Peterson said, "When I'm in a congregation where somebody uses it in the Scripture reading, it makes me a little uneasy. I would never recommend it be used as saying, 'Hear the Word of God from *The Message*.' But it surprises me how many do. You can't tell people they can't do it. But I guess I'm a traditionalist, and I like to hear those more formal languages in the pulpit."[45]

Comparing *The Message* with other versions can be difficult because bigger portions of text are necessary to comprehend what Peterson is doing

---

[42] See http://www.usatoday.com/news/religion/2009–09–01-bible-translation_N.htm.

[43] See http://www.dashhouse.com/blog/2009/9/1/interview-with-douglas-moo-on-the-2011-niv.html.

[44] Maureen Girkins, the former president of Zondervan, said that "the 'divisive' TNIV and 'cherished' 1984 NIV will not be published after the newest NIV comes out." See http://www.usatoday.com/news/religion/2009–09–01-bible-translation_N.htm.

[45] See http://www.christianitytoday.com/ct/2002/october7/33.107.html?start=2.

with a certain word or phrase. For example, Luke 17:3–4 says: "Be alert. If you see your friend going wrong, correct him. If he responds, forgive him. Even if it's personal against you and repeated seven times through the day, and seven times he says, 'I'm sorry, I won't do it again,' forgive him." The phrase "if he responds" is where one usually finds the word "repent." In Matthew 27:3, Judas is described as being "overcome with remorse." John 3:16 remains in quotations marks; the adverb is understood as a reference to the extent of God's love; and Jesus is called God's "one and only" Son. First Timothy 2:12 says, "I don't let women take over and tell the men what to do. They should study to be quiet and obedient along with everyone else." First Corinthians 14 is a good example of a text that has been highly interpreted in this paraphrase. The heading of the chapter says "Prayer Language." Peterson explicitly refers to praying in tongues seven times in the first 19 verses, while verse 14 is the only one that explicitly refers to praying in tongues.

The Holman Christian Standard Bible (HCSB) is a fresh translation from the standard Hebrew and Greek texts used by most scholars today.[46] The complete Bible was published in 2003, with an update in 2009. There were two important motivations for the HCSB. First, the translators believed that Bible translations must keep up with the rapidly changing English language. Second, they recognized that significant advances in biblical research (such as the discovery of the Dead Sea Scrolls) have provided more information for Bible translators so that more accurate decisions can be made.[47] Though some have dubbed the translation a "Southern Baptist translation," about 100 scholars and English stylists from 17 denominations worked on the project. The HCSB highlights three distinctives in promoting its translation: (1) They use "Messiah" instead of "Christ" in appropriate places in the New Testament. (2) Instead of using "Lᴏʀᴅ" for the personal name of God, "Yahweh" is used in appropriate places in the Old Testament. (3) They prefer to translate the Greek word *doulos* as "slave" rather than "servant" or "bondservant."[48]

The HCSB retains "sons of God" in Matthew 5:9 and "repents" in Luke 17:3. Judas "was full of remorse" in Matthew 27:3. Women are not "to have authority" over a man in 1 Timothy 2:12. The HCSB retains the quotation marks in John 3:16 with a footnote after verse 21 stating that

---

[46] There has been confusion over which underlying manuscripts were used by the translators, but they used the United Bible Societies' *Greek New Testament* 4th corrected edition, the Nestle-Aland *Novum Testamentum Graece* 27th edition, and the *Biblia Hebraica Stuttgartensia* 5th edition.

[47] See http://hcsb.org/about.aspx.

[48] See http://hcsb.org/faq.aspx.

it "is possible that Jesus' words end" at verse 15. It translates the Greek adverb with the meaning that God was demonstrating *the way* in which he loved the world. Jesus is referred to as God's "One and Only" Son.

The final independent translation is the New English Translation (NET or NET Bible), completed in 2001. The NET Bible project began in 1995 at the annual Society of Biblical Literature meeting in Philadelphia, Pennsylvania. The original goal was to provide a digital translation that could be obtained for free on the Internet using modern English. The interdenominational committee of about 25 scholars translated from the standard Hebrew and Greek texts. The first edition was published with 60,932 translators' notes. These notes often contain technical discussions in the Hebrew and Greek text. They typically contain alternate translations (usually a more literal translation than in the text), discussions on textual variants, explanations of translation decisions, word studies, background information, and references to articles, books, and dissertations that relate to the translation and/or understanding of the verse being referenced. The NET Bible is also noted for having a unique copyright, allowing users more freedom in using the NET Bible in ministry materials.[49]

The NET Bible, which veers toward a gender-neutral translation philosophy, has "children of God" in Matthew 5:9. While "repents" is used in Luke 17:3, Judas is said to have "regretted" his actions in Matthew 27:3. John 3:16 is not in quotation marks. The adverb is understood as a reference to the manner in which God loved the world, and Jesus is called God's "one and only" Son. Paul does not allow a woman to "exercise authority" over a man in 1 Timothy 2:12. The NET Bible translates *almah* in Isaiah 7:14 as "young woman."[50]

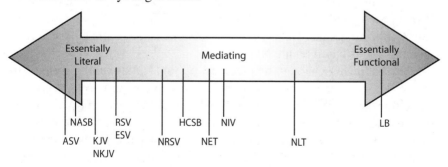

---

[49] See http://bible.org/article/preface-net-bible-first-edition for more information.

[50] Another interesting incorporation of modern scholarship in the NET Bible translation is Rom 3:22, which says that "the righteousness of God through the faithfulness of Jesus Christ for all who believe," rather than "faith in Jesus Christ," which is in the NIV, ESV, HCSB, and NLT.

Conclusion

This book has been designed to help you choose which Bible translation is best for you. The discussion on the history of Bible translation is intended to get you up-to-date on some of the issues involved in translating the Bible that have fueled passionate discussions. Our hope is that as you read through this book, you will be thinking about the translation philosophy being defended and how that philosophy is demonstrated in the translation. While philosophies vary, in the end we all want to know God more through his Word. Choosing an accurate and readable Bible is essential to that goal. However, the meaning of *accurate* and *readable* is debated.

Four translations have been chosen for this discussion. The NIV has been the best-selling Bible for many years, and the 2011 update provides a fitting opportunity to examine this translation. The resources for the NIV are too vast to mention here, but the NIV Study Bible has been an indispensable aid for many Christians since 1985. A new NIV Study Bible is currently being prepared. The ESV has been growing in popularity in recent years, receiving endorsements from many Christian leaders. It is consistently near the top five in Bible sales. Many new resources have appeared with the ESV translation, including the ESV Study Bible, the ESV Student Study Bible, the MacArthur Study Bible, and the www. ESVBible.org website. The HCSB has also been gaining popularity and steadily moving up in Bible sales. The translation also has several quality resources, including the Apologetics Study Bible, the HCSB Study Bible, and the www.MyStudyBible.com website. Finally, the NLT is one of the top-selling translations, with many resources available, including the NLT Study Bible, the NLT Life Application Study Bible, and the NLT Parallel Study Bible (a combination of the NLT Study Bible and the NLT Life Application Study Bible). The Cornerstone Bible Commentary Series includes and is based on the NLT text.

The following chapters focus on 16 passages in a parallel format so that you can compare these four major translations as they apply their Bible translation philosophy. Each translation is represented by a scholar who has served on the translation committee of that particular version. There are many ways to read these chapters as you compare the respective translation philosophies and translations. The section immediately following this chapter contains the 16 passages in a parallel format that all contributors will discuss in their chapters. You could read straight through the book, chapter by chapter. That has the benefit of giving you a coherent view of the translation being discussed. However, you will probably want to keep a finger on the 16 passages if you read it in this way.

You could also read the chapters section by section. You could read each author's description of their translation's philosophy to decide which is most convincing. Then you could read the discussion on each verse. So you could begin with Wayne Grudem's discussion of Exodus 2:5–6, then read Moo's, then Clendenen's, and then Comfort's.

We hope that by the end you have a greater understanding of how the various translations came to fruition. We hope you grow in your appreciation for all four translations as you obtain a better understanding of the distinctives of each and the labor that went into the final publishing of the English translations with your benefit in mind. We desire for you to have more clarity on the Bible you will choose for your daily devotions and study as you pursue God with all your heart, mind, soul, and strength. And we pray that your passion for God's Word increases, remembering the sacrifice of great saints of God such as John Wycliffe and William Tyndale, who gave their lives in the service of translating the Holy Scriptures into the English language.

Translation Comparison

Passages Discussed

Passage 1: Exodus 2:5–6

ESV 5 Now the daughter of Pharaoh came down to bathe at the river, while her young women walked beside the river. She saw the basket among the reeds and sent her servant woman, and she took it. 6 When she opened it, she saw the child, and behold, the baby was crying. She took pity on him and said, "This is one of the Hebrews' children."

NIV 5 Then Pharaoh's daughter went down to the Nile to bathe, and her attendants were walking along the riverbank. She saw the basket among the reeds and sent her female slave to get it. 6 She opened it and saw the baby. He was crying, and she felt sorry for him. "This is one of the Hebrew babies," she said.

HCSB 5 Pharaoh's daughter went down to bathe at the Nile while her servant girls walked along the riverbank. Seeing the basket among the reeds, she sent her slave girl to get it. 6 When she opened it, she saw the child—a little boy, crying. She felt sorry for him and said, "This is one of the Hebrew boys."

NLT   ⁵ Soon Pharaoh's daughter came down to bathe in the river, and her attendants walked along the riverbank. When the princess saw the basket among the reeds, she sent her maid to get it for her. ⁶ When the princess opened it, she saw the baby. The little boy was crying, and she felt sorry for him. "This must be one of the Hebrew children," she said.

Passage 2: Psalm 1:1

ESV   Blessed is the man who walks not in the counsel of the wicked, nor stands in the way of sinners, nor sits in the seat of scoffers; . . .

NIV   Blessed is the one who does not walk in step with the wicked or stand in the way that sinners take or sit in the company of mockers, . . .

HCSB How happy is the man who does not follow the advice of the wicked or take the path of sinners or join a group of mockers!

NLT   Oh, the joys of those who do not follow the advice of the wicked, or stand around with sinners, or join in with mockers.

Passage 3: Ezekiel 18:5–9,21–24

ESV   ⁵ "If a man is righteous and does what is just and right—⁶ if he does not eat upon the mountains or lift up his eyes to the idols of the house of Israel, does not defile his neighbor's wife or approach a woman in her time of menstrual impurity, ⁷ does not oppress anyone, but restores to the debtor his pledge, commits no robbery, gives his bread to the hungry and covers the naked with a garment, ⁸ does not lend at interest or take any profit, withholds his hand from injustice, executes true justice between man and man, ⁹ walks in my statutes, and keeps my rules by acting faithfully—he is righteous; he shall surely live, declares the Lord GOD. . . . ²¹ But if a wicked person turns away from all his sins that he has committed and keeps all my statutes and does what is just and right, he shall surely live; he shall not die. ²² None of the transgressions that he has committed shall be remembered against him; for the righteousness that he has done he shall live. ²³ Have I any pleasure in the death of the wicked, declares the Lord God, and not rather that he should turn from his way and live? ²⁴ But when a righteous person turns away from his righteousness and does injustice and does the same abominations that the wicked person does, shall he live? None of the righteous deeds that he has done shall be remembered; for the treachery of which he is guilty and the sin he has committed, for them he shall die."

NIV   ⁵ "Suppose there is a righteous man who does what is just and right. ⁶ He does not eat at the mountain shrines or look to the idols of Israel. He does not defile his neighbor's wife or have sexual relations with a woman during her period. ⁷ He does not oppress anyone, but returns what he took in pledge for a loan. He does not commit robbery but gives his food to the hungry and provides clothing for the naked. ⁸ He does not lend to them at interest or take a profit from them. He withholds his hand from doing wrong and judges fairly between two parties. ⁹ He follows my decrees and faithfully keeps my laws. That man is righteous; he will surely live, declares the Sovereign Lord. . . . ²¹ But if a wicked person turns away from all the sins they have committed and keeps all my decrees and does what is just and right, that person will surely live; they will not die. ²² None of the offenses they have committed will be remembered against them. Because of the righteous things they have done, they will live. ²³ Do I take any pleasure in the death of the wicked? declares the Sovereign Lord. Rather, am I not pleased when they turn from their ways and live? ²⁴ But if a righteous person turns from their righteousness and commits sin and does the same detestable things the wicked person does, will they live? None of the righteous things that person has done will be remembered. Because of the unfaithfulness they are guilty of and because of the sins they have committed, they will die."

HCSB   ⁵ "Now suppose a man is righteous and does what is just and right: ⁶ He does not eat at the mountain shrines or raise his eyes to the idols of the house of Israel. He does not defile his neighbor's wife or come near a woman during her menstrual impurity. ⁷ He doesn't oppress anyone but returns his collateral to the debtor. He does not commit robbery, but gives his bread to the hungry and covers the naked with clothing. [8] He doesn't lend at interest or for profit but keeps his hand from wrongdoing and carries out true justice between men. [9] He follows My statutes and keeps My ordinances, acting faithfully. Such a person is righteous; he will certainly live." This is the declaration of the Lord God. . . . [21] "Now if the wicked person turns from all the sins he has committed, keeps all My statutes, and does what is just and right, he will certainly live; he will not die. [22] None of the transgressions he has committed will be held against him. He will live because of the righteousness he has practiced. [23] Do I take any pleasure in the death of the wicked?" This is the declaration of the Lord God. "Instead, don't I take pleasure when he turns from his ways and lives? [24] But when a righteous person turns from his righteousness and practices iniquity, committing the same detestable acts that the wicked do, will he live? None of the righteous acts he did will be remembered. He will die because of the treachery he has engaged in and the sin he has committed."

NLT [5] "Suppose a certain man is righteous and does what is just and right. [6] He does not feast in the mountains before Israel's idols or worship them. He does not commit adultery or have intercourse with a woman during her menstrual period. [7] He is a merciful creditor, not keeping the items given as security by poor debtors. He does not rob the poor but instead gives food to the hungry and provides clothes for the needy. [8] He grants loans without interest, stays away from injustice, is honest and fair when judging others, [9] and faithfully obeys my decrees and regulations. Anyone who does these things is just and will surely live, says the Sovereign Lord. . . . [21] But if wicked people turn away from all their sins and begin to obey my decrees and do what is just and right, they will surely live and not die. [22] All their past sins will be forgotten, and they will live because of the righteous things they have done. [23] "Do you think that I like to see wicked people die? says the Sovereign Lord. Of course not! I want them to turn from their wicked ways and live. [24] However, if righteous people turn from their righteous behavior and start doing sinful things and act like other sinners, should they be allowed to live? No, of course not! All their righteous acts will be forgotten, and they will die for their sins."

Passage 4: Matthew 5:1–3

ESV   [1] Seeing the crowds, he went up on the mountain, and when he sat down, his disciples came to him. [2] And he opened his mouth and taught them, saying: [3] "Blessed are the poor in spirit, for theirs is the kingdom of heaven.

NIV   [1] Now when Jesus saw the crowds, he went up on a mountainside and sat down. His disciples came to him, [2] and he began to teach them. He said: [3] "Blessed are the poor in spirit, for theirs is the kingdom of heaven.

HCSB   [1] When He saw the crowds, He went up on the mountain, and after He sat down, His disciples came to Him. [2] Then He began to teach them, saying: [3] "The poor in spirit are blessed, for the kingdom of heaven is theirs.

NLT   [1] One day as he saw the crowds gathering, Jesus went up on the mountainside and sat down. His disciples gathered around him, [2] and he began to teach them. [3] "God blesses those who are poor and realize their need for him, for the Kingdom of Heaven is theirs.

Passage 5: Mark 1:40–45

ESV   [40] And a leper came to him, imploring him, and kneeling said to him, "If you will, you can make me clean." [41] Moved with pity, he stretched out his hand and touched him and said to him, "I will; be clean." [42] And immediately the leprosy left him, and he was made clean. [43] And Jesus sternly charged him and sent him away at once, [44] and said to him, "See that you say nothing to anyone, but go, show yourself to the priest and offer for your cleansing what Moses commanded, for a proof to them." [45] But he went out and began to talk freely about it, and to spread the news, so that Jesus could no longer openly enter a town, but was out in desolate places, and people were coming to him from every quarter.

NIV [40] A man with leprosy came to him and begged him on his knees, "If you are willing, you can make me clean." [41] Jesus was indignant. He reached out his hand and touched the man. "I am willing," he said. "Be clean!" [42] Immediately the leprosy left him and he was cleansed. [43] Jesus sent him away at once with a strong warning: [44] "See that you don't tell this to anyone. But go, show yourself to the priest and offer the sacrifices that Moses commanded for your cleansing, as a testimony to them." [45] Instead he went out and began to talk freely, spreading the news. As a result, Jesus could no longer enter a town openly but stayed outside in lonely places. Yet the people still came to him from everywhere.

HCSB [40] Then a man with a serious skin disease came to Him and, on his knees, begged Him: "If You are willing, You can make me clean." [41] Moved with compassion, Jesus reached out His hand and touched him. "I am willing," He told him. "Be made clean." [42] Immediately the disease left him, and he was healed. [43] Then He sternly warned him and sent him away at once, [44] telling him, "See that you say nothing to anyone; but go and show yourself to the priest, and offer what Moses prescribed for your cleansing, as a testimony to them." [45] Yet he went out and began to proclaim it widely and to spread the news, with the result that Jesus could no longer enter a town openly. But He was out in deserted places, and they would come to Him from everywhere.

NLT [40] A man with leprosy came and knelt in front of Jesus, begging to be healed. "If you are willing, you can heal me and make me clean," he said. [41] Moved with compassion, Jesus reached out and touched him. "I am willing," he said. "Be healed!" [42] Instantly the leprosy disappeared, and the man was healed. [43] Then Jesus sent him on his way with a stern warning: [44] "Don't tell anyone about this. Instead, go to the priest and let him examine you. Take along the offering required in the law of Moses for those who have been healed of leprosy. This will be a public testimony that you have been cleansed." [45] But the man went and spread the word, proclaiming to everyone what had happened. As a result, large crowds soon surrounded Jesus, and he couldn't publicly enter a town anywhere. He had to stay out in the secluded places, but people from everywhere kept coming to him.

Passage 6: Mark 16:9–20

ESV   ⁹[[Now when he rose early on the first day of the week, he appeared first to Mary Magdalene, from whom he had cast out seven demons. ¹⁰She went and told those who had been with him, as they mourned and wept. ¹¹But when they heard that he was alive and had been seen by her, they would not believe it. ¹²After these things he appeared in another form to two of them, as they were walking into the country. ¹³And they went back and told the rest, but they did not believe them. ¹⁴Afterward he appeared to the eleven themselves as they were reclining at table, and he rebuked them for their unbelief and hardness of heart, because they had not believed those who saw him after he had risen. ¹⁵And he said to them, "Go into all the world and proclaim the gospel to the whole creation. ¹⁶Whoever believes and is baptized will be saved, but whoever does not believe will be condemned. ¹⁷And these signs will accompany those who believe: in my name they will cast out demons; they will speak in new tongues; ¹⁸they will pick up serpents with their hands; and if they drink any deadly poison, it will not hurt them; they will lay their hands on the sick, and they will recover." ¹⁹So then the Lord Jesus, after he had spoken to them, was taken up into heaven and sat down at the right hand of God. ²⁰And they went out and preached everywhere, while the Lord worked with them and confirmed the message by accompanying signs.]]

NIV   ⁹When Jesus rose early on the first day of the week, he appeared first to Mary Magdalene, out of whom he had driven seven demons. ¹⁰She went and told those who had been with him and who were mourning and weeping. ¹¹When they heard that Jesus was alive and that she had seen him, they did not believe it. ¹²Afterward Jesus appeared in a different form to two of them while they were walking in the country. ¹³These returned and reported it to the rest; but they did not believe them either. ¹⁴Later Jesus appeared to the Eleven as they were eating; he rebuked them for their lack of faith and their stubborn refusal to believe those who had seen him after he had risen. ¹⁵He said to them, "Go into all the world and preach the gospel to all creation. ¹⁶Whoever believes and is baptized will be saved, but whoever does not believe will be condemned. ¹⁷And these signs will accompany those who believe: In my name they will drive out demons; they will speak in new tongues; [18] they will pick up snakes with their hands; and when they drink deadly poison, it will not hurt them at all; they will place their hands on sick people, and they will get well." [19] After the Lord Jesus had spoken to them, he was taken up into heaven and he sat at the right hand of God. [20] Then the disciples went out and preached everywhere, and the Lord worked with them and confirmed his word by the signs that accompanied it.

HCSB   [9] [Early on the first day of the week, after He had risen, He appeared first to Mary Magdalene, out of whom He had driven seven demons. [10] She went and reported to those who had been with Him, as they were mourning and weeping. [11] Yet, when they heard that He was alive and had been seen by her, they did not believe it. [12] Then after this, He appeared in a different form to two of them walking on their way into the country. [13] And they went and reported it to the rest, who did not believe them either. [14] Later, He appeared to the Eleven themselves as they were reclining at the table. He rebuked their unbelief and hardness of heart, because they did not believe those who saw Him after He had been resurrected. [15] Then He said to them, "Go into all the world and preach the gospel to the whole creation. [16] Whoever believes and is baptized will be saved, but whoever does not believe will be condemned. [17] And these signs will accompany those who believe: In My name they will drive out demons; they will speak in new languages; [18] they will pick up snakes; if they should drink anything deadly, it will never harm them; they will lay hands on the sick, and they will get well." [19] Then after speaking to them, the Lord Jesus was taken up into heaven and sat down at the right hand of God. [20] And they went out and preached everywhere, the Lord working with them and confirming the word by the accompanying signs.]

NLT   [9] After Jesus rose from the dead early on Sunday morning, the first person who saw him was Mary Magdalene, the woman from whom he had cast out seven demons. [10] She went to the disciples, who were grieving and weeping, and told them what had happened. [11] But when she told them that Jesus was alive and she had seen him, they didn't believe her. [12] Afterward he appeared in a different form to two of his followers who were walking from Jerusalem into the country. [13] They rushed back to tell the others, but no one believed them. [14] Still later he appeared to the eleven disciples as they were eating together. He rebuked them for their stubborn unbelief because they refused to believe those who had seen him after he had been raised from the dead. [15] And then he told them, "Go into all the world and preach the Good News to everyone. [16] Anyone who believes and is baptized will be saved. But anyone who refuses to believe will be condemned. [17] These miraculous signs will accompany those who believe: They will cast out demons in my name, and they will speak in new languages. [18] They will be able to handle snakes with safety, and if they drink anything poisonous, it won't hurt them. They will be able to place their hands on the sick, and they will be healed." [19] When the Lord Jesus had finished talking with them, he was taken up into heaven and sat down in the place of honor at God's right hand. [20] And the disciples went everywhere and preached, and the Lord worked through them, confirming what they said by many miraculous signs.

Passage 7: Luke 17:3

ESV   Pay attention to yourselves! If your brother sins, rebuke him, and if he repents, forgive him, . . .

NIV   So watch yourselves. "If your brother or sister sins against you, rebuke them; and if they repent, forgive them.

HCSB   Be on your guard. If your brother sins, rebuke him, and if he repents, forgive him.

NLT   So watch yourselves! "If another believer sins, rebuke that person; then if there is repentance, forgive.

Passage 8: John 1:3–4,14,18

ESV   [3] All things were made through him, and without him was not any thing made that was made. [4] In him was life, and the life was the light of men . . . . [14] And the Word became flesh and dwelt among us, and we have seen his glory, glory as of the only Son from the Father, full of grace and truth ....[18] No one has ever seen God; the only God, who is at the Father's side, he has made him known.

NIV [3] Through him all things were made; without him nothing was made that has been made. [4] In him was life, and that life was the light of all mankind ....[14] The Word became flesh and made his dwelling among us. We have seen his glory, the glory of the one and only Son, who came from the Father, full of grace and truth .... [18] No one has ever seen God, but the one and only Son, who is himself God and is in closest relationship with the Father, has made him known.

HCSB [3] All things were created through Him, and apart from Him not one thing was created that has been created. [4] Life was in Him, and that life was the light of men ....[14] The Word became flesh and took up residence among us. We observed His glory, the glory as the One and Only Son from the Father, full of grace and truth ....[18] No one has ever seen God. The One and Only Son— the One who is at the Father's side—He has revealed Him.

NLT [3] God created everything through him, and nothing was created except through him. [4] The Word gave life to everything that was created, and his life brought light to everyone ....[14] So the Word became human and made his home among us. He was full of unfailing love and faithfulness. And we have seen his glory, the glory of the Father's one and only Son ....[18] No one has ever seen God. But the unique One, who is himself God, is near to the Father's heart. He has revealed God to us.

Passage 9: John 2:25–3:1

ESV [2:25] and needed no one to bear witness about man, for he himself knew what was in man. [3:1] Now there was a man of the Pharisees named Nicodemus, a ruler of the Jews.

NIV [2:25] He did not need any testimony about mankind, for he knew what was in each person. [3:1] Now there was a Pharisee, a man

named Nicodemus who was a member of the Jewish ruling
council.

HCSB   [2:25] and because He did not need anyone to testify about man; for
He Himself knew what was in man. [3:1] There was a man from the
Pharisees named Nicodemus, a ruler of the Jews.

NLT   [2:25] No one needed to tell him what mankind is really like. [3:1] There
was a man named Nicodemus, a Jewish religious leader who was
a Pharisee.

Passage 10: 1 Corinthians 2:1,13

ESV   [1] And I, when I came to you, brothers, did not come proclaiming to
you the testimony of God with lofty speech or wisdom . . . . [13] And
we impart this in words not taught by human wisdom but
taught by the Spirit, interpreting spiritual truths to those who
are spiritual.

NIV   [1] And so it was with me, brothers and sisters. When I came to you,
I did not come with eloquence or human wisdom as I proclaimed
to you the testimony about God . . . . [13] This is what we speak, not
in words taught us by human wisdom but in words taught by the
Spirit, explaining spiritual realities with Spirit-taught words.

HCSB   [1] When I came to you, brothers, announcing the testimony
of God to you, I did not come with brilliance of speech or
wisdom . . . . [13] We also speak these things, not in words taught
by human wisdom, but in those taught by the Spirit, explaining
spiritual things to spiritual people.

NLT   [1] When I first came to you, dear brothers and sisters, I didn't
use lofty words and impressive wisdom to tell you God's secret
plan . . . . [13] When we tell you these things, we do not use words
that come from human wisdom. Instead, we speak words given
to us by the Spirit, using the Spirit's words to explain spiritual
truths.

Passage 11: Galatians 5:2–6

ESV   [2] Look: I, Paul, say to you that if you accept circumcision, Christ will be of no advantage to you. [3] I testify again to every man who accepts circumcision that he is obligated to keep the whole law. [4] You are severed from Christ, you who would be justified by the law; you have fallen away from grace. [5] For through the Spirit, by faith, we ourselves eagerly wait for the hope of righteousness. [6] For in Christ Jesus neither circumcision nor uncircumcision counts for anything, but only faith working through love.

NIV   [2] Mark my words! I, Paul, tell you that if you let yourselves be circumcised, Christ will be of no value to you at all. [3] Again I declare to every man who lets himself be circumcised that he is obligated to obey the whole law. [4] You who are trying to be justified by the law have been alienated from Christ; you have fallen away from grace. [5] For through the Spirit we eagerly await by faith the righteousness for which we hope. [6] For in Christ Jesus neither circumcision nor uncircumcision has any value. The only thing that counts is faith expressing itself through love.

HCSB   [2] Take note! I, Paul, tell you that if you get yourselves circumcised, Christ will not benefit you at all. [3] Again I testify to every man who gets himself circumcised that he is obligated to keep the entire law. [4] You who are trying to be justified by the law are alienated from Christ; you have fallen from grace. [5] For through the Spirit, by faith, we eagerly wait for the hope of righteousness. [6] For in Christ Jesus neither circumcision nor uncircumcision accomplishes anything; what matters is faith working through love.

NLT   [2] Listen! I, Paul, tell you this: If you are counting on circumcision to make you right with God, then Christ will be of no benefit to you. [3] I'll say it again. If you are trying to find favor with God by being circumcised, you must obey every regulation in the whole law of Moses. [4] For if you are trying to make yourselves right with God by keeping the law, you have been cut off from Christ! You have fallen away from God's grace. [5] But we who live by the Spirit eagerly wait to receive by faith the righteousness God has promised to us. [6] For when we place our faith in Christ Jesus, there is no benefit in being circumcised or being uncircumcised. What is important is faith expressing itself in love.

Passage 12: Colossians 2:8–15

ESV   [8] See to it that no one takes you captive by philosophy and empty deceit, according to human tradition, according to the elemental spirits of the world, and not according to Christ. [9] For in him the whole fullness of deity dwells bodily, [10] and you have been filled in him, who is the head of all rule and authority. [11] In him also you were circumcised with a circumcision made without hands, by putting off the body of the flesh, by the circumcision of Christ, [12] having been buried with him in baptism, in which you were also raised with him through faith in the powerful working of God, who raised him from the dead. [13] And you, who were dead in your trespasses and the uncircumcision of your flesh, God made alive together with him, having forgiven us all our trespasses, [14] by canceling the record of debt that stood against us with its legal demands. This he set aside, nailing it to the cross. [15] He disarmed the rulers and authorities and put them to open shame, by triumphing over them in him.

NIV   [8] See to it that no one takes you captive through hollow and deceptive philosophy, which depends on human tradition and the elemental spiritual forces of this world rather than on Christ. [9] For in Christ all the fullness of the Deity lives in bodily form, [10] and in Christ you have been brought to fullness. He is the head over every power and authority. [11] In him you were also circumcised with a circumcision not performed by human hands. Your whole self ruled by the flesh was put off when you were circumcised by Christ, [12] having been buried with him in baptism, in which you were also raised with him through your faith in the working of God, who raised him from the dead. [13] When you were dead in your sins and in the uncircumcision of your flesh, God made you alive with Christ. He forgave us all our sins, [14] having canceled the charge of our legal indebtedness, which stood against us and condemned us; he has taken it away, nailing it to the cross. [15] And having disarmed the powers and authorities, he made a public spectacle of them, triumphing over them by the cross.

HCSB   [8]Be careful that no one takes you captive through philosophy and empty deceit based on human tradition, based on the elemental forces of the world, and not based on Christ. [9]For the entire fullness of God's nature dwells bodily in Christ, [10]and you have been filled by Him, who is the head over every ruler and authority. [11]You were also circumcised in Him with a circumcision not done with hands, by putting off the body of flesh, in the circumcision of the Messiah. [12]Having been buried with Him in baptism, you were also raised with Him through faith in the working of God, who raised Him from the dead. [13]And when you were dead in trespasses and in the uncircumcision of your flesh, He made you alive with Him and forgave us all our trespasses. [14]He erased the certificate of debt, with its obligations, that was against us and opposed to us, and has taken it out of the way by nailing it to the cross. [15]He disarmed the rulers and authorities and disgraced them publicly; He triumphed over them by Him.

NLT   [8]Don't let anyone capture you with empty philosophies and high-sounding nonsense that come from human thinking and from the spiritual powers of this world, rather than from Christ. [9]For in Christ lives all the fullness of God in a human body. [10]So you also are complete through your union with Christ, who is the head over every ruler and authority. [11]When you came to Christ, you were "circumcised," but not by a physical procedure. Christ performed a spiritual circumcision—the cutting away of your sinful nature. [12]For you were buried with Christ when you were baptized. And with him you were raised to new life because you trusted the mighty power of God, who raised Christ from the dead. [13]You were dead because of your sins and because your sinful nature was not yet cut away. Then God made you alive with Christ, for he forgave all our sins. [14]He canceled the record of the charges against us and took it away by nailing it to the cross. [15]In this way, he disarmed the spiritual rulers and authorities. He shamed them publicly by his victory over them on the cross.

Passage 13: 1 Thessalonians 1:3

ESV   remembering before our God and Father your work of faith and labor of love and steadfastness of hope in our Lord Jesus Christ.

NIV   We remember before our God and Father your work produced by faith, your labor prompted by love, and your endurance inspired by hope in our Lord Jesus Christ.

HCSB   We recall, in the presence of our God and Father, your work of faith, labor of love, and endurance of hope in our Lord Jesus Christ, . . .

NLT   As we pray to our God and Father about you, we think of your faithful work, your loving deeds, and the enduring hope you have because of our Lord Jesus Christ.

Passage 14: 1 Timothy 2:12

ESV   I do not permit a woman to teach or to exercise authority over a man; rather, she is to remain quiet.

NIV   I do not permit a woman to teach or to assume authority over a man; she must be quiet.

HCSB   I do not allow a woman to teach or to have authority over a man; instead, she is to be silent.

NLT   I do not let women teach men or have authority over them. Let them listen quietly.

Passage 15: Jude 4–5

ESV   4 For certain people have crept in unnoticed who long ago were designated for this condemnation, ungodly people, who pervert the grace of our God into sensuality and deny our only Master and Lord, Jesus Christ. 5 Now I want to remind you, although you once fully knew it, that Jesus, who saved a people out of the land of Egypt, afterward destroyed those who did not believe.

NIV   4 For certain individuals whose condemnation was written about long ago have secretly slipped in among you. They are ungodly people, who pervert the grace of our God into a license for immorality and deny Jesus Christ our only Sovereign and Lord. [5] Though you already know all this, I want to remind you that the Lord at one time delivered his people out of Egypt, but later destroyed those who did not believe.

HCSB   [4] For some men, who were designated for this judgment long ago, have come in by stealth; they are ungodly, turning the grace of our God into promiscuity and denying Jesus Christ, our only Master and Lord. [5] Now I want to remind you, though you know all these things: The Lord first saved a people out of Egypt and later destroyed those who did not believe; . . .

NLT   [4] I say this because some ungodly people have wormed their way into your churches, saying that God's marvelous grace allows us to live immoral lives. The condemnation of such people was recorded long ago, for they have denied our only Master and Lord, Jesus Christ. [5] So I want to remind you, though you already know these things, that Jesus first rescued the nation of Israel from Egypt, but later he destroyed those who did not remain faithful.

Passage 16: Revelation 3:20

ESV   Behold, I stand at the door and knock. If anyone hears my voice and opens the door, I will come in to him and eat with him, and he with me.

NIV   Here I am! I stand at the door and knock. If anyone hears my voice and opens the door, I will come in and eat with that person, and they with me.

HCSB   Listen! I stand at the door and knock. If anyone hears My voice and opens the door, I will come in to him and have dinner with him, and he with Me.

NLT   "Look! I stand at the door and knock. If you hear my voice and open the door, I will come in, and we will share a meal together as friends.

CHAPTER 2

The English Standard Version (ESV)

Wayne Grudem

Introduction: What Is the English Standard Version?

The ESV Is Derived from the King James Version Tradition

The ESV is an essentially literal translation that stands as today's direct inheritor of the great King James Version tradition. The line of descent from the KJV can be seen in the following diagram:

Figure 2: The ESV Is a Direct Descendant of the KJV Tradition

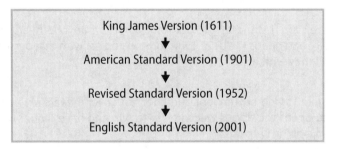

King James Version (1611)
↓
American Standard Version (1901)
↓
Revised Standard Version (1952)
↓
English Standard Version (2001)

The King James Version (called the Authorized Version in the UK) was first published 400 years ago, in 1611. It eventually became the dominant translation in the English-speaking world for more than three centuries.

It won widespread acceptance because of its intrinsic qualities: word-for-word accuracy, unparalleled literary beauty, remarkable oral readability, and an academic precision produced by the best scholarly experts of its age.

However, the English language kept changing from the form it took in 1611. English-speaking people today can still read the KJV but with difficulty, just as they can still read Shakespeare with difficulty (Shakespeare lived 1564–1616 and wrote most of his plays from 1590 to 1611, so his writings are from the same period of English as the KJV).

Eventually groups of Bible scholars began to produce revisions of the KJV, both to modernize the English and also to take advantage of scholarly advances in knowledge of Greek and Hebrew and in the discovery of older, more reliable Greek and Hebrew manuscripts of various books of the Bible.

The American Standard Version (ASV) appeared in 1901 as a major revision of the KJV, but many readers found it too woodenly literal, and it failed to gain widespread acceptance. (This was an American translation similar to an earlier British revision, the English Revised Version of 1881.)

Then in 1952 the Revised Standard Version (RSV) appeared as a revision of the ASV, and it actually reclaimed much of the literary excellence of the KJV itself. The RSV gained much wider acceptance than the ASV, but it failed to gain universal acceptance among evangelical Protestant readers because they detected some liberal bias that had crept into some verses. Nevertheless, the RSV was in many ways an excellent translation, and many evangelicals (such as the present author) continued to use it for their main personal teaching and study Bible. (For example, the RSV was the primary Bible text I quoted in my *Systematic Theology* when it was published in 1994.)

In 1989 the RSV committee issued a new translation, called the New Revised Standard Version (NRSV). I had eagerly awaited its publication, thinking I would probably change from the RSV to the NRSV as my main personal Bible. But I used it for two days and put it aside because I discovered that on nearly every page they had made gender-neutral changes that distorted the meaning of the Hebrew or Greek text.[1] So I put the NRSV away on a shelf because I decided it would not be helpful for my spiritual life to use a Bible that made me angry every time I read it. The NRSV

---

[1] See my detailed analysis of the NRSV in the booklet, "What's Wrong with Gender-Neutral Bible Translations?" (Libertyville, IL: Council on Biblical Manhood and Womanhood, 1997). Available at www.cbmw.org.

never caught on with the general public and never even rose to 1 percent of sales in the Bible market, though it is commonly used in more liberal academic circles today. Would there ever be, then, a worthy descendant of the great KJV tradition?

In 1997, Crossway Books, an evangelical publisher based in Wheaton, Illinois, obtained the rights to use the 1971 update of the RSV as the basis for a new translation in the KJV tradition, to be called the English Standard Version (ESV).[2] The ESV translation committee (called the Translation Oversight Committee) consisted of 12 members, but we made use of suggested changes to the RSV that had been submitted by a wider group of 60 specialist scholars. These consultants had been hired by Crossway to propose revisions to the RSV in the books where they had scholarly expertise (these were mostly scholars who had already published commentaries on the various books). In addition, a wider "advisory council" of 60 additional pastors and Christian leaders sent in their suggestions as well.

The ESV was first published in 2001. It changed about 8 percent of the RSV, or about 60,000 words. The remaining 92 percent is the RSV, much of which is simply "the best of the best" of the KJV tradition.

The ESV translation committee removed every trace of liberal influence that had caused such criticism from evangelicals when the RSV was first published in 1952. For example, Isaiah 7:14 was changed back to say, "Behold, the *virgin* shall conceive and bear a son." Psalm 2:12 once again says, "Kiss *the Son*," and Psalm 45:6 is once again a Messianic prediction that says, "Your throne, *O God*, is forever and ever." The important theological term "propitiation" has been restored to Romans 3:25; Hebrews 2:17; and 1 John 2:2 and 4:10.

The ESV Falls in the "Essentially Literal" Category on a Spectrum of Translations from Woodenly Literal to Highly Paraphrastic

As the following diagram shows, modern English translations of the Bible fall along a spectrum that ranges from "woodenly literal" to "highly paraphrastic." I will attempt to show in this chapter that the ESV's translation theory places it in the optimal place on this spectrum, where a high degree of literal accuracy is combined with readability and literary excellence.

---

[2] Crossway Books made a one-time payment to the owner of the RSV copyright, the National Council of Churches of Christ, to obtain the rights to use the RSV as a basis for the ESV. No additional payment is ever due, and no funds from sales of ESV Bibles go to the National Council of Churches.

Figure 3: Spectrum of Translations*

Woodenly literal-------	Essentially literal---	Mixed	Dynamic equivalence
	more word-for-word		more paraphrastic
keep Heb/Gk word order	translate the words		translate the thoughts (ideas)
Interlinear	KJV	NIV	**NLT**
	NKJV	TNIV	CEV
	NASB RSV NRSV	**NIV2011**	NCV
	ESV		The Message
	NET		
	HCSB		

*Bold font indicates translations represented in this forum.

Woodenly Literal Translations

The left side of this chart illustrates that it is possible to make a "woodenly literal" translation that just consists of putting an English word below each Greek or Hebrew word in the original text and then publishing it. In fact, this has been done. It is called an "interlinear" translation, and it is sometimes used by beginning language students. But it is hardly readable or suitable for general use. Here is an example:

> Thus for loved God the world, so that the Son the only he gave, in order that every the believing one in him not should perish but should have life eternal. (John 3:16)

Essentially Literal Translations

A better decision is to make an "essentially literal translation"—one that faithfully brings the meaning of each Greek word into English but that uses ordinary English word order and syntax. This is the next column in figure 3 above. Here is how the ESV rendered the same verse, in readable English:

> For God so loved the world, that he gave his only Son, that whoever believes in him should not perish but have eternal life. (John 3:16)

What then is an essentially literal translation? Here is my definition: An essentially literal translation *translates the meaning of every word in the original language*, understood correctly in its context, into its nearest English equivalent and attempts to express the result with ordinary English word order and style, as far as that is possible without distorting the meaning of the original.

Now sometimes one word in Hebrew or Greek must be translated with two or three words in English and other times with just a comma or a period. Still, at other times, two or three words in the original can best be translated with only one word in English. So "word for word" does not mean exactly one English word for each Hebrew or Greek word. But it does mean that every word in the original must be translated somehow. The goal in an essentially literal translation is to somehow bring *the meaning of every word* in the original into the resulting translation in English.

The reason for this emphasis on translating the meaning of every word is a belief in the importance that Scripture itself places on the very words of God. "*All Scripture* is breathed out by God" (2 Tim 3:16), and, "*Every word* of God proves true" (Prov 30:5). Jesus said, "Man shall not live by bread alone, but by *every word* that comes from the mouth of God" (Matt 4:4). "If anyone takes away from the *words* of the book of this prophecy, God will take away his share in the tree of life and in the holy city, which are described in this book" (Rev 22:19).

As the chart above indicates, the Holman Christian Standard Bible (HCSB) of 2009 falls broadly in the essentially literal range on the spectrum of translations. However, its introduction notes that they prefer the term "optimal equivalence" to describe their translation philosophy.[3] As my analysis below will show, the HCSB is somewhat closer to the NIV's "mixed" translation philosophy than the ESV, but it generally seeks to translate every word of the original faithfully.

"Formal Equivalence" Is an Inaccurate and Misleading Category
The ESV translators do not find the term "formal equivalence" to be an accurate term to describe an essentially literal translation. It puts too much emphasis on the "form" of the sentences, which refers especially to the order of words. That is a low priority in essentially literal translations, for the primary goal is to represent not just the form but the meaning of every word of the original. Therefore the first sentence about "translation philosophy" in the preface to the ESV says, "The ESV is an 'essentially literal' translation."[4]

---

[3] Introduction to the Holman Christian Standard Bible, vii.

[4] ESV Bible, preface, vii. Two other major defenses of the ESV's philosophy have also used the

It is unfortunate that some critics of the ESV continue to call it a "formal equivalence" translation. Then they reject the idea of formal equivalence because, they say, "form" must be subordinate to meaning in translation. Of course, we also believe this, so this kind of criticism of formal equivalence is just tearing down a straw man. The phrase "formal equivalence" was an invention of Eugene Nida, the pioneer of "dynamic equivalence" translations, and it is not surprising that he chose a pejorative term (one that suggests ignorant translators who do not realize that meaning is more important than form) to describe a philosophy with which he did not agree.[5]

What Is a "Dynamic Equivalence" Translation?
The NLT as an Example
On the right side of my chart above is "dynamic equivalence." A dynamic-equivalence translation translates the thoughts or ideas of the original text into similar thoughts or ideas in English and "attempts to have the same impact on modern readers as the original had on its own audience."[6] Another term for a dynamic-equivalence translation is a "thought for thought" translation, as explained in the introduction to the New Living Translation (NLT). The translators say that "a dynamic-equivalence translation can also be called a thought-for-thought translation, as contrasted with a formal-equivalence or word-for-word translation."[7] The NLT was first published in 1996 and updated in 2004 and 2007.

Another way to describe the difference is to contrast the kind of question each translator would ask in translating a text. A dynamic equivalence translator would ask, "How would people say that today?" Whereas an essentially literal translator would ask, "How did they say it then?" (with the words translated into English, of course).

A good illustration of this difference between essentially literal and dynamic-equivalence translations is actually given in the introduction to the NLT. They mention 1 Kings 2:10, which says, in the King James Version: "So David slept with his fathers and was buried in the city of David" (1 Kgs 2:10 KJV; similarly ESV). However, the NLT translates

---

term "essentially literal." See Leland Ryken, *The Word of God in English* (Wheaton: Crossway, 2002), 10, 19; and Wayne Grudem, Leland Ryken, C. John Collins, Vern S. Poythress, and Bruce Winter, *Translating Truth: The Case for Essentially Literal Bible Translation* (Wheaton: Crossway, 2005), 10, 13.

[5] I discuss Eugene Nida's translation theory on pp. 50–55 of *Translating Truth*.

[6] "Introduction," *New Living Translation* (Wheaton: Tyndale House, 1996), xli.

[7] Ibid.

this verse: "Then David died and was buried in the city of David" (1 Kgs 2:10 NLT).

The NLT translators see this as an advantage, for they say, "Only the New Living Translation clearly translates the real meaning of the Hebrew idiom 'slept with his fathers' into contemporary English."[8] The argument in favor of the NLT would be that today, when John Doe dies, English speakers don't say that John Doe "slept with his fathers." Today people would simply say that John Doe "died," so that is what the NLT has done. The translation is a "thought for thought" translation because the main thought or idea—the idea that David died and was buried—is expressed in a way that modern speakers would use to express the same idea today.

However, some details are missing in the NLT's thought-for-thought translation of 1 Kings 2:10. This dynamic equivalence translation does not include the idea of sleeping as a rich metaphor for death, a metaphor in which there is a veiled hint of someday awakening from that sleep to a new life. The expression "slept with his fathers" also includes a faint hint of a corporate relationship with David's ancestors who had previously died and are awaiting a future resurrection. But that is also missing from the dynamic equivalence translation, "then David died."

Yes, the NLT translated the main idea into contemporary English, but isn't it more accurate to translate all of the words of the Hebrew original, including the verb *shakab* (which means "to lie down, rest, sleep"), the word *'im* (which means "with"), and the word *'ab* (which means "father," or in the plural, "fathers"), since these words are in the Hebrew text as well? When these words are translated, not just the main idea but also more details of the meaning of the Hebrew original are brought over into English.[9]

Will modern readers understand the literal translation, "David slept with his fathers"? Yes, certainly. Even modern readers who have never heard this idiom before will understand it because the rest of the sentence says that David was buried: "Then David slept with his fathers and was buried in the city of David" (1 Kgs 2:10). The larger context begins in

---

[8] Ibid., xlii.

[9] This ability to convey more details of meaning is frequently evident when the ESV literally translates vivid, concrete expressions in striking metaphors, such as "bones" in Ps 35:10 or "breath" in Ps 78:33. These terms are changed to vague abstractions, such as "whole being" in Ps 35:10 or "futility" in Ps 78:33, in other versions. (I draw these examples from Kevin DeYoung, *Why Our Church Switched to the ESV* [Wheaton: Crossway, 2011], 21–22. But DeYoung acknowledges [p. 21, n. 4] that he drew many of his ideas from Ryken, *The Word of God in English*, from which I have also derived much benefit.)

verse 1, "When David's time to die drew near" (1 Kgs 2:1). Modern readers may ponder the expression for a moment, but they will understand it, and they will then have access to much greater richness of meaning that was there in the original text.[10] "Slept with his fathers" is not how we would say it today, but it is how they said it then, and we should translate it that way and convey the full richness of meaning of all the Bible's words.

The NIV Is a "Mixed" Version

The New International Version (NIV) was first published in 1978. I have put it on the chart midway between essentially literal and dynamic equivalence because it has elements of both. At times it is highly literal, but then at other times it tends toward the direction of dynamic paraphrase for the sake of better readability and easier understandability. The 2011 edition of the NIV contains this statement of its goal in the preface: "To articulate God's unchanging Word *in the way the original authors might have said it* had they been speaking in English to the global English-speaking audience *today*."[11]

What Is the Goal of Translation?

The goal of translation is not understanding how the authors might say something *today* but understanding how they actually said it *back then*. I respectfully disagree with the philosophy of translation as expressed in the NIV's preface. As a Bible translator, my goal should not be to try to imagine how Moses or Isaiah or Paul might say something if they were here today. I want to listen in on how exactly they said it *back then*. It seems to me that the NIV's philosophy here leans too far in the direction of a dynamic equivalence translation.[12]

Another way of illustrating the difference is to imagine that we had both a time machine and a language translation machine. Should our goal as translators be to use the time machine to bring David to New York City in 2011, give him the language translation machine so that he could understand and speak English, and then ask him to rewrite Psalm 23, but speaking as people would speak in New York City in 2011? Should we

---

[10] Someone might object that in today's culture "slept with his fathers" might suggest a homosexual relationship. But no reasonable reader will settle on that meaning, because David's forefathers had been dead for decades, and the immediate context talks about David dying and being buried. The highly unlikely possibility of a foolish interpretation by a careless reader should not deter translators from making the most accurate translation possible.

[11] NIV preface, v, italics added.

[12] See Ryken, *The Word of God in English*, 93–99, for a discussion of what he calls a translator's "fallacy": the idea that the important question is how *we* would say something today.

tell him, "David, just rewrite your psalm and use twentieth-first century expressions"?

No, *as a translator of Psalm 23*, I would want to use the time machine to *travel back* to ancient Israel around 1000 BC when David was writing Psalm 23. I would want to use my language translation machine to translate David's words into English and put them in ordinary English word order. It would sound something like this:

> The Lord is my shepherd; I shall not want. [2] He makes me lie down in green pastures. He leads me beside still waters. [3] He restores my soul. He leads me in paths of righteousness for his name's sake. (Ps 23:1–3 ESV)

The use of imagery concerning shepherds and sheep and pastures was common in David's time but is not as familiar today. However, I have to translate it this way because I want to know how David said something *back then*, not how I imagine he might have said something if he lived here today. The job of imagining how David would write Psalm 23 today is the job of a pastor or Bible teacher, not the job of a translator.

The Advantages of the ESV: Discussion of Specific Passages

My assigned task in the rest of this essay is to point out the advantages of the ESV in contrast with the HCSB, the NIV, and the NLT. I want to emphasize that all of these versions can be read with much spiritual benefit, and that we should be thankful to God that there are so many good translations available in English. However, the translations have differences, and as I consider the given passages, at various points I will emphasize the following six advantages of the ESV:

1. It preserves more literal accuracy in details.
2. It preserves the best of the best in the KJV tradition.
3. It has better literary excellence.
4. It preserves more of the interpretative options that were available to original readers.
5. It is not gender neutral but more accurately translates terms that refer to men and women.
6. It preserves more theological terms.

Translation Comparison

Passage 1. Exodus 2:5–6: More Literal Accuracy in Details

⁵ Now the daughter of Pharaoh came down to bathe at the river, while her young women walked beside the river. She saw the basket among the reeds and sent her servant woman, and she took it. ⁶ When she opened it, she saw the child, and <u>behold</u>, the baby was crying. She took pity on him and said, "This is one of the Hebrews' children." [I have underlined the word I will discuss, and I will follow this process throughout this essay.]

I find one of the primary advantages of the ESV to be more literal accuracy in the details of a translation. This is evident in the ESV's use of "behold" in Exodus 2:6, a word the HCSB, NIV, and NLT all omit. But it translates a word in the text, the Hebrew word *hinneh*.

In earlier translations (KJV, ASV, RSV), the word "behold" was found many times. It was the common translation used for the Hebrew word *hinneh* in the Old Testament and the Greek word *idou* in the New Testament. Both words simply mean something like "Pay attention—what follows is especially important or surprising!"

Early in our translation work on the ESV, our committee discussed what to do about "behold." We realized that in some cases there was an alternative such as "look!" or "listen!" and in a few cases that was what we used. But in hundreds of other cases, neither "look" nor "listen" seemed quite suitable (as in Exod 2:6 above). We also found that some modern translations had just decided to leave the Hebrew *hinneh* and the Greek *idou* untranslated in many places where "look" or "listen" did not seem to fit (the HCSB, NIV, and NLT simply fail to translate it here). But we believed that all the words of God are important, and we did not want to leave *hinneh* and *idou* untranslated.

After a lot of discussion, we concluded that there simply was no other English word that meant "pay attention to what follows because it is important or surprising." However, the word "behold" still carried that meaning in English.

We realized that people did not often use the word "behold" in conversation today, but we also recognized that almost everyone knew what it meant. It was in people's *passive* vocabulary rather than in their *active* vocabulary. So we decided to retain "behold" as the common translation we would use for *hinneh* in the Old Testament and for *idou* in the New Testament. We were striving for literal accuracy in the details, and we recognized that these words conveyed meaning for the original reader, meaning that we did not want today's readers to miss.

Therefore readers will find "behold" 1,102 times in the ESV. Often it seems to me to add dignity and strength to important verses in the Bible, such as the following:

> Behold, the virgin shall conceive and bear a son, and shall call his name Immanuel. (Isa 7:14)

> Behold, the Lamb of God, who takes away the sin of the world! (John 1:29)

> Behold! I tell you a mystery. We shall not all sleep, but we shall all be changed, in a moment, in the twinkling of an eye, at the last trumpet. (1 Cor 15:51–52)

> Behold, I stand at the door and knock. If anyone hears my voice and opens the door, I will come in to him and eat with him, and he with me. (Rev 3:20)

I have come to enjoy the "beholds" in the ESV. They make me pay attention to what follows and ask why the author emphasized this text. And they seem to me much stronger than the great variety of alternatives other translations use when they do translate *hinneh* or *idou* at all. For instance, in Revelation 3:20 (see above) other translations have a variety: "Listen!" (HCSB). "Here I am!" (NIV). "Look!" (NLT). It seems to me that "behold, I stand at the door and knock" is much stronger and more consistent.

In addition, now I actually notice "behold" from time to time in contemporary English, whether in a shop window with a sign that says "Behold: New low prices!" or an ad on TV that says something like, "Behold! The new Honda sedan!"

This example also shows one reason I do not put too much stock in statistical counts of word frequency such as the Collins Word Bank that was used by the NIV translators. No doubt it would show "behold" to be uncommon in modern English. But if we ask, "How did they say it back then?" we find the need to use *behold* frequently because no other single word in English today means "pay attention—what follows is important or surprising."

Passage 2. Psalm 1:1: Preserving "the Best of the Best" in the KJV Tradition

<u>Blessed</u> is the <u>man</u> who
<u>walks not</u> in the counsel of the wicked,
nor <u>stands</u> in the <u>way</u> of sinners,
nor <u>sits</u> in the seat of scoffers.

In this verse the ESV has several advantages over other translations. It seems to me that "blessed" is a better translation of the Hebrew term *'ashrē* than the HCSB's "happy" because "blessed" indicates a special kind of happiness in connection with God. I think that "blessed" is also better than the NLT's "Oh, the joys" for the same reason.

The word "man" in singular is a more accurate translation of the singular Hebrew word *'ish*, which regularly means "male human being" in the Old Testament (apart from certain idioms). Therefore "the man" is more accurate than "the one" (NIV 2011) or the plural "those" (NLT).

The ESV literally translates the common Hebrew words for "walks," "sits," and "stands" in Psalm 1:1. These metaphors accurately reflect a *process* of slowing down and then staying in the place of wicked people. This is more vivid and precise than the HCSB's "follow the advice of" and "take the path of" and "join." It is also more literal and precise than "follow the advice of" and "join" in the NLT. One might object that "stands in the way of sinners" might be misunderstood to mean "blocks their way," but that is unlikely from the context of not following evil paths.

Someone may object that the ESV's "walks not" is unnatural English and sounds strange. Why not say with the NIV, "does not walk"? The answer is that this is poetry. Poetry often inverts word order for rhythm or better flow or for emphasis. Here is where the ESV really shines, when we examine the oral sound of the translation. The ESV as a whole has better rhythm, beauty, smoothness of word flow, and ease of memorization.[13]

---

[13] See Ryken, *The Word of God in English*, 251–53, for a discussion of how many of the poetic elements of Ps 1:1 are lost in many modern translations.

When English is read aloud, what gives a piece of literature beauty and ease of readability is a regular alternation of stressed and unstressed syllables. With this in mind, compare the number and placement of stressed syllables in the second, third, and fourth lines of Psalm 1:

ESV   Psalm 1:1 Blessed is the man who

        walks not in the **coun**sel of the **wick**ed,   4 stressed
        nor stands in the **way** of **sin**ners,   4
        nor sits in the **seat** of **scof**fers;   4

HCSB   Psalm 1:1 How happy is the man who

        does not follow the ad**vice** of the **wick**ed   5
        or **take** the **path** of **sin**ners   3
        or **join** a **group** of **mock**ers!   3

NIV   Psalm 1:1 Blessed is the one who

        does not walk in **step** with the **wick**ed   5
        or **stand** in the **way** that **sinners take**   4
        or **sit** in the **com**pany of **mock**ers,   3

NLT   Psalm 1:1 Oh, the joys of those who

        do not follow the ad**vice** of the **wick**ed,   5
        or **stand** a**round** with **sin**ners,   3
        or **join in** with **mock**ers.   3

The ESV has a beautiful rhythm and flow of words. The second, third, and fourth lines each start with two stressed syllables, then alternate between unstressed and stressed syllables in a regular pattern for the rest of the line. It sounds almost musical in its beauty. The other translations do not do this. The HCSB begins the second line with a staccato rhythm of three stressed syllables in a row ("**does not fol**low"). The NIV does the same ("**does not walk**"), and so does the NLT ("**do not fol**low").[14]

At this point the perceptive reader may be wondering, how did the ESV translation committee do such a fantastic job with Psalm 1:1? The answer is, we did not. We did not touch it. We inherited it almost unchanged from the King James Version:

---

[14] An excellent discussion of the importance of rhythm in Bible translation is found in Ryken, *The Word of God in English*, 257–68. Ryken contrasts the attention to rhythm in the ESV with the apparent absence of care for rhythm in several modern translations.

1611 KJV Blessed is the man that walketh not in the counsel of the ungodly, nor standeth in the way of sinners, nor sitteth in the seat of the scornful.

1901 ASV Blessed is the man that walketh not in the counsel of the wicked, Nor standeth in the way of sinners, Nor sitteth in the seat of scoffers:

1952 RSV Blessed is the man who walks not in the counsel of the wicked, nor stands in the way of sinners, nor sits in the seat of scoffers;

2001 ESV Blessed is the man who walks not in the counsel of the wicked, nor stands in the way of sinners, nor sits in the seat of scoffers;

The KJV translators in 1611 could easily have said, "Blessed is the man that **doth not walk** in the counsel of the ungodly." That would have been ordinary word order for them. But the staccato rhythm sounded all wrong, so they put "walketh not."

In 1901 the ASV hardly touched the KJV. They only changed the word "ungodly" to the word "wicked." And so by 1901, the work of the ESV translators was nearly done, though none of us had yet been born. When the RSV came along in 1952, it just changed "walketh" to "walks" and "standeth" to "stand" and "sitteth" to "sits." They retained the best of the best in the great KJV tradition, and its poetic beauty was preserved.

Then when we came to Psalm 1:1 as we produced the ESV, we realized that the verse was already perfect. It was accurate and the English was beautiful. All we had to do was not to touch it. The ESV also preserves the "best of the best" in the great KJV tradition. Many people have asked whether any Bible translation will ever take the place of the King James Version as the accepted "standard" for the English-speaking world. My suggestion is this: If you are looking for a successor to the King James Version, consider the ESV Bible. It is a direct descendant of the King James Version (see fig. 2).

The other three translations represented in this forum (HCSB, NIV, NLT) are entirely new translations made by modern scholars and based on the original Hebrew and Greek texts.[15] This was a gigantic task, and I

---

[15] Though the NLT has as its predecessor The Living Bible [the editors, AK & DC].

admire the skill with which their committees have carried it out. But the ESV did not start from scratch to make an entirely new translation. It was a revision of a previous excellent translation, the Revised Standard Version, which was itself a descendant of the King James Bible tradition.

Even the King James Bible itself was not an entirely new translation but was based on the best readings from at least five earlier English translations. In fact, the KJV translators said in the original preface, "Truly (good Christian reader) we never thought from the beginning that we should need to make a new translation nor to make of a bad one, a good one . . . but to make a good one better, or out of many good ones one principal good one."[16]

I discovered how close the RSV (of 1952) was to the KJV when, as a college sophomore in 1967, I switched from the KJV to the RSV as my personal Bible. I had already memorized many passages in the KJV, including the 108 passages in The Navigators' "Topical Memory System." But the transition to the RSV was easy, as "thee" and "thou" readily changed to "you," and "wouldst" and "couldst" changed to "would" and "could." So much of the beautiful wording and sentence structure of the KJV was retained, and I quickly felt "at home" in the RSV. Then I used the RSV as my personal Bible from 1967 until September 2001, when the ESV came out. Once again the transition from the RSV to the ESV was easy. The ESV preserves the "best of the best" in the great King James tradition.

Passage 3. Ezekiel 18:5–9,21–24: Precise Translation of Gender Language

I will not quote this long passage here, but I think the ESV is correct to begin the section with "If a <u>man</u> is righteous." The Hebrew word *'ish* ordinarily in the Old Testament means "man" and not just "person." The HCSB, NIV, and NLT all correctly translate this as "man" in Ezekiel 18:5.

Then I think the ESV correctly switches to a non-male-oriented word in verse 21, when it says, "But if a <u>wicked person</u> turns away from all his sins that he has committed." This is because the Hebrew text has no word here meaning "man" but just an adjective, "a wicked one" or a "wicked person." The NLT incorrectly makes this plural, diminishing the emphasis on individual responsibility in the Bible: "But if <u>wicked people</u> turn away

---

[16] Eroll Rhodes and Liana Lupas, eds., *The Translators to the Reader: The Original Preface of the King James Version of 1611 Revisited* (New York: American Bible Society, 1997), 54.

from all their sins . . ." (I will discuss the translation of gender language in more detail at Luke 17:3 and Rev 3:20 below.)

Passage 4. Matthew 5:1–3: Literary Excellence and Not Capitalizing "He"

> [1] Seeing the crowds, he went up on the mountain, and when he sat down, his disciples came to him. [2] And he opened his mouth and taught them, saying: [3] "Blessed are the poor in spirit, for theirs is the kingdom of heaven."

The literary excellence of the ESV is seen in verse 3. The traditional wording, "Blessed are the poor in spirit, for theirs is the kingdom of heaven," goes directly back to the KJV. It is beautiful and accurate, and neither the ASV (1901) nor the RSV (1952) nor the ESV (2001) saw any reason to tamper with it. Its sound is both evocative and memorable, and it readily connects with several other Old Testament and New Testament statements that began with "blessed are" or "blessed is" (such as, Pss 1:1; 2:12; 32:1; 40:4; 41:1; 65:4; 84:4,5; 112:1; 119:1,2; 128:1; 144:15; Prov 3:13; 8:32; 28:14; John 20:29; Rom 4:7; Jas 1:12; Rev 1:3; 14:13; 19:9; 22:14). The NIV similarly sticks with the tradition here, but the renderings "The poor in spirit are blessed" (HCSB) and "God blesses those who are poor and realize their need for him" (NLT) lose something of the richness and beauty of this verse.

"Seeing the crowds" in the ESV is a more literal rendering of the Greek participial phrase, and it opens the possibility that it was not just "when" he saw the crowds but because he saw the crowds that he went up on the mountain to teach. In verse 2, "he opened his mouth" again is a literal translation of the Greek text, which is preserved in the ESV.

The ESV does not capitalize pronouns referring to God, but Matthew 5:1–3 is one of many examples where the HCSB capitalizes "He" and other pronouns referring to Jesus or to God or the Holy Spirit: "When He saw the crowds, He went up on the mountain, and after He sat down, His disciples came to Him" (Matt 5:1 HCSB).

Such capitalization was not done in the King James Version or the RSV, ESV, NIV, or NLT. The question of capitalizing pronouns that refer to God is simply a matter of stylistic preference in English. Nothing in the original Hebrew or Greek texts represents such a practice, for those texts did not make any distinction between capital letters and lowercase letters—all the letters were the same.

Some readers may feel that it helps them know when a pronoun refers to God rather than somebody else in the context, but there are actually not many cases where the context does not immediately make it clear. For example, no reader doubts that Matthew 5:1 is talking about Jesus. Other readers may feel that it attaches a level of reverence to these pronouns, but it may be said in response that the original authors did not do this, and they probably felt that the content of the Bible itself honored God appropriately.

Another reason against capitalizing these pronouns is that there are so many thousands of pronouns that refer to God in the Bible that this practice makes for a cluttered-looking text (see the HCSB of Matt 5:1 above, for example). It does not seem to me that meaning is affected in any significant way, whichever decision is made. On this question the ESV has stuck with the practice of the primary translations in the great KJV tradition.

Passage 5. Mark 1:40–42: Leprosy or a Skin Disease?

> [40] And a <u>leper</u> came to him, imploring him, and kneeling said to him, "If you will, you can make me clean." [41] <u>Moved with pity</u>, he stretched out his hand and touched him and said to him, "I will; be clean." [42] And immediately the <u>leprosy</u> left him, and he was made clean.

The difference between "moved with pity" (ESV) and "was indignant" (NIV) is based on a close judgment call between two different sets of Greek manuscripts, but it seems to me that the Greek manuscript evidence supporting "moved with pity" is more diverse and substantial than that supporting "was indignant."

While some might argue that the words "leper" and "leprosy" found in the ESV represent too narrow a range of skin diseases, on the other hand, the translation "a serious skin disease" (HCSB) is so broad and vague as to be unhelpful to the reader. There is much to be said for the ESV's decision to keep the term "leprosy" (as the NIV did and the NLT).[17]

---

[17] The ESV has a note at Mark 1:40: "*Leprosy* was a term for several skin diseases; see Leviticus 13."

In verse 45, the ESV's "people were coming to him" seems preferable as a rendering of the imperfect tense of the Greek verb, indicating continual but uncompleted action over a period time.

Passage 6. Endings to Mark's Gospel

I think the ESV and the NIV have made the best decision on a difficult question: Was the section we now call Mark 16:9–20 part of what Mark originally wrote in his Gospel? New Testament scholars on all sides of this question will admit that a decision is not easy because there is evidence on both sides.

Many ancient Greek manuscripts include these verses. But a significant number of early and reliable manuscripts of Mark's Gospel do not include them, and a number of other early copies of Mark either include special marks indicating that the verses are doubtful or else say the verses are not found in the copies in Mark they are using. In addition, the vocabulary, grammar, and style of these verses seem significantly different from the Gospel of Mark, particularly in Greek, but even to some extent in English.

Therefore the ESV translation committee decided to enclose these verses in double brackets and to precede them with a note that says, "[Some of the earliest manuscripts do not include 16:9–20.]". This seems to me to be a fair decision that does not exclude these verses but also shows that there is considerable question about them.

It should be noted that no significant point of doctrine is affected by either including or excluding these verses. Everything taught in them can be deduced from other places in the New Testament as well, and the verses do not contradict anything taught elsewhere in the New Testament.

Passage 7. Luke 17:3: The Translation of Gender Language

Before I discuss the translation of "brother" as "brother and sister" in Luke 17:3, I will include some general comments about translating gender language. My point will be that another advantage of the ESV (and the HCSB as well) is that the ESV accurately translates words with masculine meaning in Greek and Hebrew into words with masculine meaning in English.

What Is the Heart of the Issue in Translating Gender Language?

In the discussion over the translation of gender language in the Bible today, the question is not whether a translation has *more* or *fewer* male-specific words, nor is the question whether we *want* more or fewer male-specific words in the Bible. What we *want* should have nothing to do with a translation!

The proper question, rather, is this: When the original Greek or Hebrew word *meant* a male person, do we faithfully show that meaning in English?

Some Changes in Gender Language Are Appropriate

Some appropriate changes to gender language should be made when older versions are updated. If there is no male meaning in the original Greek or Hebrew, then we should not use a male-oriented term in English to translate it. Here is one example of a good change that was made in Matthew 16:24 from the 1971 RSV to the 2001 ESV:

RSV   Then Jesus told his disciples, "If any <u>man</u> [Gk. *tis*, "anyone"] would come after me, let him deny himself and take up his cross and follow me."

ESV   Then Jesus told his disciples, "If <u>anyone</u> would come after me, let him deny himself and take up his cross and follow me."

It was right for the ESV to change "any man" to "anyone" because the Greek word *tis* did not mean "any man" and did not have a masculine meaning but simply meant "anyone." This is an example where a word had a *grammatically* masculine gender but not a masculine *meaning* in Greek.

But the NLT and 2011 NIV Have Gone Too Far

Recent gender-neutral Bibles, however, have gone too far with this process and have removed thousands of examples of the words "man," "father," "son," "brother," and "he/him/his" in places where the original Hebrew or Greek meant a male human being or meant a single individual person. They have replaced these words with gender-neutral terms the original Greek or Hebrew simply did not mean, as shown on the following chart:

Figure 4: Replacements of Male-Specific Words
with "Gender-Neutral" Terms in the 2011 NIV

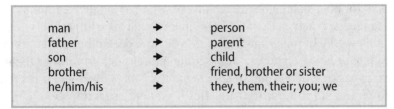

man	→	person
father	→	parent
son	→	child
brother	→	friend, brother or sister
he/him/his	→	they, them, their; you; we

These substantial changes in gender language are in some ways more significant than they were with the TNIV, when readers could still buy the old 1984 NIV if they did not agree with the TNIV. But now there is no choice of NIVs because the 1984 edition has been discontinued, and the 2011 NIV is the only one available.

I should also note that the HCSB and the ESV generally agree on the translation of gender language, so I will not generally include the HCSB in my discussion in this section.

Luke 17:3: Improperly Adding "and Sister" to the NIV
One example of the gender-neutral changes that I object to in the NIV is found in Luke 17:3:

ESV   If your <u>brother</u> [Gk. *adelphos*] sins, rebuke him, and if he repents, forgive him,

The Greek here is not difficult or controversial, and the translations of the ESV, the HCSB, and the 1984 NIV were exactly the same in every word. But in the 2011 NIV, the verse has been changed to say, "If your brother <u>or sister</u> sins against you, rebuke <u>them</u>; and if <u>they</u> repent, forgive <u>them</u>." The problem with the translation "brother or sister" is that the Greek word *adelphos* in singular means "brother." It does not mean "sister," and it does not mean "brother or sister." A different Greek word means "sister," the word *adelphē*; and it does not occur in this verse. It was not part of what Jesus said.

Now at this point someone with some knowledge of Greek might object, saying, "But the *masculine plural* form *adelphoi* often means 'brothers and sisters.'" And I agree that that is correct. But that does not affect the meaning of the *singular* word *adelphos*, and in this verse the word is singular.

The *plural* form can mean "brothers and sisters" because of the way singulars and plurals function in many languages that have grammatical genders for nouns and adjectives. Anyone who has studied a common foreign language (such as French, German, or Spanish) will probably realize how this works in many languages. If you are speaking about a group of *male human beings*, you use a masculine plural noun to refer to them. If you are speaking of a group of *female human beings*, then you use a feminine plural noun to refer to them. But if you are speaking about a *mixed group* of both male and female people, then you use the *masculine plural form* of the noun. This is just the way plurals work when you have to make a choice. And it happens that way in Greek, too, so that the *plural* form *adelphoi* often will mean "brothers and sisters."

However, you never use a masculine *singular* noun to mean a "male or a female person." Never in the ancient Greek world would you see a woman walking down the road and say, "There goes an *adelphos*" (using the masculine singular form of the word). That is the form Jesus uses in Luke 17:3, and it does not mean "brother or sister."

In fact, there is an easy way to say "brother or sister" in Greek. There is an example of it in James 2:15, "If a *brother or sister* is poorly clothed." The Greek phrase is *adelphos ē adelphē* ("brother or sister"). But Jesus did not say that in Luke 17:3.

Another objection might be that the Bauer-Danker-Arndt-Gingrich *Greek-English Lexicon of the New Testament* (BDAG) defines *adelphos* to mean not only "brother" but also in meaning (2), "fellow member, member, associate."[18] Does not this give justification for translating it "brother or sister" or "another believer" (as in the NLT)?

My response is to say that the person who makes this objection is not reading the Bauer *Lexicon* carefully enough because that second meaning is described as a "figurative extension of meaning 1" (which is "brother"). Therefore, for the original readers, the masculine singular sense of "brother" was always present even with this additional figurative meaning, "member." At any rate, the NIV did not translate this word as "fellow member" or anything like that. They translated it more specifically as "brother or sister," which is equivalent to something like "male or female fellow member," which is something *adelphos* never means.

---

[18] Walter Bauer, *A Greek-English Lexicon of the New Testament and Other Early Christian Literature*, 3rd ed, rev. and ed. F. W. Danker, W. F. Arndt, and F. W. Gingrich (Chicago: University of Chicago Press, 2000), 18. BDAG is the abbreviation.

Anybody can also do a word study to demonstrate this. The singular Greek term *adelphos* appears 428 times in the Greek New Testament together with the Greek translation of the Old Testament (the Septuagint), and 428 out of 428 times it refers to a male human being, a "brother." If *adelphos* can mean "brother or sister," then I wonder if someone would please show me one place in the Bible where this *singular* form is used to speak of a female person. I do not think it exists.

If you are doing a word study on a particular word in the Bible, and 428 times out of 428 examples it has the same meaning, I think you are safe in saying that it takes this meaning 100 percent of the time. The singular word *adelphos* simply means "brother." It does not mean "brother or sister."

Therefore, Jesus did not say "brother or sister" in Luke 17:3. But the NIV says "brother or sister." It seems to me they are adding words to the Bible that Jesus did not say. And Jesus did not say "another believer" (NLT). He said "brother," and we should not change what he said.

Application Is Different from Translation

At this point someone might object, "But the verse also certainly *applies* to a sister who sins!" Of course it does. The Bible has many gender-specific examples that *apply* to both genders. The parable of the prodigal son (Luke 15:11–32), for example, also *applies* to prodigal daughters. But we don't translate it as the parable of the prodigal "son or daughter" because the words do not mean prodigal "son or daughter." Readers understand that the parable also *applies* to prodigal daughters. They understand that easily from an accurate translation that simply speaks of the prodigal "son."[19] *Translation* is different from application.

The parable of the persistent "widow" (Luke 18:1–8) also *applies* to teaching men to be persistent in prayer, but we don't translate it by saying, "And there was a widow or widower in that city." People can read a story about a person of one gender and easily make the application to someone of the other gender. People get it.

Here is another example, this one from the Ten Commandments: "You shall not covet your neighbor's wife" (Exod 20:17). I am thankful the 2011 NIV did not change this verse, but on the same principle they used to change "brother" to "brother or sister," should they not also change this commandment to say, "You shall not covet your neighbor's wife or

---

[19] The word "prodigal" is not actually found in the text of Luke 15:11–32 but is used as a common summary of the story, which just refers to the "younger son."

husband"? After all, maybe somebody will read "You shall not covet your neighbor's wife" and think, *Well, I guess it's OK then to covet my neighbor's husband.* Will that happen?

No, of course not. Bible readers are not that foolish. Readers understand that when the Bible uses a specific female example to teach a general truth, it naturally *applies* to men as well. And when it uses a specific male example to teach a general truth, it naturally *applies* to women as well. That is not difficult for readers to understand.

Are We Willing to Let the Bible Use Specific Male Examples to Teach a General Truth?

Here is the heart of the dispute over gender language in the Bible: The Bible uses both male and female individual examples to teach a general truth, but it has many more male-specific examples than female ones, examples where the author holds up one male individual to teach a general truth. Should we just go ahead and change all of these male-specific examples to be gender inclusive when we translate the words of Scripture? If Jesus said "brother," should we just go ahead and change it to "brother or sister" or "believer"? No, we should not. Translators should not change Jesus' words and tamper with what he said.

This same procedure affects thousands of verses in the NLT and 2011 NIV.[20] "Brother" wrongly becomes "brother or sister" or some other gender-neutral expression 63 times in the 2011 NIV. Then there are many other verses where "man" is incorrectly changed to "person," and "father" is changed to "parent," and "son" is changed to "child." Here are two more examples: 1 Samuel 18:2 speaks of David not returning to his "father's house," but in the new NIV this is changed to "family," even though the Hebrew words for "father" (*'ab*) and house (*bayit*) are in the verse (it is missing from the NLT). Or, in Nahum 3:13 the prophet Nahum prophecies judgment on Nineveh by saying, "Your troops are women." But apparently it was thought unacceptable to speak in this negative way about women serving as soldiers, so the new NIV has changed this to "Your troops—they are all weaklings," even though the ordinary Hebrew word for "women" (*nashîm*) is in the text. There are many other such changes.

---

[20] Detailed information about such changes in the 2011 NIV can be found at www.cbmw.org. A study published there by the Council on Biblical Manhood and Womanhood claims that the 2011 NIV corrected 933 of the problematic translations found in the 2005 TNIV but that the 2011 NIV still has 2,766 inappropriate translations of gender language that do not accurately render the meaning of the original Hebrew or Greek text.

One final problem with the gender-neutral tendencies of the 2011 NIV has to do with a diminishing of the Bible's emphasis on individual, personal relationship to God through changing singulars ("he, him") to plurals ("they, them"). I will discuss this below, in connection with Revelation 3:20.[21]

Passage 8. John 1:3–4,18: "In Him Was Life"

[3] All things were made through him, and without him was not any thing made that was made. [4] In him was life, and the life was the light of men. . . .[18] No one has ever seen God; the only God, who is at the Father's side, he has made him known.

In verse 4, the translation "In him was life" (ESV) is literal and accurate while the NLT's translation, "The Word gave life to everything that was created," is an extensive interpretation that has been added to the text while regrettably excluding the more profound truth of the verse—that Christ had in himself the eternal, uncreated life of God.

The ESV's translation "of men" in verse 4 is a direct and literal translation of the Greek text (plural genitive of *anthrōpos*). It seems to me that the ESV here is more accurate than "everyone" (NLT) or "all mankind" (NIV), both of which include the idea of "all," which is not in John's Greek text. The NIV and NLT expand the meaning to say explicitly that Jesus enlightens *all people*, not just believers (this idea is in v. 9, but not in v. 4).

In verse 18, the difference between calling the Son of God "the only God" (ESV) and "the One and Only Son" (HCSB) is based on a difference in Greek manuscripts, but more recently discovered early papyrus manuscripts favor the remarkable reading "the only God," adopted by the ESV. The NLT's reading "the unique One, who is himself God" is based on the same manuscripts as the ESV but expresses a more expanded explanation of the meaning. The NIV's translation "the one and only Son, who is himself God" is an expanded paraphrase that seems to want to translate both of the differing manuscript traditions (one reading "Son" and one reading "God") rather than just one or the other. All these translations, except the HCSB, agree that the person being talked about is God the Son, the second

---

[21] Another significant analysis of the gender language of the 2011 NIV is found in Vern Poythress, "Gender Neutral Issues in the New International Version of 2011," *Westminster Theological Journal* 73 (2011): 79–96.

Person of the Trinity, and that the verse calls him "God" (the HCSB has this in the footnote).

Passage 9. John 2:25–3:1: Preserving an Evident Connection When the Same Greek Word Is Used

[Jesus] . . . [25] needed no one to bear witness about man, for he himself knew what was in <u>man</u> [Gk. *anthrōpos*]. [3:1] Now there was a <u>man</u> [Gk. *anthrōpos*] of the Pharisees named Nicodemus, a ruler of the Jews.

The ESV rightly picks up the intentional connection between the use of "man" (Greek *anthrōpos*) in John 2:25 and John's use of the same Greek word just three words later in the Greek text (John 3:1) to refer to Nicodemus, "a man of the Pharisees." (The HCSB also does this.)

John is telling us that Jesus knew what was in every human being (every "man"), and therefore certainly Jesus knows the heart of this "man" named Nicodemus who was coming to see him. But the NIV partially obscures the connection because they translate the first occurrence as "mankind" and the second occurrence as "man." The NLT is even more troubling because it completely fails to translate the entire Greek phrase that is rendered in English "for he himself knew what was in man." Perhaps they thought it was redundant, but the additional statement is there in Greek, and it should be included in English as well.

This is an example of how an essentially literal translation such as the ESV will often show consistency in translating key terms, especially within a single author. Of course this cannot be done 100 percent of the time because the range of meanings a Hebrew or Greek word will take in different contexts frequently does not exactly match the range of meanings a single English word would have. However, using the same word in English is often possible and beneficial because the author wanted the reader to see the connection in his frequent repetition.

Another clear example of this consistency is the use of the word "abide," which represents an important concept in 1 John. It translates the Greek word *menō*, which can mean "remain, stay, abide, persist, continue to live, await." The ESV decided to retain "abide" 23 out of 24 times where *menō* occurs in 1 John (the exception is 2:19, with "continued"). For example, "Whoever says he *abides* in him ought to walk in the same way in which he walked" (1 John 2:6). An English reader can easily trace the uses of "abide" through the entire epistle of 1 John.[22]

In the NIV *menō* is translated five different ways: "live," "remain," "continue," "reside," and "be." English readers cannot see the connection in John's frequent use of this important word. The NLT similarly uses five different words: "live," "remain," "continue," "stay," and "be." The ESV more consistently translates such key terms.

Wild Card:[23] Romans 3:25: Retaining Theological Terms Such as "Propitiation"

As an essentially literal translation, the ESV is willing to preserve more theological terms. One example is seen in Romans 3:25:

> [Christ Jesus] whom God put forward as a <u>propitiation</u> [Gk. *hilastērion*] by his blood, to be received by faith.

The Greek word *hilastērion* means "a sacrifice that bears God's wrath and turns it to favor." This was a common term in the ancient world where, even in pagan religions, people were familiar with the concept of sacrifices that would turn away the wrath of an offended deity. This was the term the New Testament writers used in several key verses to speak of Jesus' death as "propitiation" (Rom 3:25; Heb 2:17; and 1 John 2:2 and 4:10).

No other English word than "propitiation" means "a sacrifice that bears the wrath of a deity," but the word "propitiation" has that meaning. This presents us with two choices. We can simply abandon the word and thereby give up (or make much more difficult) the idea of teaching people this important concept, central to the doctrine of Christ's atoning death for us. Or we can retain the word and thereby retain this important concept in the New Testament. It is difficult to teach the concept to people who do not even have this word in their Bibles. For this reason the ESV and the HCSB have retained the word "propitiation" and thereby retained the ability of pastors to explain this doctrine that is at the heart of our understanding of salvation.

The NIV has given up the term "propitiation" and has substituted the more vague expression "sacrifice of atonement." The NLT has used the

---

[22] I found this example of *menō* in 1 John and several other examples in this essay from DeYoung, *Why Our Church Switched to the ESV*, 23.

[23] Each author was given the option of including a "wild-card" verse that the others were not told about.

phrase "sacrifice for sin." Both of them are devoid of the concept of bearing the wrath of God against sin, a concept being challenged by a number of writers today and one that is crucial for a correct understanding of salvation in the New Testament.

I do not have space to discuss other terms with theological implications here, but I would mention that in contrast to some of the other versions in this forum, the ESV retains "saints" as a term for Christians, shows a pattern of literally laying on of hands in passages such as Mark 6:2 and Acts 5:12 and retains "spirit" in verses like Acts 17:16 and 2 Corinthians 2:13. One advantage of the ESV is that it retains such theological terms.

Passage 10. 1 Corinthians 2:1–13

I do not object to the NIV's translation of 1 Corinthians 2:1, "And so it was with me, brothers and sisters." The NLT is similar, with "dear brothers and sisters." The meaning "brothers and sisters" is an acceptable sense of the plural Greek word *adelphoi* (as I explained above in the discussion of Luke 17:3). But it seems to me another acceptable solution is the one taken by the ESV using "brothers" in the text and adding a footnote that says, "Or *brothers and sisters.*" The HCSB has "brothers" in the text with a note similar to the ESV.

Passage 11. Galatians 5:2–6

It seems to me that the expression "faith working through love" (ESV, HCSB) is more literal and precise than "faith expressing itself through love" (NIV) or "faith expressing itself in love" (NLT). The Greek verb *energeō* simply means "work, be at work, be active, operate, be effective." Perhaps Paul means that faith is "expressing itself through love," but maybe his thought is not that faith is expressing itself at all but is remaining hidden and is simply energizing and empowering love. The ESV and the HCSB are less interpretative and leave open to the reader more of the interpretative options that were available to the original reader.

Passage 12. Colossians 2:11: Preserving Interpretative Options and Translating "Christ" Rather than "Messiah"

> In him also you were circumcised with a circumcision made without hands, by putting off the body of the flesh, by the circumcision of Christ.

Colossians 2:11 shows another benefit of an essentially literal translation, namely, preserving more of the interpretative options that were available to the original reader. In this verse the ESV simply translates the genitive phrase "by the <u>circumcision of Christ</u>." Does this mean "the spiritual circumcision that Christ performed on you" or "the spiritual circumcision that comes when you trust in Christ" or something else? The original readers had to ponder that question as they read what Paul wrote.

The NIV decides for the reader that one of the possible meanings is correct, and so it says, "You were circumcised by Christ" (Col 2:11 NIV). There was an explicit way to say that in Greek, but that is not what Paul said. The NLT goes even further with a detailed explanation: "Christ performed a spiritual circumcision—the cutting away of your sinful nature" (Col 2:11 NLT), all this to translate a brief Greek expression that literally says, "the circumcision of Christ." The NIV and NLT remove some interpretative options that were available to the original readers.

The HCSB uses the term "Messiah" in Colossians 2:11: "the circumcision of the Messiah," rather than using the word "Christ" to translate Greek *christos*. The HCSB promotional material indicates that the HCSB committee considers it an advantage to have translated the Greek word *christos* as "Messiah" rather than "Christ" in contexts where a Jewish background is particularly in view. And so the HCSB translates the same Greek word *christos* as "Messiah" 116 times in the New Testament but as "Christ" 405 times in the New Testament.

Is this helpful? It does highlight the Messianic background to the Greek word for "Christ," and one legitimate meaning of the word *christos* is "anointed one" (or therefore, "Messiah"). But the disadvantage of this translation is that readers do not evidentially see that "Messiah" and "Christ" are representing the same Greek word, where two different English names are used. And how do we know when a specifically "Jewish background" is in view, especially since, by the time the epistles were written, most of the churches had mixed backgrounds of both Jews and Gentiles that had come into the church and become Christians? So the translation seems inconsistent.

In addition, it seems that at some point in the early New Testament church, the name *christos* came to be used more as a name or title of Christ than simply meaning "anointed one." Therefore I think it better to follow the majority of English translations today and to translate the word *christos* consistently as "Christ," as the ESV has done.

Passage 13. 1 Thessalonians 1:3: Preserving Interpretative Options

Another example of preserving interpretative options is seen in 1 Thessalonians 1:3:[24]

> remembering before our God and Father your <u>work of faith</u> and <u>labor of love</u> and <u>steadfastness of hope</u> in our Lord Jesus Christ.

The Greek phrases in 1 Thessalonians 1:3 are simple genitive constructions that might have a variety of meanings. The range of meanings is similar to the possible meanings in our English phrases "work of faith," "labor of love," and "steadfastness of hope." Therefore the ESV and the HCSB, by retaining these phrases literally, preserve for modern readers the opportunity to think through the question, "Just what kind of 'work of faith' did Paul mean?" Just as the original readers would have wondered that, so modern readers have to ponder that question and think about the phrase in its context and in light of what else Paul has said about work and faith.

However, the NIV has taken away the options and decided that only one of them is the correct one: "your work produced by faith." So in this case the readers are not even aware that other options are available. They just think Paul is talking about work that resulted from the faith the Thessalonians had.

But then readers turn to the NLT, and they find that it says something completely different: "your faithful work." This is not work "produced by faith" but work done faithfully, reliably, dependably, obediently. This is also a possible meaning, but it too might not be the correct one. In any case, the readers of the NLT only have one interpretative option available to them as well.

And so it is with many genitive phrases and with dozens of other examples in the NIV and NLT. In the interest of making the translation immediately understandable to modern readers, the translators of the NIV and NLT have decided on one "correct" interpretation of expressions that have several possible legitimate interpretations in Greek.

I am not saying the ESV and HCSB never do this kind of thing. It certainly is a judgment call. Sometimes translators agree that only one of the

---

[24] I got the idea for mentioning 1 Thess 1:3 from DeYoung, *Why Our Church Switched to the ESV*, 12–13. Excellent discussions of the importance of preserving ambiguity that is in the original text are found in Ryken, *The Word of God in English*, 208–11.

options really has legitimate claim as a possible interpretation, and then that is what they will put in the text. But my point is that an essentially literal translation like the ESV has the advantage of doing this less often than other translations. Our translation committee consciously attempted to leave open the interpretative options that would have been available to the first readers whenever we thought legitimate alternatives could be justified from the Greek or Hebrew text.

Passage 14. 1 Timothy 2:12: Are Women Told Not to "Exercise Authority" or Not to "Assume Authority"?

I do not permit a woman to teach or to <u>exercise authority</u> over a man; rather, she is to remain quiet.

This is another verse that is translated accurately in the ESV, but by contrast it shows the gender-neutral tendencies of the 2011 NIV. To my mind this is the most objectionable verse of all because it is a key text that has been under much scrutiny for the last 30 years in the debate over whether women can be pastors and elders in churches. The NIV in 1 Timothy 2:12 has adopted a translation ("assume authority") that has never before been seen in any major English translation (except the discontinued TNIV).

I do not object to the 1984 NIV here, which had a meaning similar to the ESV: "I do not permit a woman to teach or to <u>have authority</u> over a man; she must be silent." But now the 2011 NIV has made a significant change: "I do not permit a woman to teach or to <u>assume authority</u> over a man; she must be quiet." What is the difference? Now any woman who becomes a pastor can just say, "I'm obeying this verse because I didn't 'assume authority' on my own—I waited until the church gave it to me."

I realize that the verse still says that Paul does not permit a woman to "teach" men, and that alone should prevent women from seeking the role of a teaching pastor. But I also recognize that egalitarian interpreters are quick to claim that Paul is only prohibiting one thing, "assuming authority in order to teach," and so they will soon claim that both verbs are only prohibiting teaching or having authority *that has been wrongly self-assumed,* not teaching or having authority that has been given by the church or the elders. I think these are incorrect interpretations, but my point is that the

2011 NIV has made it much more difficult to argue against them from the English text.

The NIV's translation committee claims "assume authority" is "a particularly nice English rendering because it leaves the question open."[25] They mean that "assume authority" could be understood in either a negative way (meaning "*wrongly assume authority* on one's own initiative") or a positive way (meaning "*begin to use authority* in a rightful way").

But I think the translation is simply wrong. Why? Because it allows people to give a negative sense to the Greek verb *authenteō*, which is not supported by the most relevant evidence and which no other modern English translation has ever done (except the discontinued TNIV).[26]

For nearly 20 years I have watched as evangelical feminists have tried one novel idea after another, always seeking to give a negative sense to this important verb in 1 Timothy 2:12 so they could argue that there was still a *rightful* use of authority Paul was not prohibiting. As I summarized the arguments in 2004, I noted that David Scholer claimed that *authenteō* implied "violence and inappropriate behavior." Craig Keener said it meant "a domineering use of authority." Rebecca Groothuis suggested it meant "take control by forceful aggression." Leland Wilshire said it meant "instigate violence." Richard and Catherine Kroeger proposed different meanings, such as "cultic action involving actual or representational murder," teaching that would "proclaim oneself the author of a man," or even "thrust oneself (in pagan sexual rituals)."[27]

The reason evangelical feminists sought to discover a negative sense for the word was evident: If Paul was only prohibiting women from somehow *misusing* authority, then the verse would not stop women from being pastors. Paul would be saying, "I do not permit a woman to *misuse* authority in order to teach a man," but that would imply that *rightful* use of authority as a pastor was just fine. If someone wanted to dismiss the verse's implications in this way, any negative meaning would do, and many were proposed.

Now the TNIV and the 2011 NIV have come up with yet another negative meaning, "I do not permit a woman to teach or to *assume authority* over a man; she must be quiet" (1 Tim 2:12). This meaning was also

---

[25] "Updating the New International Version of the Bible: Note from the Committee on Bible Translation" (booklet distributed by the Committee on Bible Translation at the Evangelical Theological Society meeting in Atlanta, GA, November 2010), 7. Available at www.niv-cbt.org.

[26] See also the negative rendering of *authenteō* in the KJV.

[27] See quotations in Wayne Grudem, *Evangelical Feminism and Biblical Truth* (Sisters, OR: Multnomah, 2004), 305–6.

proposed by Philip B. Payne in his book *Man and Woman, One in Christ.*[28] He claims the verse means "I am not permitting a woman to assume authority to teach a man."[29] He says, "The false teachers were teaching their own unauthorized doctrines with *self-assumed, not delegated, authority.* . . . This prohibition does not, however, restrict teaching by authorized women, such as Priscilla (2 Tim 4:19)."[30]

However, there are significant objections to the translation "assume authority":[31]

1. An exhaustive survey of 82 ancient examples of this verb by H. Scott Baldwin found that it overwhelmingly indicated a neutral or positive concept of ruling or reigning, not a negative idea.[32] Although Baldwin concludes that one possible meaning was "assume authority," he warns that he does not intend this to be understood in a negative sense: "Meaning 3a, 'to assume authority over,' is a positive term that appears to imply that one moves forward to fill the leadership role."[33] Therefore Baldwin's study cannot rightly be used in support of the NIV's rendering, which will frequently be taken in a *negative* sense of wrongly taking self-assumed authority.

2. A study by Andreas Köstenberger of 100 parallel examples of the same sentence structure in Greek (the structure "neither X nor Y") showed that in every example, both of the actions were viewed positively (as in "they neither sow nor harvest") or negatively (as in "neither break in nor steal"). But in 1 Timothy 2:12, the verb "teach" represents an activity that is viewed positively in Paul's writings, and therefore the verb "exercise authority" must also be an activity that is viewed positively.[34]

3. A massive study not only of the verb *authenteō* but also of several cognate terms by Al Wolters concludes, "There seems to be no basis for

[28] Philip B. Payne, *Man and Woman, One in Christ* (Grand Rapids: Zondervan, 2009), 361–97.

[29] Ibid., 395.

[30] Ibid., 396 (emphasis added).

[31] See Grudem, *Evangelical Feminism and Biblical Truth*, 304–18, for a fuller discussion of these objections.

[32] H. Scott Baldwin, "A Difficult Word: Authenteō in 1 Timothy 2:12," in *Women in the Church: A Fresh Analysis of 1 Timothy 2:9–15*, ed. Andreas Köstenberger, Thomas Schreiner, and H. Scott Baldwin (Grand Rapids: Baker, 1995), 65–80 and 269–305.

[33] Ibid., 75.

[34] Andreas J. Köstenberger, "A Complex Sentence Structure in 1 Timothy 2:12," in *Women in the Church*, 81–103. See also Köstenberger's response to inadequately-grounded criticisms by Philip B. Payne in *Journal for Biblical Manhood and Womanhood* (Fall 2008), 5 (available at http://www.cbmw.org/ images/jbmw_pdf/13_2/odds%20ends.pdf).

the claim that *authenteō* in 1 Timothy 2:12 has a pejorative connotation, as in 'usurp authority' or 'domineer.'"[35]

4. In a recent article, Al Wolters finds fresh new evidence for this verb from a previously misdated papyrus. He argues again that *authenteō* did not have a negative sense in examples close to the time of the New Testament and that the "ingressive" sense ("begin to exercise authority") is found only in the aorist tense, not in the present tense as in 1 Timothy 2:12.[36] This implies that both the "positive" sense and the "negative" sense of the NIV's "assume authority" are incorrect.

5. Another problem with all of these negative meanings is that they cannot adequately explain why Paul prohibits only women and not men from this activity. Why would he say, "I do not permit *a woman* to teach or to misuse authority"? Would it not also be wrong for *men* to misuse authority?

Why, then, does the 2011 NIV use the translation "assume authority"? The NIV's translation committee says that the benefit is that this "leaves the question open." But leaving a verse open to an incorrect interpretation is not a virtue.

I think the NIV committee failed to appreciate that evangelical feminists who want to become pastors are not going to take "assume authority" in a positive sense at all. They will uniformly take it to prohibit a wrongful "self-assumed authority" and then say they are not "assuming authority" on their own but just accepting it from the church. Consequently, 1 Timothy 2:12 in the NIV has become useless in the debate over women's roles in the church. In any church that adopts the 2011 NIV, no one will be able to answer their argument using this English Bible.

The Council on Biblical Manhood and Womanhood is surely correct to say:

> This verse alone in the 2011 NIV gives evangelical feminists the most important advance for their cause in the last thirty years. But the translation is simply incorrect, as many writers have demonstrated in extensive scholarly discussion elsewhere, and as all other modern English translations agree.[37]

---

[35] Al Wolters, "A Semantic Study of *authentēs* and Its Derivatives," *Journal of Greco-Roman Christianity and Judaism* 1 (2000): 170–71. (This journal is so far only available online; see http://divinity.mcmaster.ca/pages/ jgrchj/index.html.)

[36] Al Wolters, "An Early Parallel of *authentein* in 1 Timothy 2:12," *Journal of the Evangelical Theological Society* 54.4 (December 2011): 673–84. I am grateful to Al Wolters for providing me with a pre-publication copy of this article.

[37] Council on Biblical Manhood and Womanhood, *An Evaluation of Gender Language in the 2011*

Because of these changes in gender language, it is not surprising that in June 2011, the Southern Baptist Convention overwhelmingly passed a resolution calling the 2011 NIV "an inaccurate translation" and said, "We cannot commend the 2011 NIV to Southern Baptists or to the larger Christian community."[38]

Passage 15. Jude 5

The surprising translation "that <u>Jesus</u>, who saved a people out of the land of Egypt, afterward destroyed those who did not believe" (Jude 5 ESV) is also adopted by the NLT ("<u>Jesus</u> first rescued the nation of Israel from Egypt"). This is based on a judgment about different Greek manuscripts. The HCSB and NIV have the phrase "the Lord" instead of the word "Jesus."

I think the ESV and NLT have made the right decision in this case. The Greek manuscripts that have the reading "Jesus" are older, more reliable, and more diverse. In addition, this is a "more difficult" reading (that is, it is more likely to have been changed by scribes who puzzled about it), and it is the reading that best explains the other manuscripts (because scribes would easily switch "the Lord" for "Jesus," but it is hard to understand why they would switch in the other direction). Therefore, this reading meets the criteria usually used to decide such questions among Greek manuscripts. Theologically, it reminds us that the same Jesus who walked the earth during the period of the Gospels is also the eternal Son of God who was actively at work in the world during the time of the Old Testament.

Passage 16. Revelation 3:20: Loss of "He" and "Him" and Emphasis on Personal Relationship with God

"He" and "Him" in Revelation 3:20

> Behold, I stand at the door and knock. If anyone hears my voice and opens the door, I will come in to <u>him</u> and eat with <u>him</u>, and <u>he</u> with me.

This is a troubling example of the damage done to a translation when it is trying every way possible to avoid the unacceptable words "he" and "him."

Edition of the NIV Bible, 6 (found at www.cbmw.org). CBMW also objects to feminist bias in the translation of 1 Cor 14:33–34 (which now implies a limited local regulation) and Rom 16:7 (which now makes Junia unambiguously an apostle).

[38] See http://www.bpnews.net/bpnews.asp?id=35565.

The ESV has translated the verse accurately because the three words "him," "him," and "he" accurately represent the three occurrences of the masculine singular Greek pronoun *autos* ("he, him") in the Greek text.

But if you are trying to avoid "he" and "him" because they are thought to be objectionable today, then changes have to be made. So the NIV changes "him" to the awkward expression "that person," which sounds distant and impersonal, and simply draws attention to itself as a sort of gender-neutral, politically correct terminology. In addition, the NIV has to say, "and they with me," and the reader wonders if it is a personal relationship with Jesus anymore, or if it includes the whole group of all the people included in "if anyone hears my voice" in the earlier part of the sentence. The idea of personal relationship with Jesus is obscured. A similar loss of personal relationship through a change to plurals is seen in John 14:23, where the "anyone" will make readers think of a plural group that Jesus and the Father will come to.

Furthermore, part of the verse is left out of the NIV's translation of Revelation 3:20. In the Greek text Jesus clearly says, "I will come in to him." But the new NIV decides to leave out "to him" altogether.[39]

The NLT also wanted to avoid the words "him" and "he," so they changed it to "if you hear my voice." But the reader does not know if the "you" is singular or plural. Once again personal relationship with Jesus and the individual believer is obscured. And once again "to him" is completely omitted. The NLT's idea of sharing a meal "as friends" is a nice thought, but nothing in the Greek text speaks about friendship. This is just the NLT's attempt to recover some personal nuance to the verse even though the idea of Jesus eating with an individual person is no longer found.

A Broader Loss of Emphasis on an Individual's Relationship with God
Does this kind of change from "him" to "them" make any difference? Of course it does. The Bible's emphasis on an individual's personal relationship with God and personal responsibility to God is of great importance. But in the 2011 NIV, the singular words "he/him/his" in such verses were found to be objectionable because they were too "masculine" sounding. And so they were changed to plurals such as "they" or "them" or to "you" or something else more than 2,000 times. (This does not count the

---

[39] The Greek phrase is *pros autōn*.

times when the NIV was using "them" in a "singular" sense in specific contexts.)[40]

When a translation makes this many changes, the Bible's emphasis on the relationship between the individual person and God is significantly blunted. This is distorting one strand of the Bible's teaching—the strand that uses a large amount of individual male examples to teach a general truth. The 2011 NIV found that kind of teaching to be objectionable, and it has removed it more than 2,000 times from the Bible.

It is interesting and somewhat baffling, however, that the 2011 NIV still used "he" occasionally in sentences like this: "Blessed is the one who does not condemn <u>himself</u> by what <u>he</u> approves" (Rom 14:22). The NLT, on the other hand, used the plural "those"/"they" in Romans 14:22. Psalm 34:19, which was widely criticized in the TNIV because of the loss of the singular in a Messianic prophecy, has now been corrected in the 2011 NIV: "The righteous person may have many troubles, but the LORD delivers <u>him</u> from them all."

This is a change from the 2005 TNIV. That edition removed, as far as I know, every instance of "he" used in a generic sense in statements like this where a singular male example is used to teach a general truth. But now in the 2011 NIV they have used it occasionally but rarely. The apparent reason is that the Collins Bank of English, a database of more than 4.4 billion words, showed that this construction was still used about 8 percent of the time.[41]

This indicates to me the weakness of simply depending on the Collins Bank of English and their perception of frequency of English usage. Even if this construction only occurs 8 percent of the time in English, what if the use of such masculine singular pronouns in Greek and Hebrew occurs 100 percent of the time in this kind of construction in the Bible? Shouldn't we then translate it accurately 100 percent of the time in verses like John 14:23?[42]

A construction that occurs 8 percent of the time is still frequent in English. It means that people can still understand such an expression quite well, and it is the most accurate representation of the original statement in Greek in verses like John 14:23.

---

[40] See the detailed list of verses at www.cbmw.org.

[41] "Summary of Collins Corpus Report," available at www.NIV-cbt.org, 2.

[42] More detailed analysis and criticism of the use of the Collins Bank of English is found in Poythress, "Gender Neutral Issues in the New International Version of 2011," 89–95.

Some Respected Authorities Consider Singular
"They" Unacceptable in Formal English

In addition, a use of "they" in a singular sense is still considered by many experts and many ordinary readers to be unacceptable in written English today. For example, the 2010 edition of *The Chicago Manual of Style*, the most authoritative guide to English usage today, says: "Many people substitute the plural *they* and *their* for the singular *he* or *she*. Although *they* and *their* have become common in informal usage, neither is considered acceptable in formal writing, so unless you are given guidelines to the contrary, do not use them in a singular sense."[43] The latest edition (2009) of the *Associated Press Stylebook* says: "Use the pronoun *his* when an indefinite antecedent may be male or female: *A reporter tries to protect his sources.* (Not *his or her* sources . . .)."[44]

I mention these authorities to say that the NIV has clearly taken one side of a disputed matter in English today. It certainly was not a necessary matter of modern English usage that led the NIV translators to decide to use "they" in a "singular" sense when translating masculine singular pronouns in Hebrew or Greek in the Bible. And when the context makes readers think (as in John 14:23) that "they" should be understood in a plural sense, the translation wrongly loses the focus on the individual person that was there in the original Hebrew or Greek text.

Which Pronouns Can You Now Trust?

There is yet a more serious problem that comes when the NIV and NLT change many hundreds of examples of "he/him/his" to something like "they" or "you" (see Luke 16:13, for example, where "he" has become "you" in the NIV and NLT). The problem is not only the hundreds of verses that were changed but also the lack of confidence that readers now will have in every example of "they" and "you" in the NIV and NLT.

Pastors and Bible study leaders can no longer be confident that they can make a point based on the third-person plural pronouns ("they/them/their") or the second-person pronouns ("you/your/yours") in the NIV and NLT because these words might not accurately represent the actual meaning of the Greek or Hebrew text. This affects not just the hundreds of pronouns that were changed from singulars but *all* the second-person pronouns and all the third-person plural pronouns, a total of around 40,000 pronouns in each of these versions. Maybe the original was a plural ("them"), but then

---

[43] *Chicago Manual of Style*, 16th ed. (Chicago: University of Chicago Press, 2010), section 5.227, 303.
[44] *Associated Press Stylebook and Briefing on Media Law* (New York: Basic Books, 2009), 131.

again maybe "them" is a gender-neutral substitute for an underlying mascu-line singular pronoun ("he"). How can ordinary readers know? They can't unless they check the Greek or Hebrew text in every case, and who is going to do that? Do Bible readers really want to study or memorize or teach from a text where tens of thousands of pronouns are thrown into doubt?

Because the ESV and the HCSB followed a philosophy of accurately translating masculine singular pronouns in Hebrew and Greek with mas-culine singulars in English ("he/him/his"), these two translations are much more trustworthy in rendering the tens of thousands of pronouns that occur in the Bible.

Conclusion

Out of several good translations today, I prefer the ESV for the following reasons:

1. It preserves more literal accuracy in details.
2. It preserves the best of the best in the KJV tradition.
3. It has better literary excellence.
4. It preserves more of the interpretative options that were available to original readers.
5. It is not gender neutral but more accurately translates terms that refer to men and women.
6. It preserves more theological terms.

I believe the ESV has these advantages because it is an excellent example of an essentially literal translation. It takes seriously the responsi-bility to translate faithfully every word of God that he gave us in the Bible. "Man shall not live by bread alone, but by *every word* that comes from the mouth of God" (Matt 4:4).

CHAPTER 3

The New International Version (NIV)

Douglas J. Moo

History of the NIV

Howard Long was a businessman and a committed Christian. His work and travels brought him into contact with many unbelievers, and Howard had a passion to let them know about the good news of Jesus Christ. But he had a problem. In talking with people who had not been brought up in the church, Howard discovered that the King James Version of the Bible, the Bible that had nourished his faith, simply did not communicate with his business associates. Written in an English vernacular almost four centuries old, the KJV sounded almost like a foreign language to people living in the 1950s. Howard Long's frustration led him to propose to his own denomination, the Christian Reformed Church, that biblical scholars undertake a new translation of the Bible, one that would communicate God's Word clearly in modern English. After almost a decade of advocacy, discussion, and meetings, Long's vision finally took concrete shape in 1965. In that year a group of biblical scholars met and decided to undertake the task of creating a fresh translation of the Bible. These scholars called themselves the Committee on Bible Translation; and the Bible they finally produced was called the New International Version of the Bible.

Little did those initial translators know what would emerge from these small beginnings. The NIV has been the most widely used Bible in the English-speaking world for 30 years, with more than 400 million Bibles in print. Why has the NIV been so appreciated by so many readers? Because it has stuck tenaciously throughout the years to two virtues, refusing to sacrifice one to the other. The first virtue is accuracy. A Bible that does not accurately convey what the original Hebrew, Aramaic, and Greek intend to communicate would not be a Bible at all. Hundreds of the best evangelical scholars in the world have contributed to the NIV over the years, working hard to make sure it accurately communicates what God originally intended. The second virtue is readability. A translation must not only be accurate; it also must be clear and understandable. The KJV was, after all, an accurate translation. But its English is not *our* English, and so it does not communicate well. The NIV translators have worked hard to identify just the right contemporary English words that will communicate the meaning of the originals.

These twin virtues of accuracy and readability mean that translations of the Bible cannot remain static and unchanged. Again, take the KJV: it was eminently readable in its day—but it is no longer. The Committee on Bible Translation (CBT) recognized this problem of becoming outdated right from the start. And so the constitution of the CBT calls on the translators periodically to update the version in order to keep it fresh and accurate. Bible scholars keep discovering new information about the Bible and the world in which it was written. The NIV translators meet every year to monitor these developments. In addition, the English we speak and write keeps changing also. If the NIV is not to go the way of the KJV, it must keep up with changes in the language. Therefore the original NIV has been periodically updated. The NIV was first published as a whole Bible in 1978. It was updated with minor changes in 1984. Then, in 2005, a new revision was published, the Today's New International Version (TNIV). Finally, in 2011, the latest product of the work of the CBT was published. This significant update of the NIV incorporates the best from both the original NIV and the TNIV. We, the translators, pray that God will continue to use this fresh NIV to inform and convict unbelievers and to instruct and edify believers.

How Was the Updated NIV Produced?

I should say a few words about the process by which this fresh edition of the NIV was produced. From the earliest days the NIV was designed to be a Bible that would represent the entire evangelical world. The committee that produced the NIV is an independent group of scholars. Its members are chosen by the committee itself, and no denomination or publisher has any authority over the committee. Our work is sponsored by Biblica, a nonprofit organization focused on the translation and distribution of the Bible around the world, but they have no say in our translation decisions. Nor are we obligated to or pressured by a publisher, who might be concerned about producing a Bible that will sell well in a certain market. We are not controlled by any denomination or particular theological agenda. Scholars from virtually every evangelical denomination and from a wide spectrum of theological views have formed the NIV. The NIV translators, accordingly, are free of any agenda except that of translating God's Word faithfully and clearly into modern English. The CBT continues to reflect the diversity of evangelicalism. Our 15 members represent 12 different denominations. We have two women on the committee, and our members come from North America, the United Kingdom, and India. What unites the committee is a devotion to our common Lord and a deep respect for the words of Scripture our Lord has entrusted to us. The authority of God's Word is something on which we all agree. One other thing unites the committee: a deep respect for the excellent work the original translators did. We do not want to change their work quickly or without good reason. Accordingly, no change to the NIV text can be made without at least 70 percent of the members voting for it. As a result of this "conservative" voting procedure, about 95 percent of the original NIV is unchanged in the latest 2011 update.

What Approach to Translation Does the NIV Take?

A famous Italian proverb, roughly translated into English, claims "the translator is a traitor." There is some truth to this claim. Why? Because any time we translate words from one language into words of another language, we lose something. Languages differ in the way they use words and in the way they put words together to create meaning. And we simply cannot convey in one language all that might be being said in another language. Consider, for instance, alliteration: creating a certain impression by using a series of words that all begin with the same letter. The Letter to the Hebrews begins this way, with five words in its first verse all beginning with a "p" sound. Now look at English versions. Not one of them is successful in reproducing this alliteration. And the reason is not far to seek: we simply do not have five words in English that begin with the same letter and mean the same thing those five Greek words do. The point is obvious, is it not? In order to convey the *meaning* of the biblical words, we frequently have to change the *form* of those words. But where the form might be significant, we have lost something. The "translator is a traitor."

However, the situation is not as dire as this quotation might suggest. Yes, none of our translations can bring over *everything* from the original languages of the Bible. But translations, when they are well done, can bring over a lot of the meaning—enough of the sense of the original documents to give us clear indication of what God is telling us. All four of the translations at which we are looking in this book do a fine job of conveying the meaning of the original texts in English. A person can read any one of them and be sure they are hearing God's Word.

These four versions, however, do take different approaches to translation. They reflect slightly different values as far as what is really important in a translation. When we begin talking about translation "approach," or "philosophy," we hear pretty early on the word "literal." And "literal" is usually thought to be a good thing. Most of the people who ask me about the "best" translation of the Bible want to know which is the most "literal" translation. So the first thing I want to say about translation is that "literal" is not necessarily a good thing. Take an example from everyday life first. If a person from another culture were to ask me what I meant when I ordered "apple pie à la mode" at a restaurant, I could respond: "apple pie by the fashion." This is the "literal" translation of the French phrase. But do you think anyone would understand what I meant? Would not a better translation of this phrase be "apple pie with ice cream"? Or take an example from Scripture. Here is a literal translation of John 3:16:

> Thusly for loved the God the world so that the son only one he
> gave so that every one the believing into him no perish but have
> life eternal.

We might eventually figure out what this means. However, it surely is not obvious at first sight. And it is obviously not even passable English. Greek is just too different from English to allow us mechanically to put one English word in place of one Greek word and think that we will end up with English.

No translation, then, is "literal." But there is disagreement among translators about how important it is to bring over the form of the original languages into our translations. Should we try to turn Greek or Hebrew nouns into English nouns? Should we try to keep the word order of the Hebrew and Greek in English? Should we try to translate a particular Greek or Hebrew word with the same English word all the time? If the translator answers these questions positively, he or she is probably following what we call a "formal equivalent" or "word-based" philosophy. That is, one tries to find "equivalence" in form between the original biblical languages and English. At the other end of the spectrum is what is sometimes called a "dynamic equivalence" philosophy. Here the concern is with getting the meaning across as naturally and clearly as possible. A concern with reproducing forms is dropped. Greek nouns may become English verbs, Hebrew verbs may become noun phrases, and so on—as long as the meaning is being conveyed, these shifts in form are not a concern.

What is important to say about these two options, however, is that none of our translations follows either of these philosophies consistently. All of them display some concern to bring over form, and all of them are concerned to convey meaning. These versions occupy different spots on a spectrum with "formal equivalence" at one end and "dynamic equivalence" at the other:

Figure 5: Spectrums of the Four Translations

Formal Equivalence	ESV	HCSB	NIV	NLT	Dynamic Equivalence

Note how all four versions cluster together at some distance from the ends of the spectrum. I particularly want to draw attention to the distance between the spot of the ESV and the formal equivalence end of the spectrum. The ESV's claim to be essentially literal is accurate enough, but we have to recognize the degree of modification involved in the word *essentially*. The ESV frequently departs from the "form" of the original; it must if it is to *translate* the text. But the important point is this: *Each of these versions is making decisions about whether to keep the form of the original or not.* Every "form" in the original must be evaluated by the translator and a decision made about whether that form can or should be kept in the English or not. The ESV translators more often decide that the form can, in fact, be kept; the NLT translators, on the other hand, are most willing to drop the form. The HCSB decides less often than the ESV to keep the form of the original; and the NIV, slightly less often (but only slightly!) than the HCSB. What governs the translators' decisions about whether to keep the forms of the original or not? Meaning, of course. Or, perhaps better:

the kind of English into which one wants to translate. The ESV translators are so concerned with keeping the form of the original that they are content if their translation is in *understandable* English. The NLT translators, on the other hand, place a high value on translating into *easy* English, and in pursuing this virtue, they are willing more often to jettison form. The NIV and HCSB translators occupy a mediating position, retaining the form of the original as long as the result is *natural* English.

From personal experience I can tell you how hard the NIV translators work to come up with English translations that will *both* convey meaning in English *and* retain the form of the original (where it matters). But we are willing to depart from form if it is necessary to do so in order to achieve "natural" English. The NIV is often criticized for these kind of decisions. Two questions in particular are raised.

First, are we not "changing God's words"? Yes, of course we are—as does every English translation. "God's words," his inspired words, are in Hebrew, Aramaic, and Greek. By definition, translations change *every one* of "God's words" the minute they put them into English. The real question is this: Does a given translation accurately convey the *meaning* of God's words in contemporary English?

Second, versions such as the NIV are also sometimes criticized for not providing in English enough of the form of the original to provide a translation that can be a good basis for study or preaching. What may be said in reply? A point that is not always appreciated is this: *All* of our translations depart regularly from the form of the original. Consider the following chart. I have underlined in each version places where the English departs from the form of the Greek.

Philippians 2:6

ESV who, <u>though he was</u> in <u>the</u> form <u>of</u> God, did not count <u>equality with</u> God <u>a thing to be grasped,</u>

NIV Who, being in <u>very nature</u> God, did not consider <u>equality with</u> God <u>something to be used to his own advantage;</u>

HCSB who, existing in the form of God, did not consider <u>equality with</u> God <u>as something to be used for His own advantage.</u>

NLT   Though <u>he was</u> God, he did not think <u>of</u> <u>equality</u> <u>with</u> God <u>as</u>
      <u>something to cling to</u>.

The point, of course, is that each of the versions departs regularly from
the form of the original. *No* translation can come even close to providing
in English the kind of basis for study that we would really need. Here is
another example of this issue: the single Greek word *sarx* is translated with
12 different English words or phrases in the ESV, the most "literal" of our
four versions (and I am sure the other three are similar). This is no criticism of the ESV—simply a reminder that no English translation, if it is
going to be at all readable, can provide reliable information about the form
of the original. One might respond that at least some English versions
provide a bit more of that kind of information. Yes, but at a cost—the cost
of readability. The more an English translation sticks to the form of other
languages, the less it will truly be *English*.

Let me say again, each of the four versions at which we are looking in
this book does a credible job of conveying the Word of God into English.
They take slightly different approaches in the way they do it. This brings
great benefit to English students of the Bible because we have so many
excellent translations to compare and from which to learn. But my job in
this essay is to commend to you the NIV as an excellent modern English
translation that deserves to be read, preached from, and studied. There is
a reason the NIV has been the most popular English Bible for decades: it
follows a "mediating" translation approach that pays careful attention to the
form of the original while putting that original into natural, comprehensible
English. When we work on the NIV, we do pay attention to the form of the
original, and we try to retain that form in English—but only *if it is significant and if it is possible to do so while still using natural English.*

What About Gender Decisions?

We on the CBT were excited to have the opportunity to
update the NIV. Most of us were unhappy with the decision to keep publishing the NIV alongside the TNIV in
2005. And we were overjoyed to be able to bring these
two streams of our translation work back into one single
current: an updated NIV. We had been preparing for years
for such an update, considering suggestions for revision from scholars and
laypeople all over the world and adding our own revision ideas to the hop-
per. In obedience to the mandate that our charter gives us, we had been

monitoring advances in biblical scholarship and developments in English in order to keep the NIV up-to-date, making sure it would be both accurate and clear. I will have an opportunity below to illustrate many of these changes as I consider specific passages, but here I need to pave the way for some of that discussion by talking about our approach to the translation of gender.

When we were given the task of making final revisions for an NIV update to be released in 2011, the committee pledged to look especially carefully at what kind of English expressions we would use to refer to men and women. One reason we made this pledge is because the TNIV received a lot of criticism for the way it handled this matter. We accordingly agreed to revisit every decision about gender we had made in preparing the TNIV. But the more important reason we made this pledge is because we recognized that our charter required us to do so. Our charter requires us to keep the NIV up-to-date in order to make sure it continues to use the English that people are actually writing and speaking. And the biggest "structural" change in English between 1984 and 2011 was clearly the question of how gender is expressed.

This is not the place to pursue all the issues regarding the translation of gender in the Bible, but let me begin with our motivation since some have called this into question. Our decisions about gender were part and parcel of our single overall agenda—to put God's Word accurately into modern English. *No other agenda informed our gender decisions.* In every case our procedure was a simple and straightforward one: (1) decide whether the original text was inclusive (men and women included) or exclusive (men only or women only); (2) decide on the English words that would clearly communicate that meaning. I want to say a few words about each of these points.

1. Determining the gender intention of the original authors is not always easy. The problem is that the biblical languages use the masculine *form* of words to refer both to men only and to men and women together. Take, for instance, the Greek word *anthrōpos*. This word is masculine in form, but it can mean either "man" (as opposed to a woman) or "a human being." All modern versions of the Bible therefore translate the word both ways, depending on the context. The same is true with pronouns in the biblical languages. Their masculine third-person singular pronouns function much the way the pronoun *he* used to work in English. One could only know from context whether "he" referred to a man (e.g., "Larry is diligent; he is a hard worker") or to men and women equally (e.g., "The believer has

been regenerated. He has a new life"). There are, of course, some words in both Greek and Hebrew that undeniably refer to either a man (or men) or a woman (or women). But many of the most common words can function either exclusively (men as opposed to women) or inclusively (men and women equally). The actual words and the form of the words do not tell us which it is. Translators must make this judgment for themselves. We will see several examples of this debate in the verses we discuss below. However, to repeat: the first step in gender translation is to decide what the original documents intend.

2. Once we decide whether the original text has an inclusive or exclusive intention, we must next figure out how to say this clearly in modern English. But what is "modern English"? Every translation must make a basic decision at this point. Translations function to transfer meaning from a source (in this case the original text of Scripture) to a "receptor," or audience. Translation will not work unless one knows the audience. For instance, a children's Bible that uses college-level English might be good at identifying the meaning of the original, but it would hardly be an effective translation. The NIV, as we suggested above, seeks to translate into "natural" modern English. To be more specific, we want to use English that will be widely understood by people in Africa and India as well as people in North America, by believers and unbelievers, by people with Ph.D.s and those with only a high-school education.

Now what does all this have to do with gender translation? A lot. I frequently run into people who say, "I don't know why you can't use 'he' in a generic sense; I do it all the time." Others object, "How could you possibly use 'man' for the human race? 'Man' excludes women." The problem is that all of us speak a different English. My English, as someone raised in middle America, with a Ph.D., teaching in a college, is different from the English spoken by a high-school-educated farmer in Mississippi or the English spoken by the owner of a secretarial agency in India. How is one to determine, then, how gender is being used in English "in general"? By doing careful research about the state of the language in general. Toward this end the CBT commissioned a major study of gender in modern English. This study was carried out by Collins Dictionaries, which owns the largest databank of English in the world: more than 4.4 billion words. At our request the researchers at Collins developed sophisticated software that enabled them to query that database about the way gender is being expressed in contemporary English. The "Collins Report" gave the

CBT clear, detailed information about the state of English—a resource that no other translation has had available.

What did the Collins Report tell us about modern English? We do not have space here to provide the full report.[1] But three of its findings are especially interesting and will be significant for some verses I discuss below.

1. English speakers around the world are using a variety of terms to refer to men and women together and for the human race collectively. Plural words such as "people," "human beings," and "humans" are widely used. When it comes to terms that focus on humans in a collective sense, "man," "mankind," "humanity," and "the human race" are all being used.

2. The gender-neutral pronoun "they" ("them"/"their") is by far the most common way English-language speakers and writers today refer back to singular antecedents such as "whoever," "anyone," "somebody," "a person," "no one," and the like. Even in evangelical sermons and books, where the generic "he," "him," and "his" are preserved more frequently than in other forms of communication, instances of what grammarians are increasingly calling the "singular they" ("them" or "their") appear three times more frequently than generic masculine forms. In other words, most English speakers today express themselves in sentences such as these: "*No one* who rooted for the Chicago Cubs to be in a World Series in the last sixty years got *their* wish. *They* were disappointed time and time again."

3. The pronoun "he" (and its related forms) is no longer widely used in a generic sense. Yes, "he" is still being used generically by some authors, but our research makes clear that this is no longer a "natural" English option to refer to men and women equally. Most English speakers hear the word *he* as having a masculine orientation. The implications for translation are extremely significant. Translators who regularly use *he* in verses that address both men and women equally are, in effect, mistranslating: they are introducing in English a masculine orientation or nuance that is not present in the original.

In the light of these and other findings, the CBT adopted a set of guidelines that we applied during the NIV update process. These guidelines arise not from some ideological agenda or from personal experience; they are based on solid data. All data, of course, must be interpreted, and the CBT had to look carefully at specific contexts to decide how to apply the findings of the Collins Report. Our decisions were driven by this research,

---

[1] The full report may be found at http://www.niv-cbt.org/information/collins-corpus-report.

and our concern was always fidelity to what the original texts were saying. Where those texts indicate an exclusive reference, we used the appropriate modern English exclusive term; where they indicated an inclusive reference, we used the appropriate modern English inclusive term.[2]

Translation Comparison

Now let's see how the NIV has fleshed out these principles in actual texts.

Passage 1. Exodus 2:5–6

> [5] Then Pharaoh's daughter went down to the Nile to bathe, and her attendants were walking along the riverbank. She saw the basket among the reeds and sent her female slave to get it. [6] She opened it and saw the baby. He was crying, and she felt sorry for him. "This is one of the Hebrew babies," she said.

The four versions on which we are focusing in this book all translate this text in about the same way. Three minor differences might be noted.

First, the NIV and the HCSB refer specifically to "the Nile," while the ESV and NLT have simply "river." Either is an acceptable translation. Because of the location of the incident, the river involved probably was the Nile, and the Hebrew word used here often refers to it. But "river" or "stream" is also acceptable.

Second, the versions differ on whether the women with Pharoah's daughter were "attendants" (NIV; NLT), "young women" (ESV), or "servant girls" (HCSB). The authoritative Hebrew lexicon, HALOT,[3] suggests the meaning "attendants" here, but they note that the word can also mean "young unmarried girls." "Servant girls" seems to be an appropriate contextual translation also.

Third, the four versions handle the first part of verse 6 differently:

ESV   When she opened it, she saw the child, and behold, the baby was crying. She took pity on him . . . .

NIV   She opened it and saw the baby. He was crying, and she felt sorry for him.

---

[2] For more detail on the NIV update, our procedures, and responses to critics, see www.niv-cbt.org.

[3] L. Koehler, W. Baumgartner, and J. J. Stamm, *The Hebrew and Aramaic Lexicon of the Old Testament*, trans. and ed. M. E. J. Richardson, 5 vols. (Leiden: Brill Academic, 1994–2000).

HCSB   When she opened it, she saw the child—a little boy, crying. She felt sorry for him . . . .

NLT   When the princess opened it, she saw the baby. The little boy was crying, and she felt sorry for him.

Two trends in our translations are evident here. First, the ESV typically tries to reproduce the form of the original at the expense of modern English. "Behold" translates a particular Hebrew word, but the word chosen is out-of-date English. Nobody today speaks like that. Second, the NLT tries to help the reader negotiate the story by making explicit the antecedent of the pronoun at the beginning of the verse ("the princess"). A bit more complicated is the phrase rendered "a little boy, crying" in the HCSB. This version sticks closest to the Hebrew here. But each of the other versions seems to convey the sense of the passage adequately; the follow-up pronoun in the NIV and the ESV ("him") makes clear that the baby was male.

Passage 2. Psalm 1:1(–3)

¹ Blessed is <u>the one</u>
who does not walk <u>in step with</u> the wicked
or <u>stand in the way that sinners take</u>
or sit in the company of mockers,
² but whose delight is in the law of the Lord,
and who meditates on his law day and night.
³ <u>That person</u> is like a tree planted by streams of water,
which yields its fruit in season
and whose leaf does not wither—whatever <u>they</u> do prospers.

Four translation decisions in the NIV of Psalm 1:1 deserve mention. First, we had to decide how to translate the Hebrew word in verse 1 that denotes the person to whom the blessing is promised. The Hebrew word used here can refer either to a male (as opposed to a woman) or to a human being. The Hebrew dictionaries make this clear, and the ESV and HCSB tacitly recognize this fact by removing any male connotation in their translation of this word elsewhere in the Psalms (for the ESV, see 12:2; 41:9; 49:2; 62:9; 87:5; 109:16; 119:24; for the HCSB, 12:2; 41:9; 49:2,7; 62:12; 76:5; 78:25; 87:5; 92:6; 109:16; 119:24). Clearly, then, the word in itself does not have a masculine sense.

One can only know from context what is intended. Advocates of the translation "man" sometimes argue that the original text refers to a "blessed"
male, who then becomes representative of all people. So "man" should
be kept in Psalm 1:1 even though the verse ultimately includes men and
women equally. The problem with this approach is twofold. First, how do
we know the original author was referring to a male? As we have seen, the
Hebrew word does not tell us this, and nothing in the context makes this
clear. Second, keeping "man" here gives the wrong impression to modern English readers. As the Collins Report shows, English speakers today
"hear" the word "man" when applied to an individual as having a masculine connotation. This is how people today would then "hear" Psalm 1:1,
and it is not at all clear that they would make the interpretive leap to conclude that "man" here ultimately includes men and women equally. The
NIV "the one" and the NLT "those" make this point clear.

Why, however, does the NLT use a plural and the NIV a singular form?
This raises our second issue. The plural form in verse 1 is chosen by the
NLT translators because of the pronouns that refer back to this opening
verse later in the psalm. As you can see if you read further in the ESV and
the HCSB, the pronouns they use are "he" and "his." But these pronouns
carry a masculine sense in most modern English. Moving to the plural is
one way to avoid this problem; "they" and "their" have no gender bias.
The NIV often follows the pattern of the NLT in moving to plurals. This
does not violate appropriate translation theory since the point is how best
accurately to convey the meaning of the original. A singular followed by
"he" can give the impression that the text is restricted to males; a plural, it
is argued, can remove the individuality intended in the original. The point
is: a choice has to be made, and moving to a plural in a general blessing
of this kind is not a big problem. The psalms often express blessings in
the plural without anyone thinking the text has lost individual application:
e.g., Psalm 84:4: "Blessed are those who dwell in your house; they are
ever praising you." However, while using a plural form in English is an
acceptable translation option, the NIV follows a different route. A singular is kept in verse 1 of Psalm 1 and then followed up (in v. 3) with "that
person" and "they." The latter translation uses the so-called "singular" or
"distributive" "they." See our discussion of Ezekiel 18 for more information about this pronoun and its use in the NIV.

A third element in the NIV translation of Psalm 1:1 worthy of note is
our apparent "dropping" of the word "counsel" (ESV) or "advice" (HCSB;
NLT) in line two. But the NIV has not overlooked the Hebrew word used

here. Rather, we translate it in our language of "walk in step with." As a recent commentator on the Psalms explains, "[The English translation] 'counsel' could give the impression that [the Hebrew] refers to 'advice' the faithless give, but more likely it denotes intentions they formulate, into which they seek to draw other people."[4] It is just this idea that the NIV has captured in its language of "walk in step with."

The NIV translation of the third line in Psalm 1:1 provides an example of a key virtue of the NIV: its attempt to avoid what we call "biblish," a kind of English that has become traditional in Bible translation but that does not communicate well to the majority of English speakers. The original NIV translated this line in Psalm 1:1 as "or stand in the way of sinners." But think about this for a moment: why would it be a bad thing to "stand in the way of" sinners? The English metaphor "stand in the way of" means to keep someone from doing something. Should not the righteous be doing just that? Here, then, is a case where the traditional biblical language says just the opposite of what the text wants to say. The NIV, HCSB, and NLT recognize this problem and translate differently to avoid it.

Passage 3. Ezekiel 18:5–9,21–24

⁵ Suppose there is <u>a righteous</u> man who does what is just and right. ⁶ He does not eat at the mountain shrines or look to the idols of Israel. <u>He</u> does not defile his neighbor's wife or have sexual relations with a woman during her period. ⁷ <u>He</u> does not oppress anyone, but returns what <u>he</u> took in pledge for a loan. <u>He</u> does not commit robbery but gives <u>his</u> food to the hungry and provides clothing for the naked. ⁸ <u>He</u> does not lend to them at interest or take a profit from them. <u>He</u> withholds his hand from doing wrong and judges fairly between two parties. ⁹ <u>He</u> follows my decrees and faithfully keeps my laws. <u>That man</u> is righteous; <u>he</u> will surely live, declares the Sovereign Lᴏʀᴅ. . . . ²¹ But if <u>a wicked person</u> turns away from all the sins they have committed and keeps all my decrees and does what is just and right, <u>that person</u> will surely live; <u>they</u> will not die. ²² None of the offenses <u>they</u> have committed will be remembered against <u>them.</u> Because of the righteous things <u>they</u> have done, <u>they</u> will live. ²³ Do I take any pleasure in the death of <u>the wicked</u>? declares the Sovereign Lᴏʀᴅ. Rather, am I not pleased when <u>they</u>

---

[4] John Goldingay, *Psalms*, vol. 1: *Psalms 1–41*, Baker Commentary on the Old Testament Wisdom and Psalms (Grand Rapids: Baker, 2006), 82.

turn from their ways and live? [24] But if a righteous person turns from their righteousness and commits sin and does the same detestable things the wicked person does, will they live? None of the righteous things that person has done will be remembered. Because of the unfaithfulness they are guilty of and because of the sins they have committed, they will die.

These two passages from Ezekiel 18 beautifully illustrate the gender choices the updated NIV has made. The Hebrew text in both these passages uses masculine forms. The first paragraph introduces a righteous "man"/"person" (Hebrew *ish*) and then follows up with third singular masculine verbs, pronouns, and adjectives through the rest of the paragraph. The second passage simply uses masculine participles, verbs, and pronouns throughout. On the basis of the word *ish* in verse 5, it could be argued that the former paragraph focuses on an individual male person. As we have seen in our comments on Psalm 1:1, this is certainly not clearly the case. Nevertheless, the translators of all four of our versions decided the reference here was probably to a male. Why? Look at verse 6: the person being described "does not defile his neighbor's wife or have sexual relations with a woman during her period." And so they render "man" in verse 5 and use masculine pronouns in the rest of the paragraph.

No such definite gender indicator is found in the second paragraph. Accordingly, all four versions begin in verse 21 with a nongender-specific reference: "a wicked person" (NIV; ESV), "the wicked" (HCSB), "wicked people" (NLT). And in verse 24, they translate "righteous person" (NIV; ESV; HCSB)/"righteous people" (NLT). The ESV and HCSB refer back to these two individuals in the rest of the paragraph with the pronouns "he" and "him." By doing so, they suggest to the modern English reader that the reference in this paragraph is to a wicked male individual. To repeat the point we have made in several places already: the Collins Report shows that "he," "his," "him," and "himself" have a definite masculine connotation in contemporary English. The NLT and NIV translators recognize this fact about modern English. They do not think any such masculine connotation is intended in this paragraph. But how can one express this in English? Here one of the biggest problems in the development of English comes into play.

As we have noted, the pronoun *he* and its other forms used to do double duty: it could refer to a single male person or to a single person of any gender. This latter generic sense of *he* has certainly not disappeared from

English. However, it is less common than it used to be, and research shows that most people now hear this word as having a definite masculine connotation. What, then, does the translator do when a third-singular word in Hebrew or Greek is generic? There is no generic third-singular pronoun in English. If we are talking about a person, we must use either *he* or *she*—and both now have clear exclusive gender connotations. One option translators employ is to shift to plural constructions because "they" is not gender specific. This is the route the NLT takes in our passage: they translate "wicked people" in verse 21 and "righteous people" in verse 24. They then follow up with plural pronouns. This is often a good option, and the NIV does this often as well.

In this passage, however, the NIV has chosen a different option. While we do not see a big problem in moving from singulars in Greek and Hebrew to plurals in English, preserving the singular of the original can be a virtue in some texts. In this text the NIV has accomplished this by using "wicked person" in verse 21 and "righteous person" in verse 24 but then referring back to these two individuals with "that person" (vv. 21b and 24b) and with the pronouns "they" and "their." But wait a minute, you might object: how can the singular "person" be followed by the plural pronoun "they"? In fact, as English dictionaries make clear, *they* (and *them, their, themselves*) have been used for centuries in a "singular," or "distributive," sense. Authoritative guides to modern English recognize this trend and recommend this construction. Note the comments, for instance, in *The Cambridge Guide to English Usage*: "[I]n ordinary usage *he/his/ him* seems to be losing its capacity to be generic." "All this evidence from different quarters of the English-speaking world shows that singular use of **they/them/their** after indefinites is now well established in writing." "The appearance of singular **they/them/their** in many kinds of prose shows its acceptance by English writers generally. It recommends itself as a gender-free solution to the problem of agreement with indefinite pronouns and noun phrases."[5] The Collins Report backs up this conclusion with data. It shows that, by a wide margin, the normal way for English-speakers today to follow up a general word such as "one," "person," "each," "every," etc., is with a "singular 'they.'" The updated NIV therefore uses this combination often. We are thereby able to "get the best of both worlds": we keep a singular construction, but we make clear that it is intended to be inclusive.

[5] Pam Peters, *The Cambridge Guide of English Usage* (Cambridge: University Press, 2004), 244, 538. See also, e.g., Bryan A. Garner, *Garner's Modern American Usage* (Oxford: Oxford University Press, 2003), 718; Sidney Greenbaum, *The Oxford English Grammar* (Oxford: University Press, 1996), 20.

Passage 4. Matthew 5:1–3

> [1] Now when Jesus saw the crowds, he went up on a <u>mountainside</u> and sat down. His disciples came to him, [2] and <u>he began to teach them</u>. He said: [3] "Blessed are <u>the poor in spirit</u>, for theirs is the kingdom of heaven."

Three differences among the four versions are worth brief mention. First, the ESV and HCSB have Jesus going up "on the mountain," whereas the NIV and NLT translate "on a/the mountainside." The Greek word is usually translated "mountain," but it can also refer, in certain contexts, to a mountainous area or to some part of a mountain. Since the place indicated here is one where Jesus teaches both his disciples (5:1) and "the crowds" (7:28), it is probably a flat plateau somewhere on the slope of the hills that jut out from the Sea of Galilee. Luke describes this same location as "a level place" somewhere below the upper parts of the mountain (Luke 6:17; see v. 12). "Mountainside" might be a slightly better way of describing this place, but either of the options certainly gets the idea clearly enough.

Second, in place of the simple "he [Jesus] began to teach them" in the NIV, HCSB, and NLT, the ESV translates, "he opened his mouth and taught them." This translation sticks more closely to the actual Greek words used here, but it raises the problem of idioms. Every language and culture has its own set of idioms, and these are often hard to translate into another language. (I remember the puzzled expression on a Korean student's face when I advised him "to bury the hatchet.") The Bible is no exception—it uses a lot of idioms. Many of these idioms simply cannot be translated without losing the meaning entirely: none of our versions translate "dig the ears" (e.g. "open the ears to hear") in Psalm 40:6. But translators differ about whether they should try to preserve idioms that could be understood. "Open his mouth" is just such an idiom. It is widely used in the Old Testament with the meaning "begin to speak" (see, e.g., Job 3:1; Isa 5:14; Ezek 3:2), and some interpreters think Matthew's use of the phrase is intended to remind us of Moses (see Exod 4:15, where God promises to "put words in [Moses'] mouth" [the Greek version, the Septuagint, has "open his mouth"]). However, the phrase is certainly not modern English. As so often happens, then, translators must make a decision. Should we preserve the "biblical" style by keeping the idiom? Or should we drop the idiom and make the idea clear to a modern English reader? I prefer the second of these options here.

A third difference among our versions is the way the "poor" who receive God's blessing are described. ESV, HCSB, and NIV stick pretty closely to the Greek: "poor in spirit." The NLT, however, renders "those who are poor and realize their need for him." Here is another decision that must be made: stick closely to the Greek structure at the risk of leaving the average English reader puzzled about what "in spirit" means, or keep "in spirit," which may not communicate clearly? I think the latter option is preferable here. Translators have to be careful not to introduce unintended ideas into the text that are not there. The NLT is open to criticism on this point. Their rendering could suggest that Jesus has two ideas in mind: actual material poverty and the humility that forces a person to recognize their need for God. It is possible that this is what the Greek here actually intends, but this is not, in my view, probable.

Passage 5. Mark 1:40–45

40 A man with leprosy came to him and begged him on his knees, "If you are willing, you can make me clean." 41 Jesus was indignant. He reached out his hand and touched the man. "I am willing," he said. "Be clean!" 42 Immediately the leprosy left him and he was cleansed. 43 Jesus sent him away at once with a strong warning: 44 "See that you don't tell this to anyone. But go, show yourself to the priest and offer the sacrifices that Moses commanded for your cleansing, as a testimony to them." 45 Instead he went out and began to talk freely, spreading the news. As a result, Jesus could no longer enter a town openly but stayed outside in lonely places. Yet the people still came to him from everywhere.

The versions display several differences in the way they translate this narrative from early in the life of Jesus, but one surely stands out. At the beginning of verse 41, ESV, HCSB, and NLT refer to Jesus' "pity" or "compassion" as the motivation for his cleansing of the man with leprosy. But the NIV says that "Jesus was indignant." How in the world could there be such a big difference in translation? The answer is that the versions are translating different Greek texts.

The difference here reveals an important but somewhat hidden part of the translation process—translators must decide just what Greek words they are going to translate. The problem is that we do not have one single "inspired" Greek New Testament. Rather, we have thousands of manuscripts that we have to sift through and compare. Where these manuscripts have different "readings" of the Greek, we must decide which one is most likely to have been the original word, or words, the biblical author wrote down. Now, in God's providence, we have so much good information about the Greek text that we can usually be pretty sure about what the original Greek actually was. And even when we have doubt about the original, we should not worry. The differences are so minor that no important New Testament teaching is ever in doubt.

Still, there are differences, even if minor, and they do affect the meaning of some specific texts. The variant reading in Mark 1:41 is a good example. Most of the Greek manuscripts here have a verb that is accurately rendered in the ESV, HCSB, and NLT as "have compassion"/"pity." The other option, the Greek word that means "be angry" or "indignant," is found in only one Greek manuscript (and several others in other languages). Why in the world, then, you might be asking, did the NIV decide to base its translation on this word? Simply because of a basic principle of textual criticism: prefer the reading that can best explain the others. In other words, we have to ask this question: as scribes copied the Gospel of Mark over the centuries, would they have been more likely to put the Greek word for "anger" in place of the one for "compassion"? Or the reverse? The answer is clear: they would have been far more likely to substitute "compassion" for "anger." The Gospels frequently refer to Jesus' compassion as the motivation for his healings. Scribes would know this and would tend to use that language here also. Moreover, the idea of Jesus' being "angry" does not fit the context very well. For this reason the great majority of recent commentators on the Gospel of Mark have decided that the original Greek here referred to Jesus' anger.[6] As he saw what the man with

---

[6] I have 14 Mark commentaries in my home library. Thirteen of them prefer the word for "anger": D. E. Nineham, *The Gospel of St. Mark*, Pelican New Testament Commentaries (New York: Penguin, 1963), 86; Vincent Taylor, *The Gospel According to St. Mark* (London: Macmillan, 1966), 187; C. E. B. Cranfield, *The Gospel According to Saint Mark*, Cambridge Greek Testament Commentary (Cambridge: Cambridge University Press, 1966), 92; William L. Lane, *The Gospel According to Mark*, New International Commentary on the New Testament (Grand Rapids: Eerdmans, 1974), 84; Joachim Gnilka, *Das Evangelium nach Markus*, Evangelisch-Katholischer Kommentar zum Neuen Testament II.1 (Neukirchen-Vluyn: Neukirchener, 1978), 92–93; David E. Garland, *Mark*, The NIV Application Commentary (Grand Rapids: Zondervan, 1996), 75; Hugh Anderson, *The Gospel of Mark*, New Century Bible (Greenwood, SC: Attic, 1976), 96–97; Morna D. Hooker, *The Gospel According to Saint Mark*, Black's New Testament Commentaries (Peabody, MA: Hendrickson, 1991), 79; Robert A. Guelich, *Mark 1:1–8:26*, Word Biblical Commentary 34A (Dallas: Word, 1989), 72; Joel Marcus, *Mark 1–8*, Anchor Bible Commentary 27 (New York: Doubleday, 2000), 206; Robert H. Stein, *Mark*, Baker Exegetical Commentary on the New Testament (Grand Rapids: Baker, 2008), 110–11; R. T. France, *The Gospel of Mark*, New International Greek Testament Commentary (Grand Rapids: Eerdmans, 2002), 115; James R. Edwards, *The Gospel According to Mark*, Pillar Commentary (Grand Rapids: Eerdmans, 2002), 70. The lone dissenter is H. B. Swete, *Commentary on Mark* (Grand Rapids: Kregel, 1977), 29.

leprosy had suffered, Jesus responded initially with "anger" or "indignation" at the terrible plight of people in this sin-ravaged world.

The point I am making here is not that the NLT, ESV, and HCSB are wrong in putting "compassion" or "mercy" in their texts—the textual critical issue is a tough call, and the major printed editions of the Greek New Testament (the United Bible Societies 4th ed. and the Nestle-Aland 27th ed.) both have the Greek word for "compassion."[7] My point, rather, is that the NIV option is defensible, representing as it does the view of most scholars on the Gospel of Mark. The NLT, to its credit, while putting "moved with compassion" in the text, includes the alternative in a footnote. The ESV and HCSB do not even mention this alternative, failing to alert the English reader to the reading that most scholars consider the original.

Passage 6. Ending of Mark's Gospel

Perhaps the most significant textual problem in the entire New Testament is the question of how the Gospel of Mark ends. As in Mark 1:41, the problem is that our early New Testament manuscripts do not agree. Some of them end the Gospel with 16:8. Others include what is known as a "short ending," which is around two verses in length. Still others have a "longer ending," numbered verses 9–20 in our Bibles. This "longer ending" is found in the majority of manuscripts and was included in the King James Version (and the NKJV, which follows the same text as the KJV did). Because this "longer ending" is found in so many manuscripts, it is not surprising that some scholars think it was an original part of Mark's Gospel. But the great majority of scholars disagree. Why?

One of the key principles of textual criticism is that manuscripts must be "weighed" and not just "counted." It is not the number of manuscripts that matters but the quality of those manuscripts. The date of a manuscript is, of course, important in assessing its quality. But just as important is its "genetic" status. Textual critics group New Testament manuscripts into "families." Manuscripts are put into different families based on common elements they share. The long ending of Mark is found mainly in manuscripts that come from one "family," a family that seems to follow a New Testament textual tradition that is not as old as the other families. The KJV

---

[7] Although Metzger, in his commentary, notes that it was a close call for the committee (Bruce M. Metzger, *A Textual Commentary on the Greek New Testament*, 2nd ed. [New York: United Bible Societies, 2002], 65).

translators had access mainly to manuscripts from this family. Discoveries since the KJV, however, have given textual critics many more manuscripts from other families that are earlier than this so-called "majority text." This is why the great majority of textual critics today are convinced that verses 9–20 could not have been part of Mark's Gospel when it was first written. (Other factors, such as differences between the style of these verses and Mark's usual style, are also important.)

All four of our versions appear to agree that neither the "long ending" nor the "short ending" were original, but they have different ways of indicating it. The NLT and the HCSB are the most subtle in making this point. These versions use the same form of heading used throughout the Gospel of Mark before verses 9–20. They use the same font that is used in the rest of the Gospel. They do place these verses within single brackets, but readers could easily miss their import. The only clear clue to the status of the text comes in their footnotes on these verses. The NLT warns readers that "[t]he most reliable early manuscripts of the Gospel of Mark end at verse 8." The HCSB is much less clear, simply saying that "[o]ther manuscripts omit bracketed text"—a note that could be read as saying that the text they print is the original. The ESV goes a bit further. It encloses the text in double brackets, and adds a note before the text: "Some of the earliest manuscripts do not include 16:9–20." The NIV most clearly marks this text as suspect. It includes a line between verse 8 and verse 9, puts the text of verses 9–20 in a different font, and includes this note, in brackets, in the text itself: "The earliest manuscripts and some other ancient witnesses do not have verses 9–20." The NIV translators have kept the variant in the text because of its length and importance in the history of the New Testament text. A strong case could be made for treating this variant reading like any other and putting it in a footnote. But at least the NIV makes quite clear that verses 9–20 do not belong to the original Gospel of Mark. It communicates much better than NLT and HCSB and a bit better than the ESV the status of this text (according to the great majority of contemporary scholars).

Passage 7. Luke 17:3(–4)

³ So watch yourselves. "If your <u>brother or sister</u> sins <u>against you</u>, rebuke them; and if they repent, forgive <u>them</u>. ⁴ Even if they sin against you seven times in a day and seven times come back to you saying 'I repent,' you must forgive them.

The four versions offer three alternatives in translating the word *adelphos* in this verse. The ESV and HCSB translate "brother" and use masculine singular pronouns to follow up. The NLT translates "believer" and follows up with "that person." The NIV uses "brother or sister" and the pronouns "them" and "they." Why has the NIV translated the single word *adelphos* with "brother or sister" instead of "brother"? Simply because the English language has changed. When the NIV was translated 30 years ago, pastors could address their congregations as "brothers," and just about everyone would understand that the reference was to both men and women. But today? Would not people assume that only men were intended? Do you not hear your pastor saying "brothers and sisters" just about all the time? The fact is that Jesus clearly intends the word that is used here to refer to both men and women equally.[8] In modern English we do not communicate this with the word "brother" but with "brother or sister." The NLT solves this problem by using "believer." The word *adelphos* certainly comes to mean something like "fellow religionist" in places in the New Testament. Here, however, the NIV translators thought Jesus might have been connoting the idea of a spiritual "familial" relationship.

Some have protested, arguing that while the plural *adelphoi* can refer to men and women, the singular form of the word does not. Yet this protest is not cogent, as a glance at texts such as 1 John 3:15–17, 1 Corinthians 8:11–13, and James 4:11 reveals (I am quoting the ESV to make my point):

> [15] Everyone who hates his brother is a murderer, and you know that no murderer has eternal life abiding in him. [16] By this we know love, that he laid down his life for us, and we ought to lay down our lives for <u>the brothers</u>. [17] But if anyone has the world's goods and sees <u>his brother</u> in need, yet closes his heart against him, how does God's love abide in him? (1 John 3:15–17)

> [11] And so by your knowledge this weak person is destroyed, the <u>brother</u> for whom Christ died. [12] Thus, sinning against your <u>brothers</u> and wounding their conscience when it is weak, you sin against Christ. [13] Therefore, if food makes my <u>brother</u> stumble, I will never eat meat, lest I make my <u>brother</u> stumble. (1 Cor 8:11–13)

---

[8] The Greek dictionaries agree; see, e.g., Louw and Nida: "The masculine form ἀδελφός may include both men and women" (Johannes P. Louw and Eugene A. Nida, eds., *Greek-English Lexicon of the New Testament Based on Semantic Domains*, 2 vols. [New York: United Bible Societies, 1988, 1989], 11.23).

> Do not speak evil against one another, <u>brothers</u>. The one who speaks against a <u>brother</u> or judges his <u>brother</u>, speaks evil against the law and judges the law. But if you judge the law, you are not a doer of the law but a judge. (Jas 4:11)

Does it make any sense at all to think that the plural "brothers" in these passages refers to believing men and women, whereas the singular "brother" refers to a male believer only? No; in these cases the singular *adelphos* identifies one individual from the group of *adelphoi*. And since the plural has no particular focus on males, the singular does not either.

To be sure, the NIV recognizes that the New Testament text sometimes illustrates a point by putting before us a particular example. In these cases we are happy to translate *adelphos* simply as "brother" (see, for example, Matt 7:3–5). But when the text, as in Luke 17:3 (and 1 John 3:15–17), is stating a general principle, we prefer to make clear the applicability of that principle to both male and female believers equally.

Once we used "brother or sister" as our translation at the beginning of the verse, we then had to decide what pronouns to use to refer back to this phrase. The NIV translators have avoided using "he" and "him" in this verse because we are convinced that most modern English speakers no longer "hear" these words as generic. The English language has changed, and Bible translations must change along with it. To be sure, this change has not taken place uniformly everywhere. We all speak a slightly different form of English. Some of us perhaps still think that "he" is straightforwardly generic and cannot understand what all the fuss is about. But a Bible translation must seek to use the language that most people are using, and the Collins Report has conclusively shown that the generic use of "he," "him," and "his" is no longer a natural English idiom for the majority of English-speakers. We have therefore chosen to use the pronouns "they" and "them" in a singular, or distributive sense—a usage that has a long history in English and that is now the preferred way to follow up an initial generic singular reference (see again my comments on Ezekiel 18).

One other translation decision in the NIV deserves quick mention. Of our four versions, only the NIV adds "against you" in verse 3 to describe the kind of sin to which Jesus refers. The KJV and the NKJV also have this phrase. They include it because some of the early Greek texts have an equivalent phrase. We do not think those texts are the best texts, but we do think they point the way to the correct meaning of verse 3. Verse 4, which is closely attached to verse 3, makes clear that the issue in this context is not "sinning" in general but sinning against a particular person. The commentaries agree that this is the idea in verse 3 (and note also the somewhat parallel texts in Matt 18:15 and 21).[9] We think, therefore, that there is every reason to believe the verb "sin" here has the particular connotation "sin against someone else." Translation should reflect meaning; once the translator decides this is the meaning, "sins against you" is the accurate rendering.

Passage 8. John 1:3–4,14,18

> [3] Through him all things were made; without him nothing was made that has been made. [4] In him was life, and that life was the light of all <u>mankind</u>. . . . [14] The Word became flesh and made his dwelling among us. We have seen his glory, the glory of <u>the one and only Son</u>, who came from the Father, full of grace and truth. . . . [18] No one has ever seen God, but <u>the one and only Son</u>, who is himself God and is in closest relationship with the Father, has made him known.

Our four versions make a number of different translation decisions here. But the issue of most interest to the readers of this book, I suspect, will be the differing translations of the word *anthrōpōn*. This word is the standard word in Greek to refer to a person of indeterminate gender or to people of mixed gender. This latter issue is the one important here because the word is plural. The ESV and HCSB therefore render "men." I am pretty sure the translators of these versions intend this word to be read generically, applicable equally to men and women: Jesus is the "light" for men and women equally. The question is whether their translation succeeds in communicating this in modern English. I doubt it. The evidence from the Collins Report (see my introduction) makes clear that most people today use "men" to refer to "men as opposed to women."[10] The NIV and the NLT avoid this mistranslation in different ways: the NIV using "mankind" and the NLT "everyone." However, it might be objected, does not the NIV perpetuate the gender problem by using "mankind"? We do not think so.

[9] See, e.g., Robert H. Stein, *Luke*, New American Commentary 24 (Nashville: B&H, 1992), 429; John Nolland, *Luke 9:21–18:34*, Word Biblical Commentary 35b (Dallas: Word, 1993), 838; Joseph A. Fitzmyer, *The Gospel According to Luke x–xxiv*, Anchor Bible 28a (Garden City, NY: Doubleday, 1985), 1139–40; Darrell L. Bock, *Luke 9:51–24:53*, BECNT (Grand Rapids: Baker, 1994), 1387.

[10] It is somewhat puzzling why the ESV and HCSB use "men" in verse 4 but then, in a similar text, do not use the word "man" in verse 9 ("The true light, who gives light to [enlightens] everyone [*panta anthrōpon*]").

Our research, again, shows that this word, along with "man," is still being widely used to refer to the human race in general.

In verses 14 and 18, we encounter a Greek word that is difficult to understand and translate: *monogenēs.* The word originally meant "the only one born" (to a set of parents), hence the KJV translation "only begotten." But the word came to mean "pertaining to what is unique in the sense of being the only one of the same kind or class."[11] The modern versions get this idea across by using words or phrases such as "only" (ESV) or "one and only" (NLT in v. 14; NIV; HCSB) or "unique" (NLT in v. 18). The translations handle the word in verse 14 in basically the same way; the differences among them are only stylistic. But we have a more substantial difference in verse 18, where the NIV and the HCSB refer to "the one and only Son," the ESV to "the only God," and the NLT to "the unique One, who is himself God." Complicating the matter here is a textual variant; some manuscripts have the Greek word for "Son" and others do not. One might then think that the NIV and the HCSB are following this variant Greek text. I do not know what the HCSB is doing here, but I can say that the NIV is not following that variant text. We translate "one and only Son" because we think the simple word *monogenēs* here implies the word "Son." So, with the HCSB and the NLT, we take this word to stand by itself as a way of referring to Christ, with the word for "God" functioning as a further description of Christ. The ESV, on the other hand, takes *monogenēs* as an adjective ("only God"). Each of these renderings, it seems to me, is quite defensible.

Passage 9. John 2:25–3:1

> [2:25] He did not need any testimony about <u>mankind</u>, for he knew what was in <u>each person</u>. [3:1] Now there was a Pharisee, a <u>man</u> named Nicodemus who was a member of the Jewish ruling council.

This text illustrates a common dilemma faced by translators—whether to focus on meaning or on form. Adding in transliterations of three of the words in the text will make the issue clearer:

> He did not need any testimony about mankind [*anthrōpou*], for he knew what was in each person [*anthrōpō*]. [3:1] Now there was

---

[11] Louw and Nida, *Greek-English Lexicon*, 58.52.

a Pharisee, a man [*anthrōpos*] named Nicodemus who was a
member of the Jewish ruling council.

It is easy to see that John is using the same Greek word three times in these
verses. The relationship among these three words may be something that one
would want English readers readily to see. This relationship is clear in the
ESV and HCSB, which translate each occurrence of this Greek word with
"man." By doing so, these versions help the English reader see that John
may well intend to introduce Nicodemus as a particular "man" to which the
general statement in verse 25b applied: Jesus, indeed, knew what is in "each
man," as his dialogue with this one particular "man" will reveal.

The relationship among these three key instances of the same word is
not so clear in the NIV and NLT. The latter collapses the two clauses in verse
25 into one and therefore translates only one instance of *anthrōpos*, rendering it "mankind." Then, in 3:1, the NLT refers to Nicodemus as a "man."
The NIV keeps all three occurrences of the word, rendering it, successively,
"mankind," "person," and "man." There is no doubt that something is lost
in the NIV translation here—the wordplay is not nearly as clear. But I want
to stress that something is gained as well. As we have noted repeatedly, the
word "man" when applied to an individual person no longer is a term that
includes both men and women. Now, to be sure, the ESV and HCSB translations seem to be using "man" at the end of verse 25 to refer to the human
race as a whole (this is what "man" means earlier in the verse, and an indefinite article would have needed to signal a shift to an individual person—that
is "a man"). But it is questionable if this is what John intends. It is perhaps
more likely that he wants to emphasize in verse 25b that Jesus knew what
was in each individual "man," or person. And, if this is the meaning, "man"
becomes a problematic translation because it suggests the reference is to a
male human being rather than to a human being generally.

Passage 10. 1 Corinthians 2:1,13

[1] And so it was with me, <u>brothers and sisters</u>. When I came to you,
I did not come with eloquence or human wisdom as I proclaimed
to you <u>the testimony</u> about God.... [13] This is what we speak, not
in words taught us by human wisdom but in words taught by the
Spirit, <u>explaining spiritual realities with Spirit-taught words</u>.

Two matters in the translations of 1 Corinthians 2:1 call for comment. First
is the difference between "brothers" in ESV and HCSB and "brothers and

sisters" in NIV and NLT. We commented briefly on the Greek word involved (*adelphos*) in our explanation of Luke 17:3. In this verse we have a characteristic use of the word in the plural to address a general Christian audience. This word can refer to a male as opposed to a female (e.g., a brother as distinguished from a sister). But, as the major dictionaries recognize, the word also comes to be used for men and women equally.[12] Translating this word "brothers" when the word is used in this way suggests in modern English that the reference is exclusively to, or particularly to, Christian males. I find that pastors instinctively recognize this, often amending the text they are reading in public (if it has "brothers") to "brothers and sisters." To get across the intention of the authors of the New Testament, then, "brothers and sisters" is a better translation. The NIV usually chooses this way of rendering the word, adding a footnote to make clear what is going on: "The Greek word for *brothers and sisters* (*adelphoi*) refers here to believers, both men and women, as part of God's family" (to avoid clutter, this footnote is placed on the first occurrence of the word in every book, with reference to the other places in the book where it occurs).

Another difference in our translations is easily spotted: NIV, ESV, and HCSB have "the testimony of/about God," while the NLT has "God's secret plan." Why the difference? Because our Greek manuscripts have two different words here, words that would easily become confused because they look (and sound) so much alike: *martyrion* ("testimony") and *mystērion* ("mystery," or "secret plan"). A decision between the two is not easy. Commentators disagree. A good case can be made for either word, and each certainly fits this context.

In verse 13 of 1 Corinthians 2, the issue is how to translate the last clause of the verse. This issue has been debated for years by scholars, and it must be said that no clear agreement has been reached. It is hard, therefore, to fault any of the versions for the decisions they have made. What is clear is that Paul is talking about "spiritual realities" (NIV)/"spiritual truths" (ESV and NLT)/"spiritual things" (HCSB). But what is ambiguous is whether these spiritual matters are being *interpreted for* the benefit of "spiritual people" (ESV, HCSB) or are being *explained by means of* "Spirit-taught words" (NIV) or by the "Spirit's word" (NLT). I think each translation here can be defended on exegetical grounds. But I would like to point out that each translation has had to make significant interpretive

---

[12] Walter Bauer, *A Greek-English Lexicon of the New Testament and other Early Christian Literature*, 3rd ed, rev. and ed. F. W. Danker, W. F. Arndt, and F. W. Gingrich (Chicago: University of Chicago Press, 2000), 18, says, "The pl. can also mean **brothers and sisters**" (commenting on extrabiblical usage).

decisions simply to translate the passage into English at all—a reminder that interpretation in translation is unavoidable.

Passage 11. Galatians 5:2–6

> [2] Mark my words! I, Paul, tell you that if you let yourselves be circumcised, Christ will be of no value to you at all. [3] Again I declare to every man who lets himself be circumcised that he is obligated to obey the whole law. [4] You who are trying to be justified by the law have been alienated from Christ; you have fallen away from grace. [5] For through the Spirit we eagerly await by faith <u>the righteousness for which we hope</u>. [6] For in Christ Jesus neither circumcision nor uncircumcision has any value. The only thing that counts is faith expressing itself through love.

This passage illustrates the way the NIV balances attention to the form of the original with a concern to communicate in clear and natural English. On the one hand, the NIV introduces many fewer interpretive paraphrases into its translation than does the NLT. The NLT language of "to make you right with God" in verse 2 and "to find favor with God" in verse 3 is introduced without express warrant in the Greek. The NLT translators may well respond that the context (see esp. v. 4) makes clear that this is the issue—surely Paul is not condemning all circumcision. He himself circumcised Timothy (Acts 16:1–3). Yet it is not entirely clear that being "right with" God or "finding favor" with God exhausts Paul's reasons for opposing circumcision. In the argument of Galatians 3:7–4:7, Paul focuses on the issue of becoming the children of Abraham. This idea may well overlap significantly with the matter of being "right with God" (see 3:7). But the two may not be identical, and introducing the idea of being "right with God" in verses 2–3 here might introduce a restriction that Paul did not intend. Note that in 3:3, Paul scolds his readers for thinking they can be perfected "by means of the flesh." "Flesh" there almost certainly includes reference to circumcision. Here in 2:2–3, then, Paul may be warning the Galatians about trying to find perfection, or "ultimate justification," by means of circumcision. But the NLT suggests that the issue is initially getting into relationship with God.

In these verses the NIV is content to express Paul's warnings in language that sticks fairly close to Paul's Greek. But sticking to Paul's Greek is, as we have seen, not always a way of providing the best translation. Verse 4 illustrates this point. The ESV, true to its overall approach, retains the order of the clauses in English that we have in the Greek: "You are severed from Christ, you who would be justified by the law; you have fallen away from grace." This translation certainly gets the idea across, but the sequence of clauses is awkward. The other three versions reverse the order of the first two clauses (see the NIV above). This makes for more natural English, and nothing is lost. There is no reason to think the order of Paul's clauses carries any particular significance.

One other translation decision gives us a peek into the differences in translation philosophy among these four versions. In verse 5, the ESV and the HCSB translate "the hope of righteousness," whereas the NIV has "the righteousness for which we hope" and the NLT, "the righteousness God has promised us." These latter two translations make clear that the "righteousness" Paul refers to here is future (although I am not sure I like the NLT rendering "[what] God has promised" for "hope" [Gk. *elpis*]). The issue here is how to translate a Greek genitive construction. In this construction the Greek puts two nouns together in a relationship, but the particular relationship they have to each other is a matter of interpretation. Perhaps the closest English equivalents are phrases such as "fire hose" or "houseguest." We instinctively unpack these phrases to mean "a hose used for putting out fires" and "a guest staying in one's house." So here Paul refers to "hope righteousness," leaving it unclear whether he means "a hope [for something] that is based on righteousness" or "a hope that we will receive righteousness." The ESV and HCSB are content with the English "of" construction here. This translation for the Greek genitive is sometimes preferred because it is claimed to be the "literal" rendering. This is not true: the Greek has no preposition between the nouns. The most that can be said about the "of" translation of the genitive is that it sometimes can preserve an ambiguity— once the translator has decided the Greek really is ambiguous. However, this English phrase is often not as open-ended as some have suggested. I would argue that most English readers would take "hope of righteousness" to mean a hope for righteousness. In any case the NIV and NLT follow the majority of interpreters and make clear for the reader the relationship between these words Paul probably intended.

Passage 12. Colossians 2:8–15

[8] See to it that no one takes you captive through hollow and deceptive philosophy, which depends on human tradition and the elemental spiritual forces of this world rather than on Christ.

> [9] For in Christ all the fullness of the Deity lives in bodily form, [10] and in Christ you have been brought to fullness. He is the head over every power and authority. [11] In him you were also circumcised with a circumcision not performed by human hands. Your whole self ruled by <u>the flesh</u> was put off <u>when you were circumcised by Christ</u> [or *"put off in the circumcision of"*], [12] having been buried with him in baptism, in which you were also raised with him through your faith in the working of God, who raised him from the dead. [13] When you were dead in your sins and in the uncircumcision of your <u>flesh</u>, God made you alive with Christ. He forgave us all our sins, [14] having canceled the charge of our legal indebtedness, which stood against us and condemned us; he has taken it away, nailing it to the cross. [15] And having disarmed the powers and authorities, he made a public spectacle of them, triumphing over them by the cross.

I could spend lot of time talking about this text: its Greek is difficult, and it has some fascinating and important theological teaching. But I must restrict myself to three points about translation this text beautifully illustrates.

One of the most difficult words in Paul's letters to understand and translate is *sarx*. This word occurs in verse 11 in our text, where the ESV, HCSB, and NIV translate "flesh" and the NLT "sinful nature." The "original" NIV (and the TNIV) had "sinful nature" here and in many other passages where the word *sarx* appeared. But we decided to drop this translation for the updated NIV. We translators had heard a lot of criticism of this translation over the years, and we finally decided the criticism was justified: "sinful nature" created connotations unintended by Paul. However, I also want to make clear that nothing in principle is inappropriate in translating *sarx* with any variety of English words. To argue that the word "means" "flesh" and that any other rendering therefore departs from the "literal" meaning is to commit the semantic fallacy of thinking words have a single stable meaning that can be reproduced with a single word in another language. As I have argued in the introductory section, it is impossible to produce a translation that follows what we call a "concordant" approach. By "concordant," I mean the replacement of every Greek or Hebrew word with a single equivalent English word. Only if a given Greek or Hebrew word perfectly matched a particular English word could such a translation approach be possible. But this just does not happen (or happens rarely). In the case of *sarx*, as I noted above, all four of our translations use a wide variety of expressions to translate it in various contexts.

A second, related issue is the way our versions handle the contested word in verse 8, rendered in the NIV "the elemental spiritual forces." Our four versions reflect the two main lines of interpretation, the HCSB rendering "elemental forces of the world," while the other three introduce a reference to "elemental spirits" (ESV) or "elemental spiritual forces" (NIV) or "spiritual powers" (NLT).[13] But what is interesting is the variety in the rendering of this same word, *stoicheia*, elsewhere in the New Testament (Gal 4:3,9; Heb 5:12; 2 Pet 3:10,12). The NIV is the only version that maintains any degree of concordance, using a form of "element" in each place; the other three use a variety of English expressions.[14] Please understand: I am not quarreling with the decision to translate this same phrase differently in these verses since a respectable number of scholars argue for a different referent in these different texts. But here is a place where the NIV preserves a more "concordant" rendering than either the ESV or the HCSB, and this is not an isolated instance. The translators of each of these versions have to make tough decisions about how to bring over Hebrew and Greek words into English. No version will consistently provide the kind of concordant translation that someone wanting to study the nuance of particular Greek and Hebrew words would require.

Third, I would like to look again at yet another genitive construction, in this case one that occurs at the end of verse 11. A simple rough-and-ready translation would be "Christ circumcision." Opinion about this genitive is divided. Some commentators think Paul is referring to Christ's own "circumcision"; that is, he is using the word metaphorically to depict the crucifixion as the place where Christ "stripped off" his own "body of flesh." But other interpreters are convinced that Paul is referring (again, metaphorically) to a circumcision that believers experience when they are converted, and their own "body," or "self," dominated by the flesh is "stripped off." If we follow the first interpretation, the genitive *Christou* would denote the object of circumcision: "the circumcision performed on Christ." The second interpretation, on the other hand, would reverse this relationship: the circumcision would be one performed "by Christ" (a "subjective" genitive). The NIV and the NLT opt for this latter interpretation, putting the subjective genitive interpretation in their texts. The ESV and the HCSB translate simply "of Christ" and "of the Messiah"

---

[13] ESV, TNIV, and NLT provide the alternative interpretation in a footnote.

[14] ESV: "elemental spirits" (Col 2:8,20); "elementary principles" (Gal 4:3,9); "principles" (Heb 5:12); "heavenly bodies" (2 Pet 3:10,12). HCSB: "elemental forces" (Col 2:8,20; Gal 4:3,9); "principles" (Heb 5:12); "elements" (2 Pet 3:10,12). NLT: "spiritual powers" (Col 2:8,20); "[basic] spiritual principles" (Gal 4:3,9); "basic things" (Heb 5:12); "elements" (2 Pet 3:10,12).

respectively. Here, it might be argued, the ESV and the HCSB have provided the English reader with a rendering that keeps the options open, thus avoiding the interpretation that has crept into the NIV and NLT. There is something to be said for this viewpoint.

However, on the other hand, (1) it might just be questioned whether the translation "circumcision of Christ" is really open-ended in English. My own suspicion is that the English reader would tend to read this as an objective genitive: a circumcision performed on Christ. In any case, I think it unlikely that they would interpret it to mean a circumcision performed "by" Christ. So what looks at first like a neutral rendering that leaves options open may, in fact, preclude one significant option. (2) The ESV and HCSB rendering has, moreover, an important downside: the verse as it now stands in these versions is going to make little sense to the average English reader. Consider the ESV: "In him also you were circumcised with a circumcision made without hands, by putting off the body of the flesh, by the circumcision of Christ." This is tough for anyone to negotiate without considerable help. Well, it is sometimes said, let the reader get the help: no one said the Bible is easy; why "dumb it down"? The point is well taken in general; the Bible is full of cultural baggage and language that simply cannot be put into simple modern English without unacceptable loss of meaning. Yet readability must be a factor in the decisions translators make, recognizing that many people will not have access to the help they need to understand the text. Many Christians simply do not have the ability to read study notes or commentaries and do not have regular access to good preaching and teaching—to say nothing of unbelievers who are trying to understand the Bible. Advocates of "word-based" approaches sometimes sound a bit like medieval priests, not worrying about whether the common Christian can understand the Bible and insisting that it is the job of the priestly caste—in this case the preacher—to make the Word understandable. Now I know no one really advocating this; I am exaggerating to make a point. But there is a point: translators must juggle the often-conflicting values of providing the English reader with (1) a text that serves as something of a window into the underlying ambiguities of the Greek, Hebrew, and Aramaic; and (2) a text that is comprehensible. In this case the NIV has chosen the second route. But please do not overlook the footnote in the NIV text. In a sense the NIV has got the best of both worlds: it translates into comprehensible English and provides the reader with both interpretive options.

Passage 13. 1 Thessalonians 1:3

We remember before our God and Father your work <u>produced by faith</u>, your labor <u>prompted by love</u>, and your endurance <u>inspired by hope</u> in our Lord Jesus Christ.

Here we meet up again with our old friend the genitive construction—in fact, three of them. Paul remembers the Thessalonian Christians' "faith work," "love labor," and "hope endurance." Clearly this straightforward translation of the three phrases does not enable the English reader to get a good sense of what Paul means. The ESV and HCSB therefore put the preposition "of" between the two words in each case: "work of faith," "labor of love," "steadfastness/endurance of hope." The English "of + object" construction is what beginning Greek students are taught to use to translate the genitive construction. As I mentioned earlier, however, it is not the "literal" rendering, since there is no preposition in the Greek. However, the "of" construction does have one advantage: it often leaves open the precise relationship between the two nouns in the genitive construction. Advocates of a more "literal" or "word-based" translation philosophy therefore argue that the genitive construction in Greek should usually be translated with the English "of" construction in order to keep all the interpretive options open. The translator, it is argued, should pass on to the English reader the ambiguity of the original text. Readers and students of the Bible should have the opportunity of making up their own minds about what the Greek is saying.

I agree that the translator should preserve ambiguity—where it is possible. Translators often face situations in which it is simply impossible to preserve an ambiguity that is found in the biblical languages. For instance, in Luke 16:8 a genitive construction is used to denote the manager in Jesus' parable. Using "of" to join these nouns in English would yield "the manager of unrighteousness" (*ton oikonomon tēs adikias*). This does not communicate well in English, and so all four versions "interpret" the genitive and translate "the dishonest/unrighteous manager" (NLT has "dishonest rascal"—where they got the word "rascal," I have no idea). In other contexts it will be possible to use an "of" construction to preserve the ambiguity of the original. For instance, in the "original" (1984) NIV, the important Pauline phrase "God righteousness" (*dikaiosynē theou*) was translated "righteousness from God." The translators decided the genitive *theou* ("of God") indicated the source of righteousness, and so they translated accordingly. But scholars have carefully scrutinized this phrase (which occurs eight other times in Paul) over the last three decades, and they have not reached any consensus about just what the phrase means. In the updated NIV, therefore, we chose to translate with the more open-ended "of" construction to preserve more of these interpretive options for the English reader. "The righteousness of God" is now found in the NIV.

So what about 1 Thessalonians 1:3? Why has the NIV not used the open-ended "of" construction here? Because these three genitive constructions are not really ambiguous. The significance of these genitives is clear. Paul uses the genitives to indicate the thing that produces each of these virtues: faith produces work, love leads to labor, and hope stimulates endurance. The standard grammars and commentaries agree; indeed, I could find no commentator on 1 Thessalonians who held any other view of these genitives.[15] In other words, there really is no ambiguity in the case of these genitives. A translation should therefore appropriately bring out this sense.

Passage 14. 1 Timothy 2:12

> I do not permit a woman to teach or <u>to assume authority</u> over a man; she must be quiet.

Few New Testament verses have been debated with as much passion as this one over the last 30 years. The reason is not hard to discover; perhaps no other New Testament verse speaks as significantly to the question of what roles women should have in the church than this one. "Complementarians" (if I may use this popular though somewhat artificial label) insist that the verse imposes certain permanent restrictions

---

[15] See, e.g., Nigel Turner, *Syntax*, vol. 3 of *A Grammar of New Testament*, by James Hope Moulton and Nigel Turner (Edinburgh: T&T Clark, 1906), 211; Friedrich Blass and Albert Debrunner, *A Greek Grammar of the New Testament and Other Early Christian Literature*, trans. Robert Walter Funk (Chicago: University of Chicago Press, 1961), 90; Daniel B. Wallace, *Greek Grammar Beyond the Basics: An Exegetical Syntax of the New Testament* (Grand Rapids: Zondervan, 1996), 106; Charles A. Wanamaker, *The Epistles to the Thessalonians: A Commentary on the Greek Text*, The New International Greek Testament Commentary (Grand Rapids: Eerdmans, 1990), 75; F. F. Bruce, *1 & 2 Thessalonians*, Word Biblical Commentary 45 (Waco, TX: Word, 1982), 12; Leon Morris, *The First and Second Epistles to the Thessalonians*, New International Commentary on the New Testament (Grand Rapids: Eerdman, 1991), 39–43; Abraham Malherbe, *The Letters to the Thessalonians: A New Translation with Introduction and Commentary*, Anchor Bible 32B (New York: Doubleday, 2000), 108; Gene Green, *The Letters to the Thessalonians*, Pillar New Testament Commentary (Grand Rapids: Eerdmans, 2002), 88–91; Ernest Best, *A Commentary on the First and Second Epistles to the Thessalonians*, Harper's New Testament Commentaries (New York: Harper & Row, 1972), 67; Gordon Fee, *The First and Second Letters to the Thessalonians*, New International Commentary on the New Testament (Grand Rapids: Eerdmans, 2000), 24–26; and see also the note in the NET Bible.

on the ministry of women. Egalitarians, on the other hand, are not convinced this is the correct interpretation of the verse. We must, of course, bypass much of that exegetical and theological debate as we focus on the issue we are concerned with—the NIV translation of the verse.

A quick comparison with the other three versions we are considering in this book reveals only one significant difference among them: whereas the ESV, HCSB, and NLT have the essentially synonymous translations "have" or "exercise authority," NIV has "assume authority." The English expressions are attempts to render a single Greek word, *authentein*. This word comes from a rare verb: it does not occur anywhere else in biblical Greek, and it is found only a few times in Greek literature written at or before Paul's day. Interpreters and translators therefore have little solid evidence to inform their decisions about this verb. For this reason scholars are divided about what meaning to give the word. The paucity of evidence and the disagreement among scholars made our translation of this word in the NIV a difficult decision. Why did we opt for "assume authority"—especially when most of the modern versions translate "have" or "exercise" authority?

First, this is the meaning the recognized authority on the meanings of New Testament words gives to the word. The Greek English lexicon of Bauer, Arndt, Gingrich, and Danker (BDAG) claims the word means: **"to assume a stance of independent authority, *give orders to, dictate to*."**[16] We were also impressed that scholars on both sides of the complementarian/egalitarian divide have identified "assume authority" as a possible meaning for the word in this verse.[17] They note that other words that come from this same root often have the idea of "initiating" an action: hence "assume [take on, enter into] authority."

A second factor we thought important in deciding how to translate this rare word was a basic principle of linguistics that can be put in the form of a simple question: why has an author used a particular word? In this case the question is relevant because Paul elsewhere uses a verb (and a phrase) that clearly means "have" or "exercise" authority. Of course, Paul could

---

[16] Walter Bauer, *A Greek-English Lexicon of the New Testament and Other Early Christian Literature*, 3rd ed, rev. and ed. F. W. Danker, W. F. Arndt, and F. W. Gingrich (Chicago: University of Chicago Press, 2000), 150.

[17] See H. Scott Baldwin, "A Difficult Word: αὐθεντεῖν in 1 Timothy 2:12," in *Women in the Church: A Fresh Analysis of 1 Timothy 2:9–15*, eds. Andreas J. Köstenberger, Thomas R. Schreiner, and H. Scott Baldwin (Grand Rapids: Baker, 1995), 65–80 (see p. 80); Philip B. Payne, *Man and Woman, One in Christ: An Exegetical and Theological Study of Paul's Letters* (Grand Rapids: Zondervan, 2009), 361–97.

be using a different word here to mean the same thing; authors certainly do this. But we were not sure in this case that this consideration explained Paul's use of so rare a word. We concluded that Paul probably chose this unusual word to say something a bit different than if he had used his regular word for "have authority"; and, as we have seen, the nuance of "initiating" authority makes good sense in light of other occurrences of this word and forms of the word.

To summarize: our translation "assume authority" follows the acknowledged standard source for the meanings of New Testament words; it is a meaning for which other careful scholars have argued; and it fits this context. Our decision to translate the word this way has nothing to do with any particular modern ideological or theological agenda; we are simply following the evidence as we see it. Some critics of this translation suggest that our translation rests on bad scholarship and is a capitulation to a "feminist" or "egalitarian" agenda. Nothing could be further from the truth. Was Calvin an "egalitarian" because he translated the word this way? And, in terms of scholarship: anyone who claims that the meaning of this rare word has been established is simply not being fair to the diversity of views in the scholarly community. We just cannot be sure about it. Moreover, the English "assume authority" is certainly not incompatible with a "complementarian" reading: as a quick Google search will show you, the phrase has the sense simply of "moving into a position or situation of authority" over others. As Scott Baldwin, in an essay in a book that strongly advocates a "complementarian" reading of this verse, says, "'to assume authority over' is *a positive term* that appears to imply that one moves forward to fill the leadership role."[18]

Passage 15. Jude 4–5

[4] For certain individuals whose condemnation was written about long ago have secretly slipped in among you. They are ungodly people, who pervert the grace of our God into a license for immorality and deny Jesus Christ our only Sovereign and Lord. [5] Though you already know all this, I want to remind you that the Lord at one time delivered his people out of Egypt, but later destroyed those who did not believe.

---

[18] Baldwin, "Difficult Word," 75 (emphasis added).

This passage is the opening salvo Jude fires in his battle against false teachers, who are threatening the spiritual health of the Christians to whom he writes. Verse 4 is a long and complex single sentence in Greek, and it is instructive to see the way our versions handle it. The ESV, in typical fashion, keeps the single sentence and follows closely the sequence of the Greek. Each of us has our own idea about what constitutes good English style. I will only say that, for me, the ESV reads awkwardly. By following the Greek so closely, the ESV ends up simply not being good, natural English. The separation of the relative clause "who long ago were designated" from its referent ("certain people") is not easy to navigate. The phrase "ungodly people" is stuck in and interrupts the natural flow of the English. The HCSB "fixes" both these problems: it moves the relative clause up so that it immediately follows its referent ("some men, who were designated"); and it breaks the long sentence with a semicolon, using a pronoun ("they") to pick up the subject and continue the sentence. The NIV follows this same pattern, breaking the verse into two sentences. The NIV "written about" is also, it seems to me, an improvement on the ESV/HCSB "designated" (as well as translating the Greek verb more accurately!). As we would expect, the NLT departs the furthest from the sequence of the Greek in the interest of producing an accessible English rendering. They not only divide the verse into two sentences, but they shift the clause about "condemnation . . . written long ago" from the opening part of the verse to the second part of the verse. Yet the NLT may go too far in its rearrangement. They not only move this clause to the end of the verse, but they also link this clause to the next one with a "for." In the NLT, then, the condemnation of these people comes because "they have denied our only Master and Lord, Jesus Christ." But this is a connection the Greek text simply does not make.

Verse 5 is shorter and less complicated, and it reads pretty well in all four of the versions. My own admittedly subjective view is that the NIV improves the English style a bit by putting the clause "though you already know all this" at the front of the verse rather than having it interrupt the main clause ("I want to remind you that") as in the other three versions. An interesting textual issue is reflected in the difference between "the Lord" in NIV and HCSB and "Jesus" in ESV and NLT. Some manuscripts have simply the Greek equivalent of "Lord" (*kyrios*), while others have the name "Jesus." The NET also has "Jesus," while most of the other versions have "Lord" (CEB; NAB; NASB; NRSV; NJB; NKJV). The textual issue is complicated and not easy to decide; one can make a good case for either "the Lord" or "Jesus." Because the textual decision is difficult, it is important that the alternative be reflected in a footnote—as the NIV, the ESV, the HCSB, and the NLT do.

Passage 16. Revelation 3:20

> Here I am! I stand at the door and knock. If <u>anyone</u> hears my voice and opens the door, I will come in and eat with <u>that person</u>, and <u>they</u> with me.

We have here a final text that falls into the pattern we have observed throughout this book: the ESV and HCSB are comfortable in using masculine singular pronouns—"I will come in to him and eat [have dinner] with him, and he with me"—whereas the NIV and NLT choose other words. The NLT uses a second-person pronoun and then a first-person plural pronoun: "If *you* hear my voice and open the door, I will come in, and *we* will share a meal together as friends." Some might object that this takes an inappropriate liberty with the text—the Greek, after all, is in the third-person singular throughout. But this objection misses the larger issue. As we have repeatedly noted, masculine third-person singular pronouns in modern English carry distinctly masculine connotations. Are these connotations present in the Greek of this text? Certainly not. Jesus here addresses *any* believer, without any reference to their gender. Using the masculine pronouns "he" and "him," then, can import a masculine orientation into this text that was never intended. Translators legitimately, then, will seek to find translation options that do not have this problem. English pronouns in the first and second person ("you," "we") are not "marked" for gender, and so they more accurately reflect Jesus' intention to include all believers equally in his promise.

The NIV takes a different tack, following up "anyone" with "that person" and "they." "That person," of course, maintains the singular of the original text without being gender specific. And "they" has its common "singular" or "distributive" sense: in this context it modifies "that person." I have noted this use of the "singular" "they" in several other passages (Psalm 1; Ezekiel 18; Luke 17:3), and I will not repeat here what I say about its widespread usage in modern English again. But I might briefly deal with the criticism that the shift to "they" in texts like this might cause confusion to the reader. In other words, the English reader or listener might be misled into thinking some new group of people has suddenly popped up. In some contexts, to be sure, this can be a problem. The NIV translators have been careful to analyze each text to see if this becomes a problem. In this text I do not think this problem arises. Modern English speakers have become so accustomed to this "singular" "they" that they usually have no problem in figuring out what is going on. Indeed, most of us use this kind of construction all the time without even realizing it—it has just become part of the way we speak. We say, "Anyone who wants to eat needs to wash *their* hands"; or, "The person who wants to make a good impression should comb their hair." The NIV uses this natural modern English way of speaking to preserve the singular focus in Revelation 3:20 without giving the false impression that males are somehow given special attention here. Rather, just as in the case of Bible translations, each believer is invited to make *their* own decision.

Chapter 4

The Holman Christian Standard Bible (HCSB)

E. Ray Clendenen

The HCSB project began in 1998 under the supervision of B&H Publishing. The first full-text Bible was published in 2004. A second edition was released in 2009 and is available in the HCSB Study Bible, on MyStudyBible.com, and in many styles of printed Bibles.

Principles of Optimal Equivalence

Terms such as "optimal equivalence" must be described positively as well as negatively. I will attempt to do this, but it must be done in the context of the two major alternative translation philosophies: formal equivalence and functional equivalence.[1]

Distinguished from Formal Equivalence

Usually referred to as "literal," this translation philosophy is better described as formal equivalence for two reasons.[2] First, the term "literal" is a slippery one. It is often equated with word-for-word translation, and

---

[1] Eugene Nida, the originator of the term "dynamic equivalence," later responded to some misunderstanding by changing the designation to "functional equivalence." See Jan de Waard and Eugene A. Nida, *From One Language to Another: Functional Equivalence in Bible Translating* (Nashville: Thomas Nelson, 1986), vii–viii.

[2] Some have argued that the term "formal equivalence" is pejorative, implying that such translations are more concerned with form than meaning. That certainly is not my intent, and it is not what "formal equivalence" means.

yet such translations do not really follow the word order of the Hebrew and Greek texts, which would be incomprehensible in English. No translation is truly literal. At best they can be "essentially literal," as the ESV admits.

Another problem with "literal" is that it is often equated with "true," "real," "basic," or "accurate." For example, Merrill Tenney claimed that the word *embrimaomai* in John 11:33 "means literally 'to snort like a horse' and generally connotes anger."[3] Did Jesus really snort like a horse when faced with the death of Lazarus? The only evidence that this is the meaning of *embrimaomai* is that the word is found with that meaning in writings such as the fifth-century BC playwright Aeschylus. But that usage has nothing to do with John's use of it to describe Jesus. The word "literal" is used here to bless an exegetical fallacy, and the layman has no recourse but to accept it because "literal" in the popular evangelical dialect is thought to mean "true" or "real." The word "literal" is not a silver bullet.

Another problem with "literal" is that sometimes people try to make a distinction between a "translation" and an "interpretation." They want a version that *just translates* the Bible rather than *interpreting* it, and they think that is what a literal translation does. But this is a false dichotomy. There is no such thing as a translation that does not interpret. The first step in translation is to understand the text to be translated. The second step is to render that text in the new language in such a way the reader will understand what the text means. That is interpretation.

For example, the HCSB of 2 Samuel 19:7 includes the statement, "Go out and encourage your soldiers."[4] A note is attached to the word "encourage" that says, "Lit *speak to the heart of.*" This gives a word-for-word translation of the idiom. We might expect an "essentially literal" translation like the NASB or ESV to render the idiom as is. But, in fact, every major English translation renders the phrase with a functional equivalent. Both the NASB and the ESV have "go out and speak kindly to your servants" (the NASB has a note giving the literal, but the ESV does not).

The second reason the term "formal equivalence" is better is that this translation philosophy means so much more than "word for word." A formal equivalence translation has five basic characteristics. It seeks, where possible, to translate the source texts (1) word for word; (2) using the same grammatical structures as the original; (3) preserving the idioms; (4) using the same translations of the same words and phrases in similar contexts,

---

[3] Merrill C. Tenney, "The Gospel of John," in *The Expositor's Bible Commentary*, vol. 9: *John-Acts* (Grand Rapids: Zondervan, 1981), 119.

[4] All references to the HCSB and the other translations are to the latest editions.

especially if they are in close proximity; and (5) usually relying heavily on translation notes to call attention to textual variants and alternate interpretations, to explain difficult terms and expressions, and to describe rhetorical features (such as plays on words) that are impossible to render in English.[5]

A formal equivalence translation philosophy might be said to have a higher tolerance for grammatical structures that do not sound as natural in English as other structures would. Rather than "How would we say that in English?" the "literal" translator asks, "Can I keep the lexical and grammatical structures the same and still make sense in English?" It results in many translations that are *possible* but not "optimal."

Now how does *optimal equivalence* differ? Optimal equivalence has the same five characteristics but adds one more. Instead of "where possible," optimal equivalence aims at these same characteristics while not sacrificing *naturalness of expression*. For example, although "truly, truly, I say to you," is comprehensible, it is not the way most people talk. Therefore, the HCSB has "I assure you." "Literal" does not mean "accurate." How many people hear Jesus say, "Truly, truly, I say to you," and understand what he meant? If an account of a crime is given in the language of seventeenth-century England and the modern-day jury does not really understand it, is it accurate? I would say no. Striving for accuracy without also striving for ease of comprehension is like shooting at a bull's eye with invisible arrows. No one can tell whether you have hit it.

Some argue that Bible translation should allow readers to get as close as possible to the texts in the original languages (called "transparency" by some), and that if the Bible text is hard to understand, it causes the reader to stop and ponder. "Leave it to the preachers to explain it." These arguments are wrongheaded. From the beginning Christianity was a *translated* faith. Jesus apparently spoke mainly in Aramaic, but almost all we have of his words are in Greek—the common Greek understood by the most people. Unlike Islam, carrying the Christian message across cultures has always involved *translating* the Scriptures into the languages of those cultures, not forcing the people to learn Greek, Hebrew, and Aramaic. And what should and does cause readers to stop and ponder is the profoundness of the message, not the difficulty of the language. There are enough difficult

---

[5] The HCSB has almost 8,000 translation notes, and the ESV has more than 6,000. In addition, the HCSB has a glossary of about 150 "bullet notes," that is, explanations of frequently occurring terms that are simply marked with a bullet at the first occurrence per chapter. This device saves the addition of more than 3,000 repetitive translation notes (of which the ESV has many). By comparison, the TNIV has about 3,000 notes, and the NLT has more than 4,000 (again, with many repetitions).

passages in the Bible (see 2 Pet 3:15–16) without adding to the difficulty ourselves. The grammatical subject of Bishop Westcott's famous quote should be taken seriously: "*God* was pleased to leave difficulties upon the surface of Scripture, that men might be forced to look below the surface."[6] Our job as Christians is to understand and teach (see Matt 23:13; Luke 8:16; John 3:10; 1 Cor 14:19; 2 Tim 4:2), not to lay verbal land mines to slow people down. And the idea that translators should leave in the Bible as many difficulties as possible in order to drive people to the preachers and teachers of the church would raise the hair on the necks of Martin Luther and William Tyndale, the latter of whom is said to have wanted to produce an English Bible that "a boy that driveth the plow in England" could read and understand. Translating the Bible into the common language of the people, an essential element of the Protestant Reformation, was intended to *overthrow* the clergy's monopoly on the Bible and make it possible for common people to be nourished by it.

Distinguished from Functional Equivalence

So, what is "functional equivalence"? Originally called "dynamic equivalence," Eugene Nida describes it as "the closest natural equivalent to the source-language message." By "natural" he means that the rendering must fit (1) the receptor language and culture; (2) the context of the passage; and (3) the intended audience of the translation. It must especially fit the receptor language (English in our case) in grammar and word choice.[7] Hence it is sometimes referred to as "idiomatic" translation.

Functional or dynamic equivalence, Nida says, is based on "the principle of equivalent effect." He explains that "one is not so concerned with matching the receptor-language message with the source-language message, but with the dynamic relationship, that the relationship between receptor and message should be substantially the same as that which existed between the original receptors and the message."[8] The problem here is that the translator does not always know what "effect" the original message had on the audience. What is more, in many cases in the Old Testament, we know that the effect was negative. Therefore, on the contrary, I think the translator must place *priority* on "matching the receptor-language message with the source-language message."

---

[6] B. F. Westcott, *The Bible in the Church* (Grand Rapids: Baker, 1979 [1864]), x.

[7] Eugene A. Nida, *Toward a Science of Translating: With Special Reference to Principles and Procedures Involved in Bible Translating* (Leiden: E. J. Brill, 1964), 166–67.

[8] Ibid., 159.

Optimal equivalence shares functional equivalence's commitment to naturalness of language. But it differs from functional equivalence by also treating as desirable the essential characteristics of formal equivalence. The priority for optimal equivalence is communication, which includes truth and comprehension. The message of the text and its purpose must come through.

Translation Comparison

Passage 1. Exodus 2:5–6

> [5] Pharaoh's daughter went down to bathe at the Nile while her servant girls walked along the riverbank. Seeing the basket among the reeds, she sent her slave girl to get it. [6] When she opened it, she saw the child—a little boy, crying. She felt sorry for him and said, "This is one of the Hebrew boys."

The difference in translations here comes primarily in verse 6. The issues are how to render the two synonyms, "boy" (*yeled*, used twice) and "child" (*na'ar*), and how to understand the use of *hinneh*. The two synonyms both refer to young boys of various ages, although *na'ar* can also refer to a male servant. Moses is identified three times in verse 6, then, as a baby boy. An important piece of background information that has a bearing on this verse is the pharaoh's command that Hebrew "sons" must die, though "daughters" may live (Exod 1:16). But the two midwives disobeyed and let the *yeladim*[9] live (Exod 1:17). This word is rendered either "boys" or "male children" by almost all translations. So, what happened when the pharaoh's daughter went to bathe by the Nile? She discovered several surprising things. The first was a basket or chest floating in the water among the reeds. The second was that it contained a baby. Now this point was surely not a huge surprise since we are told the baby was crying. But the word used for the child is *yeled*, the word referring to a male child, even the word used in Exodus 1:17. But what is marked with *hinneh*, a "presentative particle" that can "introduce with emotion a perception"?[10] Traditionally rendered (as in the NASB, NKJV, and ESV) as "behold" (and frequently by other translations as "look"), here it marks the recognition that this

---

[9] Plural of *yeled*.
[10] Bruce K. Waltke and Michael O'Connor, *Introduction to Biblical Hebrew Syntax* (Winona Lake, IN: Eisenbrauns, 1990), 676.

child was a crying little boy (*na'ar bokeh*). The fact that he is crying is surely no surprise, but the fact that he's a little boy is something to notice, especially since he is clearly "one of the Hebrew boys" (*miyalde ha'ibrim*). Most translations (including the ESV, NIV, and NLT) imply that the reason she "took pity" on Moses was that he was crying.

> ESV   When she opened it, she saw the child, and behold, the baby was crying. She took pity on him and said, "This is one of the Hebrews' children."

> NIV   She opened it and saw the baby. He was crying, and she felt sorry for him. "This is one of the Hebrew babies," she said.

> NLT   When the princess opened it, she saw the baby. The little boy was crying, and she felt sorry for him. "This must be one of the Hebrew children," she said.

Yet I believe the more salient fact was that he was "one of the Hebrew boys," and as such he was under a death warrant. The HCSB is the only one that clearly places the emphasis on the baby being a male, both by repetition and by the handling of *hinneh* (with an em-dash):

> HCSB   When she opened it, she saw the child—a little boy, crying. She felt sorry for him and said, "This is one of the Hebrew boys."

Passage 2. Psalm 1:1

A helpful comparison can be made of Psalm 1:1a:

> ESV   Blessed is the man who <u>walks not in the counsel</u> of the wicked,

> NIV   Blessed is the one who <u>does not walk in step with</u> the wicked,

> HCSB   How happy is the man who <u>does not follow the advice</u> of the wicked

> NLT   Oh, the joys of those who <u>do not follow the advice</u> of the wicked,

The primary difference in these translations is their rendering of the Hebrew phrase

lo'	*halak*	*ba'atsat*	*resha'iym*
not	he walks	in the advice of	wicked people

The ESV's translation of the entire clause is word for word except for the placement of the word "not."[11] However, the problem of the meaning of "walk in the counsel of" remains. It is not a common English expression and is, therefore, likely to at least slow down comprehension of the text (and increase the processing effort required of the reader).

The new edition of the NIV could be accused of not translating the word *'atsat,* "advice of." According to the major Hebrew lexicon (*HALOT*),[12] the word means either "advice" or "plan." To "walk in step with" means either, literally, to march with, or, figuratively, to pattern one's behavior after someone else. This is similar to following their advice but not the same. So the NIV has used a phrase that is functionally *similar to* the Hebrew phrase but not equivalent. The HCSB and NLT have both chosen to replace the figurative expression "walk in the advice of" with "follow the advice of." That appears to be a functional equivalent. This has no significant difference in meaning, but it has the effect of losing the parallel structure of the verse in Hebrew, which has three negated verbs: "not walk . . . not stand . . . not sit." We could argue that in this clause from Psalm 1, the ESV is "literal," the HCSB and NLT are functionally equivalent, and the NIV is a rough equivalent. Unlike the NLT and NIV, however, the HCSB retains the masculine singular "man," for the translation of Hebrew *'ish.* This is the most common Hebrew word for "man," occurring more than 2,000 times in the Old Testament, the first time being in Genesis 2:23 in opposition to *'ishah,* "woman." The NIV renders it in Psalm 1:1 by the generic "one," and the NLT pluralizes it to "those." Therefore, the HCSB might be said to follow formal equivalence except when it would interfere with accurate and unhindered comprehension: hence the term "optimal equivalence."

The remainder of the verse is likewise rendered somewhat literally by the ESV, while the others follow a functional equivalent path, with slight disagreement over what those functional equivalents are.

---

[11] The NASB is the same, except for choosing a slightly more natural rendering of the verb, which, in fact, preserves the word order better than the ESV.

[12] Ludwig Koehler and Walter Baumgartner, *The Hebrew and Aramaic Lexicon of the Old Testament,* trans. and ed. M. E. J. Richardson (Leiden: Brill, 2000).

ESV   nor <u>stands in the way of sinners</u>, nor sits in the seat of scoffers;

NIV   or <u>stand in the way that sinners take</u> or sit in the company of mockers,

HCSB   or <u>take the path of sinners</u> or join a group of mockers!

NLT   or <u>stand around with sinners</u>, or join in with mockers.

A truly literal rendering might be made as follows:

and in the path of sinners not he stands, and in the seat of scoffers not he sits.

In the first clause the ESV follows the confusing rendering of the KJV and RSV, with an idiom that means in English "to block or obstruct someone's path."[13] What it means to stand in the path of sinners is uncertain, since there is no verse in the Old Testament parallel to this. At the least, it involves association with "sinners," that is, those whose behavior violates God's instructions, God's "way." So it seems to involve participating in their sinful behavior. Those who "scoff" or "mock" refers to those who reject God and mock those who seek his ways (e.g., Prov 1:22). Their "seat" is taken to refer to their "circle"[14] or "gathering."[15] So, again, the sense involves a rather close association with the godless. All the functionally equivalent renderings have essentially the same thing.

Passage 3. Ezekiel 18:5–9,21–24

[5]"Now suppose a man is righteous and does what is just and right: [6] He does not eat at the mountain shrines or <u>raise his eyes to the idols of the house of Israel</u>. He does not defile his neighbor's wife or <u>come near a woman during her menstrual impurity</u>. [7] <u>He doesn't oppress anyone</u> but returns his collateral to the debtor. He does not commit robbery, but gives his bread to the hungry and covers the naked with clothing. [8] He doesn't lend at interest or for profit but keeps his hand from wrongdoing and <u>carries out</u>

---

[13] This is corrected in the NASB by changing "way" to "path."

[14] Hans-Joachim Kraus, *Psalms 1–59: A Continental Commentary*, trans. H. C. Oswald (Minneapolis: Fortress, 1993), 116.

[15] Peter C. Craigie, *Psalms 1–50*, Word Biblical Commentary 19 (Waco, TX: Word, 1983), 58.

true justice between men. [9] He <u>follows My statutes</u> and keeps My ordinances, acting faithfully. Such a person is righteous; he will certainly live." <u>This is the declaration of the Lord God.</u> . . . [21] "Now if the wicked person turns from all the sins he has committed, keeps all My statutes, and does what is just and right, he <u>will</u> certainly live; he <u>will</u> not die. [22] <u>None of the transgressions he has committed will be held against him. He will live because of the righteousness he has practiced.</u> [23] Do I take any pleasure in the death of the wicked?" <u>This is the declaration of the Lord God.</u> "Instead, don't I take pleasure when he turns from his ways and lives? [24] But when a righteous person turns from his righteousness and practices iniquity, committing the same detestable acts that the wicked do, will he live? None of the righteous acts he did <u>will</u> be remembered. <u>He will die because of the treachery he has engaged in and the sin he has committed.</u>

A comparison of the ESV, HCSB, NIV, and NLT of these verses reveals that the HCSB is only slightly less literal than the ESV. For example, rather than the ESV's literal "executes true justice between man and man" in verse 8, the HCSB has "carries out true justice between men." Rather than the ESV's literal "walks in my statutes" in verse 9, the HCSB has "follows my statutes." Instead of the ESV's "None of the transgressions that he has committed shall be *remembered* against him" in verse 22, the HCSB has "None of the transgressions he has committed will be held against him."[16] The remainder of that verse in the ESV is "for the righteousness that he has done he shall live." But the HCSB has reversed the word order in the clause to the more natural "He will live because of the righteousness he has practiced." The same reordering is found in verse 24. The ESV has "for the treachery of which he is guilty and the sin he has committed, for them he shall die," and the HCSB has "He will die because of the treachery he has engaged in and the sin he has committed."

Another difference one might notice between the ESV and the HCSB is the use of "shall" in the ESV and its absence in the HCSB. In traditional grammar the simple future called for "shall" only in the first person. But for the expression of determination, promise, or command, "shall" was used only in the second and third persons. In modern English, *shall* is usually encountered only in questions requesting permission or agreement (e.g., "Shall we go?") or in legal documents where "shall" expresses obligation.

---

[16] Daniel Block, *The Book of Ezekiel: Chapters 1—24* (Grand Rapids: Eerdmans, 1997), 581, explains that the Hebrew idiom here means "to charge against."

Otherwise, according to Bryan A. Garner, "shall" is "peripheral in AmE [American English]."[17] Therefore, the word is not found in the HCSB.

The NIV is less literal than the HCSB, and the NLT is still less literal. For the literal (HCSB) "raise his eyes to the idols of the house of Israel" in verse 6, the NIV has "look to the idols of Israel." The NLT uses the functional equivalent "worship." For the literal "come near a woman during her menstrual impurity" in the same verse, the NIV has "have sexual relations [NLT "have intercourse"] with a woman during her period." For the literal "defile his neighbor's wife" in verse 6, the NLT has "commit adultery." Rather than the literal negation in verse 7, "He doesn't oppress anyone," the NLT has "He is a merciful creditor." And the literal "committing the same detestable acts that the wicked do" in verse 24 is reduced to "act like other sinners" in the NLT.

One striking departure from the sense of the Hebrew in these verses is the NLT's changing of masculine singular to generic singular and then plural. After an initial "Suppose a certain man is righteous" and a series of third-person masculine singular verbs and the terms "father" and "son" in verses 5–18,[18] the NLT changes to "parent" and "child" in verse 19 with no warrant in the Hebrew text, and then to the plural "righteous people" and "wicked people" (as well as "they," "their," and "them") in verses 20b–24 on the same basis.[19] Then throughout verses 21–24, the nouns and pronouns are all plural, even though they are all singular in Hebrew.

The NIV waits until verse 20 to switch to "parent" and "child," presumably on the basis of the first clause, which uses *hannephesh*: *"The one who sins is the one who will die."* But the word *nephesh* does not change the meaning or number of the masculine singular nouns and pronouns that follow in the verse. The NIV switches to the singular "person" in verses 21–24, but they use the so-called singular "they," "their," and "them" throughout those verses. This is confusing to someone who does not use

[17] *A Dictionary of Modern American Usage* (New York: Oxford University Press, 1998), 597–98. This was a major resource of the HCSB stylists. Garner's guide to usage is based primarily on the canvassing of millions of published documents through online databases (NEXIS and WESTLAW), from which he draws about 5,600 illustrations.

[18] One loss of a masculine occurs in verse 8. The literal "justice between man and man" becomes "judging others." The NIV does something similar: "judges fairly between two parties."

[19] According to Daniel Block's note on verse 5 (*Book of Ezekiel*, 569), "The masculine 'man' is retained [in his translation] because, strictly speaking, the subjects in the chapter are all males and the crimes listed are characteristically male crimes. However, the principles enunciated apply universally, irrespective of gender." See also his translation of verses 19–24, which retains the masculine and singular of the Hebrew text throughout (ibid., 579, 581).

such a grammatical novelty, and it removes the clear masculine singular focus of the whole chapter.[20]

One final item in this passage deserves comment. The most striking thing about the HCSB here is the unusual rendering, "This is the declaration of the Lord GOD" in verses 9 and 23. The other versions have "declares the Lord GOD" (ESV), "declares the Sovereign LORD" (NIV), or "says the Sovereign LORD" (NLT). The HCSB has "[This is] the declaration of the LORD/Lord" or "This is the LORD's/Lord's declaration" about 335 times rather than the traditional "says/declares the LORD/Lord." Why the break with tradition? Regarding the HCSB, there are two reasons. The first is that the HCSB rendering is more literal. The Hebrew for "This is the LORD's declaration" is *ne'um yhwh*. The first word is a noun that means something like "oracle," "declaration," or "announcement." The noun and the following name are in a genitive relation: "declaration *of* Yahweh." The HCSB supplies "this is" to make clear what is believed to be the sense. "Says the LORD," the standard way of just indicating that God is the speaker, would be *'amar yhwh* (for example, see how both are used in Mal 1:2). The second reason for the nontraditional rendering is that according to the latest research in Hebrew discourse, this phrase was intended to be intrusive and to have two functions: (1) remind the audience that what was being said had divine authority, and (2) mark what it was attached to as especially prominent, often the conclusion of the paragraph.[21]

Passage 4. Matthew 5:1–3

[1]When He saw the crowds, He went up on the mountain, and after He sat down, His disciples came to Him. [2]Then He began to teach them, saying: [3]"The poor in spirit are blessed, for the kingdom of heaven is theirs."

The Greek New Testament makes considerable use of participles,[22] using them as the main verb of a dependent, circumstantial (adverbial) clause.

---

[20] See Block's remark in the previous note.

[21] See H. Van Dyke Parunak, "Some Discourse Functions of Prophetic Quotation Formulas in Jeremiah," in *Biblical Hebrew and Discourse Linguistics*, ed. Robert D. Bergen (Dallas: Summer Institute of Linguistics, 1994), 490, 500, 508–12; Timothy L. Wilt, "'Oracle of Yahweh': Translating a Highly Marked Expression," *The Bible Translator* 50/3 (1999): 301–4; Samuel A. Meier, *Speaking of Speaking: Marking Direct Discourse in the Hebrew Bible* (Leiden: Brill, 1992), 298–314.

[22] A Greek participle and an English participle are not the same, though they share some things in common (hence the name). Therefore, it is an error to think a Greek participle should necessarily be translated by an English participle, though a "literal" rendering may often do so.

Matthew 5:1, for example, is a short verse with four clauses. Two of them are dependent clauses with circumstantial participles, and two are independent with finite verbs.[23] They also alternate in pairs: dependent + independent, then dependent + independent.

> Dependent clauses with participles:
> When He *saw* the crowds . . . and after He *sat* down
>
> Independent clauses with finite verbs:
> He *went up* on the mountain . . . His disciples *came* to Him.

Greek, like English, puts the more prominent information in an independent clause. The two prominent events in this sentence are found in the independent clauses. The other two clauses, the dependent clauses that use participles, give supplementary information.

We might begin to express the meaning of the sentence with four propositions, marking the independent clauses with all caps.

> 1. Jesus saw the crowds.
> 2. JESUS WENT UP ON THE MOUNTAIN.
> 3. Jesus (not the disciples) sat down.
> 4. JESUS' DISCIPLES CAME TO HIM.

These four propositions, however, do not adequately account for the sentence's meaning. We must also establish the explicit or implicit relationships between them. But the first step is to acknowledge which clauses are independent and which ones are dependent. Matthew might have written:

> JESUS SAW THE CROWDS, *THEN* WENT UP ON THE MOUNTAIN,
> THEN SAT DOWN. *THEN* THE DISCIPLES CAME TO HIM.

This would have involved four independent clauses, related chronologically, with none more prominent than the others. Or Matthew could have said:

> After Jesus saw the crowds and went up on the mountain, HE
> SAT DOWN. THEN THE DISCIPLES CAME TO HIM.

This would make the first two clauses dependent and the last two independent. More important, it would place the emphasis on Jesus' sitting down

---

[23] A *finite* verb is a basic verb form, one that is not a participle or infinitive. It can take a subject, has a "tense," and can be the verb of an independent clause.

and on the disciples coming to him. One more option (there are many) Matthew had was:

> JESUS SAW THE CROWDS, causing Him to go up on the mountain and sit down. THEN THE DISCIPLES CAME TO HIM.

This would put the focus on the first and fourth clauses (and propositions). But Matthew rejected these three options, though all might be an accurate account of what happened.

Verse 2 comprises another pair of clauses like verse 1: a dependent clause followed by an independent clause. It could be rendered somewhat literally as "and opening his mouth, HE TAUGHT THEM." It is fairly well accepted that the initial dependent clause is an idiom and that the two clauses can be accurately rendered as one clause: "And/then he began to teach them." A case can be made for including verse 2 in the sentence that begins in verse 1. What is problematic is the severing of the dependent clause, "and sitting down," from the independent clause that it modifies: "his disciples came to him," and then translating the dependent clause as if it were an independent clause. The TEV is more troubling in its handling of the third clause.

The NLT, the NIV, and the TEV render the second part of verse 1 together with verse 2. The NLT has:

NLT   [1] One day as he saw the crowds gathering, Jesus went up on the mountainside and sat down. His disciples gathered around him, [2] and he began to teach them.

Similarly, the NIV has:

NIV   [1] Now when Jesus saw the crowds, he went up on a mountainside and sat down. His disciples came to him, [2] and he began to teach them.

The TEV does this as well but also renders the first clause as independent. It also renders the third clause as an adjectival (relative) clause modifying the second clause rather than the third.

TEV   [1] Jesus saw the crowds and went up a hill, where he sat down. His disciples gathered around him, [2] and he began to teach them:

This mishandling of the clauses by the NLT, the NIV, and the TEV strays from what Matthew wrote.

What Matthew chose to convey was that (1) Jesus' seeing the crowds provided the *occasion* (and perhaps even the reason) for his ascending the mountain; the latter was Matthew's first main point, or the first *event* that Matthew was especially interested in. (2) The second event was that Jesus' disciples followed him up the mountain and presented themselves before him. These two events provide the setting for the Sermon on the Mount, which is introduced in verse 2. But until Jesus sat down, the disciples may have been puzzled by what Jesus was doing. When Jesus sat down (the standard posture for a teacher), they recognized this as a teaching session and so followed him. So it was "after Jesus sat down" that the disciples followed him up the mountain. English is not a "participle heavy" language like Greek is. English loves conjunctions and adverbs. So the best way to translate this Greek into English is something like:

> When He *saw* the crowds, He *went up* on the mountain, and after He *sat* down, His disciples *came* to Him. Then he began to teach them.

The ESV follows the grammatical clues in the first two verses, though we might argue that they are taken so literally that some of the sense is obscured:

> ESV Seeing the crowds, he went up on the mountain, and when he sat down, his disciples came to him. And he opened his mouth and taught them, saying:

Then, in Matthew 5:3, the NASB, ESV, and even the NIV match the literal word order of the KJV: "Blessed are the poor in spirit, for theirs is the kingdom of heaven." That the NIV follows this rendering shows the influence tradition has even on fresh translations (as opposed to revisions of an earlier translation) that often lean toward functional equivalence. The optimal equivalence translation of the HCSB renders the same verse using "the closest natural equivalent" in word order: "The poor in spirit are blessed, for the kingdom of heaven is theirs."

Passage 5. Mark 1:40–45

[40] Then a man with <u>a serious skin disease</u> came to Him and, on his knees, begged Him: "If You are willing, You can make me clean." [41] <u>Moved with compassion</u>, Jesus reached out His hand and touched him. "I am willing," He told him. "Be made clean."

> [42] Immediately the disease left him, and he was healed. [43] Then He sternly warned him and sent him away at once, [44] telling him, "See that you say nothing to anyone; but go and show yourself to the priest, and offer what Moses prescribed for your cleansing, as a testimony to them." [45] Yet he went out and began to proclaim it widely and to spread the news, with the result that Jesus could no longer enter a town openly. But He was out in deserted places, and they would come to Him from everywhere.

According to the ESV, this passage is about a "leper" (v. 40). The NIV and NLT describe the man as "a man with leprosy," refraining from identifying him by his disease. The ESV has a note here that explains, "*Leprosy* was a term for several skin diseases; see Leviticus 13." The NIV also has a note: "The Greek word traditionally translated *leprosy* was used for various diseases affecting the skin." Likewise, the primary Greek lexicon (BDAG) gives the definition of *lepros* as "a person with a bad skin disease."[24] Translating according to the meaning of the word rather than tradition, the HCSB has "a man with a serious skin disease."

But the primary difference between the translations of these verses is the textual problem in verse 41. As Mark's testimony to Jesus' emotional state when he healed the "leper," almost all the manuscripts have the participle *splanchnistheis*, yielding the translation "moved with pity/compassion." But on the basis of one Greek manuscript and a few Old Latin translations, the NIV has followed the variant reading, *orgistheis*, from the verb *orgizō*, "to be angry." The NIV translates the participle as a simple sentence, "Jesus was indignant." As overwhelming as the manuscript evidence is against this reading being original, the textual commentary by Bruce Metzger (relating the decisions and reasoning of the textual committee) begins his discussion by noting that "it is difficult to come to a firm decision concerning the original text." Nevertheless, they determined that *splanchnistheis* was in the original.[25] Likewise, Darrell Bock judges "compassion" to be "slightly more likely to be the original sense," due to the "overwhelming" external evidence.[26] Robert Gundry also favors *splanchnistheis* on the basis of the manuscript evidence and the difficulty

---

[24] Walter Bauer, *A Greek-English Lexicon of the New Testament and Other Early Christian Literature*, 3rd ed, rev. and ed. F. W. Danker, W. F. Arndt, and F. W. Gingrich (Chicago: University of Chicago Press, 2000), 592.

[25] Bruce M. Metzger, *A Textual Commentary on the Greek New Testament*, 2nd ed. (Stuttgart: Deutsche Bibelgesellschaft, 1994), 65.

[26] Darrell L. Bock, "The Gospel of Mark," in *Cornerstone Biblical Commentary*, vol. 11 (Carol Stream, IL: Tyndale, 2005), 416.

of finding a reason for Jesus' anger. Granted that R. T. France argues in favor of *orgistheis*, he is hard pressed to explain *why* Jesus would have been angry (or indignant). His argument is essentially that if Mark wrote that Jesus was "moved with compassion," there seems no reason why it would have been changed to "was angry." Consequently, translations can only make their choice and perhaps inform the reader of the alternative in a footnote. The NIV has such a note, as does the NLT (which made the opposite decision).

Passage 6. Ending of Mark's Gospel

[8] So they went out and started running from the tomb, because trembling and astonishment overwhelmed them. And they said nothing to anyone, since they were afraid.

All modern Bible translations acknowledge the disagreement among Mark manuscripts about the ending. Some translations, such as the HCSB, only attest to the two major endings (v. 8, and vv. 9–20). Others, like the NIV, also include the so-called shorter ending (following v. 8), explaining the variation between one manuscript that ends Mark with the shorter ending and those that simply insert it between verses 8 and 9. Still other translations, such as the NLT, also include a variant addition following verse 14. Most translations simply present the variants with no explicit evaluation. The NLT explains that "the most reliable early manuscripts of the Gospel of Mark end at verse 8," although they also indicate that "the majority of manuscripts include the 'longer ending' immediately after verse 8."

Passage 7. Luke 17:1–4

[1] He said to His disciples, "Offenses will certainly come, but woe to the one they come through! [2] It would be better for <u>him</u> if a millstone were hung around his neck and <u>he</u> were thrown into the sea than for <u>him</u> to cause one of these little ones to stumble. [3] Be on your guard. If your <u>brother</u> sins, rebuke him, and if <u>he</u> repents, forgive him. [4] And if <u>he</u> sins against you seven times in a day, and comes back to you seven times, saying, 'I repent,' you must forgive <u>him</u>."

Although Jesus is speaking to his disciples (v. 1), throughout Luke 17:1–4 he is concerned with an exemplary offender. In verses 1–2, his topic is an individual who causes another to "stumble" (he does not specify the nature of the stumbling). Jesus' seriousness about someone harming another in this way is expressed not only with a strong image but also with an individual example: it would be better "for him" (*autō*) if a millstone were attached to "his" (*autou*) neck and "he" were thrown into the sea. The NIV, however, translates, "It would be better for *them* to be thrown into the sea with a millstone tied around *their* neck" (my italics). And the NLT uses second person: "It would be better to be thrown into the sea with a millstone hung around *your* neck." Presumably the reason for the change is to show that Jesus' warning does not apply only to males. However, the object of translation should be the *meaning* expressed by a text, not its *application*.

Jesus' emphasis on the individual continues in verses 3–4 with the case of someone who sins against one of his disciples. Jesus begins with an expression of the importance and perhaps difficulty of his instruction: a plural command to the group of his disciples to be on the alert or on their guard (the ESV translation "pay attention to yourselves," while fairly literal, is strange and unclear). Then Jesus describes the situation by using an individual example: "If your [sing.] brother [*adelphos*] sins." Verse 4 makes clear that the sin in view is a personal injury of some kind—"And if he [sing.] sins against you [sing.] seven times in a day"—and verse 3 describes the sinner as a "brother." The term in this context refers to a fellow believer, but he is designated by a term that speaks of spiritual kinship.[27] Thus, the NLT's "another believer" misses some of the meaning. The NIV's "brother or sister" interprets the term generically despite the consistent use of masculine pronouns throughout these verses. A note at this point declares, "The Greek word for brother or sister (*adelphos*) refers here to a fellow disciple, whether man or woman." Again, the question arises: how do we know? Joel Green's declaration that "ἀδελφός [*adelphos*] is generic"[28] is offered without justification. Johannes Beutler explains that "in translating it should be carefully noted that ἀδελφοι [*adelphoi*] (pl.) can also mean 'siblings,' i.e., 'brothers and sisters,'" but he makes no such point regarding the singular.[29]

According to Jesus, the response to this situation is "rebuke [sing.] *him* [*autō*], and if *he* [masc. sing.] repents, forgive [sing.] *him* [*autō*]." And yet the NIV renders it "rebuke *them*; and if *they* repent, forgive *them*." At

---

[27] Joel B. Green, *The Gospel of Luke*, New International Commentary on the New Testament (Grand Rapids: Eerdmans, 1997), 613.

[28] Ibid.

[29] Johannes Beutler, "ἀδελφός, adelphos, brother," in *Exegetical Dictionary of the New Testament*, ed. Horst Balz and Gerhard Schneider (Grand Rapids: Eerdmans, 1990), 1:30.

least the NLT keeps the person concerned as an individual: "rebuke that person; then if there is repentance, forgive."[30] But if Jesus had *male* sinners in mind in Luke 17:1–4, does his teaching not apply to women? Of course it does. But again, we should not confuse application with translation.

Passage 8. John 1:1–18 (especially 1:1–5,14–18)

> [1] In the beginning was the Word, and the Word was with God, and the Word was God. [2] He was with God in the beginning. [3] All things were created through Him, and apart from Him not one thing was created that has been created. [4] Life was in Him, and that life was the light of men. [5] That light shines in the darkness, yet the darkness did not overcome it. . . . [14] The Word became flesh and took up residence among us. We observed His glory, the glory as the One and Only Son from the Father, full of grace and truth. [15] (John testified concerning Him and exclaimed, "This was the One of whom I said, 'The One coming after me has surpassed me, because He existed before me.'") [16] Indeed, we have all received grace after grace from His fullness, [17] for the law was given through Moses, grace and truth came through Jesus Christ. [18] No one has ever seen God. The One and Only Son—the One who is at the Father's side—He has revealed Him.

All the translations being considered are essentially the same in John 1:1 except that the NLT has "In the beginning the Word already existed." This may be a bit more natural sounding than "In the beginning was the Word."

In verse 2, some translations move "in the beginning" after "with God" to sound more natural: "He was with God in the beginning" (HCSB, NIV). The NLT rendering, "He existed in the beginning with God," could be interpreted to suggest that He was not with God later, perhaps after the incarnation. This would be a theological error. In verse 3, the NLT removes some of the redundancy in the Greek text to sound more natural.

In verse 4, the clause "In him was life" or (HCSB) "Life was in Him" is rendered by the NLT as "The Word gave life to everything that was created." That statement is not quite true since not everything God created is alive. The more literal rendering is more accurate: the Word possesses and gives life so that everything that is alive has life *in* or *because of* him.

---

[30] Contrast the CEV: "Correct any followers of mine who sin, and forgive the ones who say they are sorry."

In verse 14, the NLT moves "full of grace and truth" (translated "He was full of unfailing love and faithfulness") from its place at the end of the verse. Although in the NLT it is an independent sentence, it follows and is therefore associated with the Word "ma[king] his home among us." But in the Greek text it follows and is associated with "His glory." According to Herman Ridderbos, "It is the fullness of that 'grace and truth' that marks the revelation of glory in the incarnate Word."[31] So it seems better to leave the phrase where it is in the Greek text. Some may also object that "unfailing love" inadequately represents the significance of "grace," which Ridderbos identifies with God's "favor, benevolence, and mercy."[32]

In verse 15, some may think that the ESV's use of "bore witness" is antiquated and that "testified" (HCSB, NIV, NLT) is a better rendering of *martureō*. Also in verse 15, the ESV's "ranks before me" is a bit unnatural. Despite the Greek preposition *emprosthen* ("before, in front of"), we would more likely say that someone ranks *higher than*. Translating "before" also implies that the following clause, "because he was before me," also uses *emprosthen*; but the Greek word for "before" there is *prōtos*. Whether the HCSB and NIV rendering, "has surpassed me," or the NLT's "is far greater than I am" is preferable to ESV's "ranks before me" is a matter of opinion. The clause reads literally "He has become before me."

In verse 16 the NIV has "grace in place of grace already given" instead of the traditional rendering "grace upon grace." This is clearly a possible translation because the phrase *charin anti charitos* uses a preposition that usually means "in place of." Yet BDAG gives the meaning as "grace after or upon grace (i.e., God's favor comes in ever new streams . . .),"[33] and Blass, Debrunner, and Funk, making the same comparison to a passage in Philo, explain the meaning as "to follow without ceasing."[34] The NIV rendering is possibly based on Stanley Porter's opinion that "the sense of replacement, possibly with reference to gospel replacing law, is to be preferred."[35] But if that is the interpretation of the phrase, which as Porter notes most commentators deny, it is strange that in the next verse where John makes the distinction between law and grace, it is not the grace of Jesus Christ replacing the grace of Moses.

---

[31] Herman Ridderbos, *The Gospel of John: A Theological Commentary,* trans. John Vriend (Grand Rapids: Eerdmans, 1997), 54.

[32] Ibid.

[33] BDAG, 88.

[34] F. Blass and A. Debrunner, *A Greek Grammar of the New Testament and Other Early Christian Literature,* trans. and rev. Robert W. Funk (Chicago: University of Chicago Press, 1961), §208.

[35] Stanley E. Porter, *Idioms of the Greek New Testament,* 2nd ed. (Sheffield: JSOT, 1994), 145.

The most difficult verse in John 1:1–18 to translate is the last one because of the textual problem. According to the critical edition of the Greek New Testament, this verse reads (literally), "No one has ever seen God; the One and Only [*monogenēs*] God [*theos*], who is in the bosom of the Father, He has expounded Him." The most widely attested variant reading has *huios*, "son," in place of *theos*. A few witnesses have *huios theou* ("Son of God"), or simply *monogenēs*, which can mean "one and only son/child" by itself (as in John 1:14; see also Luke 8:42; 9:38; Heb 11:17). But the weakness of the external evidence for these last two variants rules them out as highly unlikely.

The external evidence is divided between *theos* and *huios* since, although most of the earliest manuscripts have *theos*, they are almost all from the "Alexandrian" manuscripts. The reading *huios*, however, is found in manuscripts associated with all the other text families.[36] What is more, some early witnesses, such as the early Church fathers Cyprian, Irenaeus, and Tertullian, used a text with *huios*. Such a text was also used by some early translations: the Syriac, Old Latin, Vulgate, and Armenian versions.

Whereas the primary argument for *theos* is its internal difficulty, the reading *monogenēs huios* fits John's style since it occurs in John 3:16 and 3:18 as well as in 1 John 4:9. It also fits the immediate context, since *monogenēs* is used of God's Son in John 1:14:

> The Word became flesh and took up residence among us. We observed His glory, the glory as the One and Only Son *[monogenēs]* from the Father, full of grace and truth.

What is more, in John 1:18 itself, why would John speak of the unseeable "God" and then describe the eternal yet visible Son as "God"? Does not that introduce unnecessary confusion? The verse is teaching a distinction between the unseeable "God" and the One who makes him known. Why introduce the concept that this One who makes God known is *the One and Only* God? But these arguments (or something similar) on the basis of internal evidence convinced the majority of the committee producing the latest critical edition of the Greek text that the variant *monogenēs huios* was introduced by scribes influenced by John 3:16; 3:18; and 1 John 4:9, who were uncomfortable with the phrase *monogenēs theos*. In other words,

---

[36] See J. K. Elliott, *New Testament Textual Criticism: The Application of Thoroughgoing Principles*, NovTSup 137 (Leiden: Brill, 2010), 218. At least half a dozen witnesses from the so-called Western text, the same number of "Caesarean" witnesses, and at least a dozen Alexandrian witnesses have the reading *huios*, in addition to almost all the Byzantine witnesses.

monogenēs theos is believed to be original because it does *not* fit John's style or the immediate context—it occurs nowhere else—and it does not seem to fit John's argument, making it the more "difficult" reading. Is it not possible for a reading to be *too* difficult?

Should the textual critic allow the "more difficult reading" criterion to tyrannize the process by trumping the other kinds of evidence? David Black speaks to the issue of conflicting textual evidence:

> Of course, the greatest caution must be exercised in applying these principles. They are inferences rather than axiomatic rules. Indeed, it is not uncommon for two or more principles to conflict. Hence none of them can be applied in a mechanical or unthinking fashion. If in the end you are still undecided, you should pay special attention to external evidence, as it is less subjective and more reliable.[37]

The primary dictum in the use of internal evidence is: "The reading that best explains the origin of the other readings is probably the original reading." Could *monogenēs theos* be explained as arising from an original *monogenēs huios*? This is the minority opinion on the Greek textual committee: "It is doubtful that the author would have written [*monogenēs theos*]." The dissenter, Allen Wikgren, believed that the change from *huios* to *theos* was an early transcriptional error that occurred in the Alexandrian manuscripts. He suggested it occurred in a manuscript that used abbreviations for *huios* and *theos*, which could be confused for each other.[38] The textual critic J. K. Elliott mentions another possibility:

> On the other hand it may have been that some scribes, reflecting the theological concerns of their communities and determined to enhance Jesus' status, altered an original 'Son' (with all the subordinationist baggage that title carries) to 'God', thereby affirming his divinity and deity.[39]

The issues are difficult to sort through. But the HCSB translators chose to depart from the NA[27] text at this point and translate, "No one has ever seen God. The One and Only Son—the One who is at the Father's side— He has revealed Him."[40] Of course, a translation note explains that other

[37] David A. Black, *New Testament Textual Criticism: A Concise Guide* (Grand Rapids: Baker, 1994), 36.

[38] Metzger, *Textual Commentary on the Greek New Testament*, 170.

[39] Elliott, *New Testament Textual Criticism*, 219.

[40] Eberhard Nestle, Erwin Nestle, Kurt Aland, *Novum Testamentum Graece*, 27th ed. (New York:

manuscripts read "God" rather than "Son" and that the literal wording for "at the Father's side" is "in the bosom of the Father." How did the other versions handle the textual problem at John 1:18?

The NKJV, like the HCSB, follows the reading *huios*. The ESV, like the NASB, follows the reading *theos*. The other translations follow *theos* as well, but they interpret *monogenēs* as a noun, "only son," rather than an adjective, "(one and) only." They consider the two nouns to be in apposition, the second noun adding information about the first. This interpretation seems to strain Greek grammar a bit since it is most natural for an adjective preceding a noun to be modifying that noun rather than serving as a noun itself.

Passage 9. John 2:24–3:1

> [24] Jesus, however, would not entrust Himself to them, since He knew them all [25] and because He did not need anyone to testify about <u>man</u>; for He Himself knew what was in <u>man</u>. [3:1] There was a <u>man</u> from the Pharisees named Nicodemus, a ruler of the Jews.

One principle of formal equivalence translation is to maintain consistency, if possible, in the rendering of individual words and phrases. It is also a principle of optimal equivalence—if it can be done while maintaining a natural English style. For example, the last verse of John 2 and the first verse of chapter 3 contain three uses of the Greek word for "man" (*anthrōpos*). The translation "all men" in some translations (e.g., NASB) in verse 24 is actually inconsistent, for *pantas* simply means "all." It is plural, so the translation "all people" (ESV, NIV) or "them all" (HCSB) is actually better. The NLT rendering, "human nature," also gets more out of *pantas* than is actually there. But the use of *anthrōpos* twice in 2:25 prepares for the use of the word again in 3:1.[41] Jesus knew the hearts of men. One such man was Nicodemus. This is also apparent in the essentially literal rendering of the HCSB and ESV.

The TNIV (2005) rendered the words inconsistently:

TNIV   [24] But Jesus would not entrust himself to them, for he knew all people. [25] He did not need human testimony about <u>them</u>, for he knew what was in <u>them</u>. [3:1] Now there was a Pharisee, a <u>man</u>

American Bible Society, 1998), abbreviated as NA[27]. See Ridderbos, *Gospel of John*, 59, who supports this reading as well.

[41] See Ridderbos, *Gospel of John*, 123.

named Nicodemus who was a member of the Jewish ruling council.

The recently revised NIV improved the translation as follows:

NIV   ²⁴ But Jesus would not entrust himself to them, for he knew all people. ²⁵ He did not need any testimony about <u>mankind</u>, for he knew what was in <u>each person</u>. ³:¹ Now there was a Pharisee, a <u>man</u> named Nicodemus who was a member of the Jewish ruling council.

Yet the English Bible reader can only with difficulty make the connection since "mankind" is not "man," and "each person" misses the intentionally redundant *anthrōpos*. The NLT does something similar but collapses the clauses in 2:25 into one, so removing the repetition in another way.

NLT   ²⁴ But Jesus didn't trust them, because he knew human nature. ²⁵ No one needed to tell him what <u>mankind</u> is really like. ³:¹ There was a <u>man</u> named Nicodemus, a Jewish religious leader who was a Pharisee.

When the biblical writer has apparently emphasized a word by repetition, it is difficult to capture that emphasis in translation apart from a fairly literal translation.

Passage 10. 1 Corinthians 2:1,13

¹ When I came to you, brothers, announcing <u>the testimony of God</u> to you, I did not come with brilliance of speech or wisdom . . . . ¹³ We also speak these things, not in words taught by human wisdom, but in those taught by the Spirit, explaining <u>spiritual things to spiritual people</u>.

The only truly significant difference in verse 1 between the various translations is which of the two variants (lit., "testimony of God" or "mystery of God") is chosen. The former is the choice of the HCSB, ESV, and NIV. On the other side, the NLT favors "mystery of God." The NA²⁷ and UBS⁴ (the United Bible Society's *Greek New Testament*, 4th edition) have "mystery" (*mustērion*) in the text and list "testimony" (*marturion*) as a variant. Metzger's *Textual Commentary* defends *mustērion* "on exegetical grounds" but admits that *marturion* is "well supported." In fact, the support for *mustērion* is almost solely Alexandrian, and the support from an early papyrus (𝔓⁴⁶) is uncertain.

Although the UBS[4] gives the reading a B rating, which means the text is "almost certain," the first three editions gave it a C rating, which means "considerable degree of doubt whether the text or the apparatus contains the superior reading." In Kent Clarke's critique of UBS[4], he criticized the evaluations for a rather high percentage of readings whose probability mysteriously improved since UBS[3] with no additional manuscript evidence.[42] The Nestle-Aland edition simply has a cross in the apparatus, which "marks a change in the text from the 25th edition, where the reading so marked stood in the text. . . . These passages always represent very difficult textual decisions."[43] Finally, two modern, highly regarded English commentaries on 1 Corinthians, by Gordon Fee and Anthony Thiselton, are split on which is the best reading. Fee, a noted text critic, writes fairly strongly in favor of *marturion*.[44] The bottom line is that it should not surprise us that the translations are split on which is the best reading or that each has a note pointing out that "other/some manuscripts" read differently.

The translation differences in verse 13 come in the rendering of the final clause, "spiritual things to spiritual people" (*pneumatikois pneumatika sunkrinontes*). Its translation depends on (1) the meaning of the participle *sunkrinontes*, and (2) the gender of *pneumatikois*. The first two words are both the adjective that means "spiritual" or "of the Spirit." The first occurrence is dative plural, and either masculine (presumably referring to people) or neuter (referring to things, ideas, or words). The second is accusative plural, and is neuter.

The participle is from *sunkrinō* and can mean "combining," "comparing," or "interpreting or explaining." Most commentaries favor some nuance of the third option, which results in two main options: explaining or interpreting spiritual truths[45] (1) with spiritual words (neuter, dative of instrument), or (2) to spiritual people (masculine, dative of indirect object). Because of these issues, Craig Blomberg declares the clause to be "notoriously difficult."[46] Nevertheless, he prefers meaning (1), as do the NIV,

---

[42] Kent D. Clarke, *Textual Optimism: A Critique of the United Bible Societes' Greek New Testament* (Sheffield: Sheffield Academic Press, 1997), 84, 183–84. For example, "The problematic letter-ratings do not supply the Bible translator, the beginning student, or the working scholar with a reliable basis for assessing the certainty of the Greek text." Also see J. K. Elliott, "The Fourth Edition of the United Bible Societies' Greek New Testament," *Theologische Revue* 90 (1994): cols. 9–20.

[43] Nestle-Aland, *Novum Testamentum Graece*, 57.

[44] Gordon D. Fee, *The First Epistle to the Corinthians,* New International Commentary on the New Testament (Grand Rapids: Eerdmans, 1987), 88; cf. Anthony C. Thiselton, *The First Epistle to the Corinthians*, New International Greek Testament Commentary (Grand Rapids: Eerdmans, 2000), 207.

[45] Accusative neuter plural.

[46] Craig Blomberg, *1 Corinthians*, NIV Application Commentary (Grand Rapids: Zondervan, 1994), 64. He also says that "fortunately the overall sense remains intact on either reading."

NLT, Gordon Fee,[47] and some other commentaries. Meaning (2) is favored by the ESV, HCSB, as well as by Robertson and Plummer, Hays, and Thiselton.[48] One argument in favor of the latter view is the apparent contrast between "the spiritual" and "the natural man" (*psuchikos de anthrōpos*) in verse 14. But whichever meaning the apostle had in mind, both are true, and the alternative interpretations are cited by the various translations.

Passage 11. Galatians 5:2–6

[2] Take note! I, Paul, tell you that <u>if you get yourselves circumcised</u>, Christ will not benefit you at all. [3] Again I testify to every man who gets himself circumcised that <u>he is obligated</u> to keep the entire law. [4] <u>You who are</u> trying to be justified by the law are alienated from Christ; you have fallen from grace. [5] For through the Spirit, by faith, we eagerly wait for <u>the hope of righteousness</u>. [6] For in Christ Jesus neither circumcision nor uncircumcision <u>accomplishes anything</u>; what matters is <u>faith working through love</u>.

In verse 2, the HCSB "if you get yourselves circumcised" is the translation of two words in Greek: *ean* ("if") *peritemnēsthe* ("circumcised"). The verb *peritemnō* means to "circumcise." The form here is present middle or passive, which means to "be circumcised" or "have oneself circumcised." This sense is reflected in the ESV "if you accept circumcision," the HCSB "if you get yourselves circumcised," and the NIV "if you let yourselves be circumcised." The NLT, however, misses the sense of the verb in its attempt to divine what Paul's concern is: "If you are counting on circumcision to make you right with God." The verb speaks of an act and a resulting physical state, but the NLT renders it as a mental state and a motive (granted that the motive is borrowed from verse 4).

Verse 3 contains a declarative sentence that uses the participle form of the same verb. But the sentence changes from the second person "you" to the third person "every man" and "he." The HCSB renders the first part literally: "Again I testify to every man who gets himself circumcised." The ESV and NIV have essentially the same, but again the NLT wanders from the text, changing the declarative sentence to another conditional: "I'll say

---

[47] Fee, *First Epistle to the Corinthians*, 114–15.

[48] A. Robertson and A. Plummer, *A Critical and Exegetical Commentary on the First Epistle of St. Paul to the Corinthians*, International Critical Commentary (Edinburgh: T&T Clark, 1911), 47; Richard B. Hays, *First Corinthians* (Louisville: John Knox, 1997), 46; Thiselton, *First Epistle to the Corinthians*, 224, 264.

it again. If you are trying to find favor with God by being circumcised." I believe Paul had a rhetorical reason for switching to the third person, and normal English style should have no problem with this. Furthermore, I believe Paul had a reason for reserving the motive for the third sentence (v. 4). In verse 3, he is still focused on the *act* of circumcision.

The main question in verse 4 is whether to translate the three clauses in the same order as they are in Greek, or to switch the first two clauses for the sake of English style. The stylistic problem is that the subject of the clause is expressed in the second clause, while the double predicate is split between the first and third clauses.

> Subject = you who [want/are trying to be] justified by law
> Predicate^1 = you have been alienated from Christ[49]
> Predicate^2 = you have fallen from grace

The ESV translates literally:

ESV   You are severed from Christ, you who would be justified by the law; you have fallen away from grace.

The HCSB, like the NIV and NLT, reverses the first two clauses:

HCSB   You who are trying to be justified by the law are alienated from Christ; you have fallen from grace.

The NLT, however, again translates a declarative sentence as a conditional:

NLT   For if you are trying to make yourselves right with God by keeping the law, you have been cut off from Christ! You have fallen away from God's grace.

Translating the verse as another conditional sentence seems to weaken the forcefulness of Paul's statement.[50] The Greek text, but not the NLT, implies that some in the Galatian church were actually doing this.

A strictly literal translation of verse 5 could be "For we by the Spirit from faith the hope of righteousness we eagerly await." Clearly the object of the verb "await" is "the hope of righteousness." The latter phrase is

---

[49] That is, "you have lost the benefits provided by Christ under the new covenant." On the meaning of *katargeō* here, see Duane A. Garrett, "The Translation and Interpretation of 2 Corinthians 3," *JETS* 53 (2010), 744. Although he objects to the translation "alienated," it is difficult to find another word that concisely conveys Paul's point.

[50] We might just note that the NLT's translation philosophy keeps them from using the terms "justify" or "justification" in a theological sense anywhere in the translation.

probably a construction in which the first noun modifies the second (an "attributed genitive").[51] Christians eagerly await the righteousness we hope for. The ESV and HCSB chose to render the phrase literally, whereas the NIV unpacks it as "the righteousness for which we hope." The NLT, however, translates as if Paul were speaking of the *reason* for our hope: "the righteousness God has promised to us."

Finally, verse 6 is literally, "For in Christ Jesus neither circumcision is able for anything, nor uncircumcision, but faith through love working." The verb phrase "is able for anything" could refer to *value*, hence the ESV "counts for anything" or the NIV "has any value," or to *effectiveness*, hence the HCSB "accomplishes anything" or the NLT "there is no benefit." The final participle, "working," seems to favor the latter option, but the real problem is the final clause. "Working through love" modifies "faith," but there is no explicit verb. What does "faith working through love" do? The verb must be supplied from the previous clause. The ESV leaves the clause pretty much as is: "but only faith working through love." The other translations supply something:

HCSB   *what matters is* faith working through love.

NIV   *The only thing that counts is* faith expressing itself through love.

NLT   *What is important is* faith expressing itself in love.

The participle is from the verb *energeō*, which means to "be at work," or to "effect, produce" something. The idea of "expressing itself" might be a legitimate extension of that, but it is not really what the verb means.

Passage 12. Colossians 2:8–15 (esp. 9–12)

[8] Be careful that no one takes you captive through philosophy and empty deceit based on human tradition, based on the elemental forces of the world, and not based on Christ. [9] For the entire fullness of God's nature dwells bodily in Christ, [10] and you have been filled by Him, who is the head over every ruler and authority. [11] You were also circumcised in Him with a circumcision not done with hands, by putting off the body of flesh, in the circumcision of the Messiah. [12] Having been buried with Him in baptism, you were also raised with Him through faith in the

---

[51] See Daniel B. Wallace, *Greek Grammar Beyond the Basics* (Grand Rapids: Zondervan, 1996), 89–91.

working of God, who raised Him from the dead. [13] And when you were dead in trespasses and in the uncircumcision of your flesh, He made you alive with Him and forgave us all our trespasses. [14] He erased the certificate of debt, with its obligations, that was against us and opposed to us, and has taken it out of the way by nailing it to the cross. [15] He disarmed the rulers and authorities and disgraced them publicly; He triumphed over them by Him.

The primary differences between the translations of this passage are in verse 11. The HCSB reads fairly literally, as does the ESV:

ESV   In him also you were circumcised with a circumcision made without hands, by putting off the body of the flesh, by the circumcision of Christ.[52]

I believe the only significant difference from the ESV is their translation of the last phrase, "*by* the circumcision of Christ." Against these two literal renderings, the NIV has:

NIV   In him you were also circumcised with a circumcision not performed by human hands. Your whole self ruled by the flesh was put off when you were circumcised by Christ.

That reads more clearly than the ESV and HCSB. The NLT is even clearer:

NLT   When you came to Christ, you were "circumcised," but not by a physical procedure. Christ performed a spiritual circumcision— the cutting away of your sinful nature.

In both these translations, especially the NLT, it is clear that the Christian experiences a spiritual circumcision, a "circumcision of the heart," when he is saved, or regenerated. It is also clear that Christ is the one who performs that "circumcision" and that it involves a spiritual transformation: the removal or putting off of "your whole self ruled by the flesh," or "cutting away of your sinful nature." The NLT reminds me of *The Voyage of the Dawn Treader* when Eustace—an insufferable little boy whose greed has turned him into a dragon—gets his scales painfully pulled off by Aslan the lion. These translations are clear. My problem with them is that they are too clear.

---

[52] The HCSB renders *christos* as "Messiah" rather than "Christ" in contexts that are clearly Jewish in order to make clear the term's connection to the Old Testament promises of the Coming One (Luke 7:19).

In the first place, the NLT's "when you came to Christ" is nowhere found in the Greek text. It is extrapolated from the idea that since believers are all "circumcised" in Christ, it must happen when we first come to Christ. But the NLT places the emphasis on an event occurring at a particular time, whereas the Greek only specifies the event happened "in Him." This involves adding something not in the text and deleting something that is in the text.

Second, the NLT phrase "the cutting away" translates the noun *apekdusis*, whose meaning is given in all the major lexicons as "taking off clothes." The verb *apekduomai* is used in verse 15 of stripping the spiritual rulers and authorities of their weapons: "He *disarmed* the rulers and authorities and disgraced them publicly." What the NLT has done is to relieve Paul of his mixed metaphor: circumcision and stripping of clothes. So their clarity comes at the price of some of the verse's information and imagery.

Third, the object of the "putting/stripping off" is "the body of flesh." The clarity with which both the NIV and NLT interpret this as our sinful self totally rules out an alternative interpretation that is advocated by many scholars. C. F. D. Moule, Peter O'Brien, G. R. Beasley-Murray, Ralph Martin, James Dunn, David Garland, and Markus Barth all interpret "the body of flesh" as the physical body of Christ.[53] David Garland writes:

> The term flesh (*sarx*) does not always have a sinful implication in Paul's usage. He can use it to refer simply to the physical body without any negative connotations. All of the uses of *sarx* so far in the letter have denoted the physical flesh (1:22,24; 2:1,5) . . . "The body of flesh" is another way of saying "the physical body." The only other time this phrase occurs in the NT is in 1:22, and the NIV correctly renders it Christ's "physical body." It has the same meaning here and does not refer to a sinful nature.[54]

---

[53] C. F. D. Moule, *The Epistles to the Colossians and to Philemon*, Cambridge Greek Testament Commentary (Cambridge: University Press, 1962), 94–96; Peter T. O'Brien, *Colossians, Philemon*, Word Biblical Commentary (Waco, TX: Word, 1982), 116–17; G. R. Beasley-Murray, *Baptism in the New Testament* (Grand Rapids: Eerdmans, 1973), 152–53; R. P. Martin, *Colossians and Philemon*, New Century Bible Commentary (Grand Rapids: Eerdmans, 1982), 82–83; James D. G. Dunn, *The Epistles to the Colossians and to Philemon*, New International Greek Testament Commentary (Grand Rapids: Eerdmans, 1996), 153–58; David E. Garland, *Colossians/Philemon*, NIV Application Commentary (Grand Rapids: Zondervan, 1998), 147–49; Markus Barth and Helmut Banke, *Colossians*, Anchor Bible (New York: Doubleday, 1995), 364–65.

[54] Garland, *Colossians/Philemon*, 147–48. The same problem is found with the NLT rendering of (lit.) "the uncircumcision of your flesh" in verse 13 as "your sinful nature was not yet cut away." The

James Dunn speaks of translations that render "flesh" by such phrases as "sinful nature" as wanting "to avoid using 'flesh' at all cost and which produce unjustifiably tendentious translations." He singles out especially N. T. Wright's translation, "in the stripping off of the old human solidarities."

Finally, the last phrase of the verse, which the HCSB renders literally, "in the circumcision of the Messiah," is unclear whether the Messiah is the agent or recipient of circumcision. The NIV and NLT make clear that Christ is the agent. But all those scholars listed above believe Paul is referring here to Christ's death on the cross in which He had His "body of flesh" stripped away. I am not saying this is necessarily the correct interpretation, only that these scholars make a cogent case that should not be ignored and that a translation should allow for. The NIV does have a note attached to "put off when you were circumcised by Christ" that says, "Or *put off in the circumcision of* [Christ]." But this does little good in view of the note attached to "Your whole self ruled by the flesh": "In contexts like this, the Greek word for *flesh* (*sarx*) refers to the sinful state of human beings, often presented as a power in opposition to the Spirit; also in verse 13." The HCSB allows for the alternative interpretation with its translation.

Passage 13: 1 Thessalonians 1:3

> We recall, in the presence of our God and Father, your work of faith, labor of love, and endurance of hope in our Lord Jesus Christ

The ESV is fairly literal here except for moving "before our God and Father" from its position at the end of the verse in the Greek text. The HCSB is only slightly less literal, with its rendering of the initial participle as a finite verb (as the ESV does in v. 4) to shorten Paul's long sentence (spanning vv. 2–5). The key translation issue in this verse is how to render the three genitive phrases (HCSB): "work of faith, labor of love, and endurance[55] of hope." The ESV and HCSB leave them as genitives (that is, literal), but the NIV and NLT unpack them semantically. The NIV interprets them all as "subjective genitives."[56] That is, the second word

---

scholars listed above all consider this reference to "uncircumcision" as literal, symbolizing Gentile exclusion from divine blessing until they receive spiritual circumcision in Christ.

[55] The ESV uses the more archaic "steadfastness."

[56] See Richard C. Blight, *An Exegetical Summary of 1 and 2 Thessalonians* (Dallas: SIL, 1989), 14–16; D. Michael Martin, *1, 2 Thessalonians*, New American Commentary 33 (Nashville: B&H, 1995), 55–56; Charles A. Wanamaker, *The Epistles to the Thessalonians*, New International Greek Testament Commentary (Grand Rapids: Eerdmans, 1990), 75–76.

is understood as the subject of the verbal idea in the first word:[57] "your work produced by faith, your labor prompted by love, and your endurance inspired by hope." The NLT, on the other hand, interprets the first two as attributive genitives, in which the second noun modifies the first: "your faithful work, your loving deeds." The problem with this interpretation is that it does not work with the third one. It is interpreted as the opposite, that is, as an attributed genitive, in which the first noun acts as an adjective modifying the second: "the enduring hope you have." The inconsistency of this interpretation makes it less likely.

One final note regarding the NLT: whereas all the other translations interpret the genitive phrase "hope of our Lord Jesus Christ" as an objective genitive, that is, "hope *in* our Lord Jesus Christ,"[58] the NLT interprets it as a genitive of cause ("hope . . . because of our Lord Jesus Christ"), which is problematic since this only seems to occur with a preposition.[59]

Passage 14. 1 Timothy 2:12

I do not allow a woman to teach or <u>to have authority</u> over a man; instead, she is to be silent.

The differences in the Bible translations we are considering regarding this verse involve the meaning of the Greek infinitive "to have authority" (*authentein*). There are also hermeneutical issues regarding its syntactic and semantic relationship to the other infinitive, "to teach" (*didaskein*). But since these translations all consider the two infinitives to be parallel and equal, we will not concern ourselves with that issue here.[60]

The HCSB and NLT both render *authentein* as "to have authority." The ESV departed from its parent translation, the RSV, in translating "to exercise authority," like the NASB. The shade of difference between these two renderings is a fine one. The NIV, however, like its predecessor, the TNIV, rendered the verb "to assume authority." Although the KJV

---

[57] Another possibility is genitive of source.

[58] See Wanamaker, *Epistles to the Thessalonians*, 76.

[59] See James A. Brooks and Carlton L. Winbery, *Syntax of New Testament Greek* (Washington, DC: University Press of America, 1979), 26.

[60] For a thorough discussion, see Andreas J. Köstenberger, "A Complex Sentence: The Syntax of 1 Timothy 2:12," in *Women in the Church: An Analysis and Application of 1 Timothy 2:9–15*, ed. Andreas J. Köstenberger, Thomas R. Schreiner, and H. Scott Baldwin, 2nd ed. (Grand Rapids: Baker, 2005), 53–84.

rendered it "to usurp authority," and Goodspeed (1923) translated "to domineer over," the meaning widely accepted for some time was that Paul prohibited women from occupying an authoritative position in the church that placed them in authority over men. A controversy has been running over whether this was Paul's view. Some have defended the view that Paul simply objected to a woman either obtaining or exercising authority wrongly.

Part of the answer must come from the meaning of *authentein* and part from the context. That is, which possible meaning of *authentein* fits best here? H. Scott Baldwin has produced perhaps the most thorough study of the word's meaning in ancient Greek. Although it occurs in the New Testament only here, it is found more than 100 times in extrabiblical literature. He concludes that the word could be used with the following meanings:

1. To rule, to reign sovereignly

2. To control, to dominate [in a neutral sense]
   a. to compel, to influence
   b. to be in effect, to have legal standing
   c. to domineer, play the tyrant [found only once]
   d. to grant authorization

3. To act independently
   a. to assume authority over
   b. to exercise one's own jurisdiction
   c. to flout the authority of

4. To be primarily responsible for, to instigate[61]

Baldwin asserts that in 1 Timothy 2:12, meanings 2 or 2a are "entirely possible," and meaning 3a "could be appropriate."[62] He makes clear that by "assume authority over" he means something "positive" in that "one moves forward to fill the leadership role."[63] The question arises, however, whether the expression "assume authority over" is actually positive.

---

[61] H. Scott Baldwin, "An Important Word: Αὐθεντέω in 1 Tim 2:12," in Köstenberger, Schreiner, and Baldwin, *Women in the Church*, 49–50. Thomas R. Schreiner, "An Interpretation of 1 Tim 2:9–15: A Dialogue with Scholarship," in Köstenberger, Schreiner, and Baldwin, *Women in the Church*, 102–4, argues for "exercise authority."

[62] Ibid., 51.

[63] This elaboration of the translation "assume authority over" is found in the first edition, but not in the second. See *Women in the Church* (Grand Rapids: Baker, 1995), 75, where he also explains this meaning as "step up to the plate" or "take charge."

In fact, the expression can be found in English usage with either a negative or a positive meaning. For example:

> If the world learned one thing from Caesar, it was how *to assume authority*. He didn't go into Rome bobbing his head and looking like he might want to end the Republic. He rode in with his head up and a polished entourage bristling with weapons, and even while his old pal Pompey was calling him out, Caesar made himself the capo di tutti capi ["boss of all bosses"]. In other words, he ascended to the next level, leaving his peers watching and wondering how he did it. He marched in with one loyal legion, and seeing him coming was enough for the Senate. They fled Rome for fear of getting whacked.[64]

On the other hand, an article titled "Iraqis Assume Authority over FOB Iskan" explains that "soldiers, Iraqi Police and power plant workers gathered to transfer authority of Forward Operating Base Iskan from Coalition forces to the Ministry of Electricity during a ceremony here Feb. 22."[65]

The expression in English, then, is ambiguous. Did Paul intend to speak ambiguously? In view of his use of *didaskein*, "to teach," I would say no. He did not intend that the second infinitive carry a negative sense. And this is confirmed by the final clause, "she is to be silent" (rather than something like "she is to be humble" or to "act nice"). Paul is not speaking about a wrong use or acquisition of authority but about a woman teaching or having/exercising authority in the church over men at all.

One final objection to "assume authority" is that it speaks of *beginning* to have authority. Since "to teach" does not have an incipient sense, why would Paul use an incipient sense for the second infinitive, *unless he was speaking of wrongly obtaining authority*, which we already determined he was not?

Wildcard: 1 John 3:3

And everyone who has this hope <u>in Him</u> purifies <u>himself</u> just as <u>He</u> is pure.

The ideal for formal and optimal equivalence is that a verb be translated by a verb, a noun by a noun, a genitive phrase by a genitive phrase, an

---

[64] "Mafioso: Assume Authority," http://tinyurl.com/assumeauthority (accessed 7/30/2011). Emphasis added.

[65] See http://www.centcom.mil/news/iraqis-assume-authority-over-fob-iskan, accessed 7/30/2011.

active verb by an active verb, a singular by a singular, and so forth. The conviction is that part of the meaning is in the form. An example is provided by how various translations compare to an interlinear rendering of 1 John 3:3:

and	everyone	the one	having	the	hope	this	on
kai	*pas*	*ho*	*echōn*	*tēn*	*elpida*	*tautēn*	*ep'*

him	(he) purifies	himself	just as	that	one pure	(he) is
autō	*hagnizei*	*heauton*	*kathōs*	*ekeinos*	*hagnos*	*estin*

The translation problem in this verse is to make clear the antecedents for the pronouns, especially in the prepositional phrase "on/in him." The literal translation of the KJV illustrates the difficulty: "And every man that hath this hope in him purifieth himself, even as he is pure." The Greek is fairly clear in context that *autō*, "him," and *ekeinos*, "that one/he," refer to Christ. The believer is signified by "everyone who" (*pas ho*) and "himself" (*heauton*).

Although the translations agree on that much, they disagree on how to make it clear. The HCSB (like the NASB and NKJV) accomplishes this by capitalizing divine pronouns: "And everyone who has this hope in Him purifies himself just as He is pure." The ESV does it by changing "who has this hope in him" to "who thus hopes in him." The question is whether the action-oriented "hope in someone" is optimally equivalent to the possession-oriented "have hope in someone." The NIV and NLT remove the ambiguity by changing the focus from an exemplary individual (singular) to a generic group (plural).

NIV   All who have this hope in him purify themselves, just as he is pure.

NLT   And all who have this eager expectation will keep themselves pure, just as he is pure.

Even Eugene Nida, notable advocate of functional equivalence, acknowledged that part of the meaning can be in the form. He notes:

> The message consists of both the linguistic form and the ideational content, but it would be a serious mistake to distinguish categorically between external form and internal meaning, for

the form itself so frequently carries significant meaning, especially in terms of emphasis, focus, impact, and appeal.[66]

He later states categorically, "It is not right to speak of the Greek or Hebrew text (or a literal translation of such) as being merely 'the form' and a freer idiomatic translation as being 'the meaning.'"[67] He also offers an example: "By shifting a form into the passive to avoid a pronominal reference to God in John 1:12,[68] one seriously distorts the message about how people become God's children."[69]

Passage 15. Jude 4–5

[4] For some men, who were designated for this judgment long ago, have <u>come in by stealth</u>; they are ungodly, turning the grace of our God into promiscuity and denying Jesus Christ, our only Master and Lord. [5] Now I want to remind you, though you know all these things: The <u>Lord</u> first saved a people out of Egypt and later destroyed those who did not believe.

Verse 4 contains one finite verb, *pareisedusan* ("slip in stealthily, sneak in"[70]), translated "have crept in unnoticed" (ESV), "have come in by stealth" (HCSB), "have secretly slipped in among you" (NIV), or "have wormed their way into your churches" (NLT). The subject is "some men" (*tines anthrōpoi*), and the rest of the verse comprises four modifiers: three participle clauses and one adjective. The structure of the Greek text may be represented as follows (using the HCSB):

For some men . . . have come in by stealth

1. who were designated for this judgment long ago
2. they are ungodly
3. turning the grace of our God into promiscuity
4. and denying Jesus Christ, our only Master and Lord

The ESV, HCSB, and NIV take all four modifiers as parallel, modifying the subject, "some men/people." The NLT, however, follows the

---

[66] De Waard and Nida, *From One Language to Another*, 13.

[67] Ibid., 36.

[68] A literal translation is "But as many as received him, *he gave to them* the right to become children of God." But *The Inclusive Bible* (Plymouth, UK: Sheed & Ward, 2007) renders it, "Yet any who did accept the Word, who believed in that Name, *were empowered* to become children of God."

[69] De Waard and Nida, *From One Language to Another*, 24.

[70] BDAG, 774.

unlikely interpretation that the fourth modifier is subordinate to and gives the reason for the first modifier, even though the first and fourth clauses are separated from each other by an adjective and another clause. In fact, such an interpretation seems to be rendered impossible by the initial "and" (*kai*) that precedes the final clause and ties it closely to the previous clause. The "for" that the NLT uses at the beginning of their final clause is inexplicable.

The issue in verse 5 is a text-critical one. The first variant regards the original position of the Greek word *hapax*, "once" (also rendered "first" or "at one time"). Some manuscripts have it modifying the participle translated "know/knew." This variant is followed by the ESV (and the minority of the editors of NA[27]). Other manuscripts have it modifying the participle translated "saved/delivered/rescued," followed by HCSB, NIV, NLT (and the majority of editors of NA[27]).

The other textual problem regards the agent who "saved/delivered/rescued" Israel from Egypt. Some manuscripts have "God," some have "the Lord" (followed by the HCSB, NIV, and the majority of editors of NA[27]), and some have "Jesus" (followed by the ESV, NLT, and a minority of editors of NA[27]; one early papyrus even has "God Christ"). These text-critical issues are difficult, and the editorial committee gave their decision a D rating, which means they had "great difficulty in arriving at a decision." Therefore, differences between the various translations are to be expected.

Passage 16. Revelation 3:20

Listen! I stand at the door and knock. If anyone hears My voice and opens the door, I will come in to him and have dinner with him, and he with Me.

The HCSB differs from the ESV only in translating Greek *idou* as "Listen!" rather than "Behold," and *deipnēsō* as "have dinner with" rather than "eat with." According to the Greek lexicon (BDAG), a *deipnon* referred to "the main meal of the day."[71] In fact, it was usually "an elaborate dinner celebration"[72] (though apparently not here).

The NLT differs from both the ESV and HCSB in translating *ean tis akousē* as "if you hear" rather than "if anyone hears." This involves rendering the indefinite pronoun *tis* ("some, any, someone, anyone") and the

---

[71] BDAG, 215.
[72] Ibid.

third person verb as the personal pronoun "you" and a second person verb, thus sacrificing the rhetorical nature of "if anyone" as a general—though individual—invitation. The Greek text of verses 15–19 is clearly directed to "you [singular]," that is, the church. "The faithful and true Witness" (v. 14) could have continued speaking to "you" in verse 20 but chose instead to switch to third person, "if anyone." On what grounds is it legitimate to ignore that change?

Second, like the NIV, the NLT chooses not to translate the Greek prepositional phrase *pros auton*, "to him," which is a major clue that this is an intimate meal rather than a banquet. Finally, the NLT gives the second result of hearing Jesus and opening the door to him: "and we will share a meal together as friends." In Greek, this is literally, "and I will have dinner with him and he with me." The NLT's idiomatic translation communicates the general sense but loses the emphasis of the Greek text on the intimacy of "I . . . with him and he with me." In that same Greek text is also a hint at the divine prerogative of being the instigator, as we are necessarily the responders.

In the NIV the divine promise made to the conditional "if anyone" is "I will come in and eat with that person, and they with me." As in the NLT, "to him" and "with him" are avoided. But in their place is the awkward circumlocution "that person . . . they." For many years the exemplary masculine in this verse has been understood as having general application. It is sad that many are willing to sacrifice it for awkwardness.

Conclusion

Many other features besides its translation philosophy commend the HCSB to Bible students. A preeminent feature is that, being a fresh translation from the original texts, the HCSB translates what the text actually says rather than what tradition or political-social correctness might dictate. For example, the Hebrew phrase *ne'um yhwh*, traditionally rendered, "declares the LORD," literally means "declaration of Yahweh/the LORD." So it is rendered, "This is the LORD's declaration" (see previous comments on Ezek 18:5–9,21–24).

Second, the Hebrew and Greek terms traditionally rendered "leprosy" and "leper" are translated according to their meaning, "serious skin disease," and "a man with a serious skin disease" (see comments on Mark 1:40–45).

Third, God's name, "Yahweh," is used rather than the traditional term, "the LORD," whenever God's name is relevant in the context.

According to the *Encyclopedia Judaica*, the divine name was "regularly pronounced with its proper vowels" at least until 586 BC (when the Babylonian exile began).[73] We have archaeological evidence for this from the Lachish Letters. By the time the Old Testament began to be translated into Greek (the Septuagint) in the third century BC, Jews were avoiding the divine name and began substituting "Adonai,"[74] which translated into Greek as *kurios*, meaning "Lord." Since Jesus and the apostles and then the New Testament church used the Septuagint as their primary Bible when quoting the Old Testament Scriptures, they used *kurios* for the divine name. But the Old Testament, which is still God's Word as much as is the New Testament, reads YHWH for the divine name. But how should it be pronounced? A clue is the names that have the divine name in them, like Zechariah, which in Hebrew is *zachar-yah*, which means "YAH remembers." Scholars recognize YAH as a shortened form of the divine name. The *Encyclopedia Judaica* again says, "The true pronunciation of the name YHWH was never lost. Several early Greek writers of the Christian church testify that the name was pronounced 'Yahweh.'"[75] The Christian theologian Clement of Alexandria (d. AD 215), for example, was apparently familiar with the Jewish tradition for how the divine name was pronounced, for he regularly uses (in Greek) *'Iaoue*, which would be pronounced "Yahweh." So since we know the divine name, we think Christians should become increasingly familiar with it, so the current edition of the HCSB uses it about 600 times.

Fourth, in order to make clear that Jesus is the fulfillment of the One promised in the Old Testament (e.g., Dan 9:25–26) and that this is the reason He is called "Christ," we translate *ho christos* as "the Messiah" in the New Testament in strongly Jewish contexts (see comments on Col 2:8–15).

 Fifth, although human slavery is a terrible thing, the HCSB translates several words as "slave" whenever the context calls for it. The Hebrew words *'ebed* ("slave, servant") *shiphchah* ("female slave/servant"), and *'amah* ("female slave/servant") are rendered as "slave" about 90, 40, and 30 times, respectively (for example, in Gen 12:16; 16:1; 20:17, respectively). The Greek *doulos* is almost without exception rendered as "slave" in the HCSB (about 120 times) rather than

---

[73] Louis F. Hartman, "God, Names of," in *Encyclopedia Judaica*, ed. Cecil Roth (Jerusalem: Keter, 1972), 7:680.

[74] *Jehovah* is a medieval mixture of YHWH and Adonai.

[75] *Encyclopedia Judaica*, 7:680.

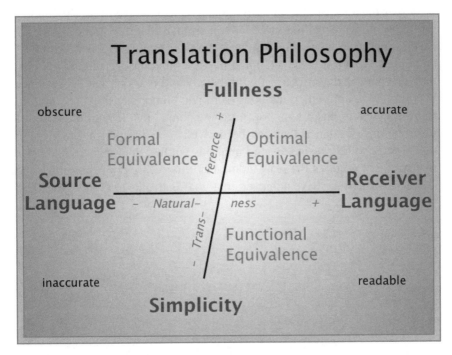

"servant" or "bondservant."[76] The exceptions are in the phrases "his servants the prophets" and "God's servant Moses" in Revelation 10:7; 11:18; 15:3. Some translations prefer "bondservant" as a term that lacks association with American slavery. The problem with that term is its quaintness and the difficulty of finding a definition for it. For example, the word does not occur in the multivolume *Anchor Yale Bible Dictionary* and only once in the *Zondervan Pictorial Encyclopedia of the Bible*, with no definition.

The optimal equivalence philosophy of the HCSB, then, makes naturalness of expression a priority, while also favoring a translation that is word for word, uses the same grammatical structures as the original,

---

[76] See BDAG, "δοῦλος," which explains that "'servant' for 'slave' is largely confined to Biblical transl[ations] and early American times." All the major Greek lexicons recognize that δοῦλος means "slave." The *Theological Lexicon of the New Testament* by Ceslas Spicq, trans. and ed. James D. Ernest (Peabody, MA: Hendrickson, 1994) even states, "It is wrong to translate *doulos* as 'servant,' so obscuring its precise signification in the language of the first century." It is sometimes said that most slaves in the ancient world were temporary debt slaves and had a much higher status than slaves in early America. But although some slaves managed to obtain their freedom, this was not always the case, and slavery still meant being owned by and at the mercy of a master. And many slaves had been prisoners of war, condemned to slavery for lawbreaking, or were born into slavery. See M. Dandamayevm and S. Scott Bartchy, "Slavery," in *The Anchor Yale Bible Dictionary* (New York: Doubleday, 1992), 58–73.

preserves the idioms (at least in footnotes), achieves consistency in rendering the same words in the same way in similar contexts, and relies heavily on translation notes. The formal features of biblical Hebrew, Aramaic, and Greek are not just the wrapping paper around the gift of God's Word; they are part of the gift. But the highest priority of optimal equivalence is communication, which includes truth and comprehension. The goal in translating every passage is not to leave behind any element of sense, of information, of nuance that can be derived from the original text using the latest scholarly resources and methods but to communicate that sense in a way that requires the least amount of processing effort possible. The degree to which we have achieved that goal is thanks to God's grace and for his glory.

CHAPTER 5

The New Living Translation (NLT)

Philip Comfort

Introduction

Before I begin an analysis of the four English translations, a few introductory remarks are in order. First, it should be noted that I was the New Testament coordinating editor and translator for the NLT. I had the privilege of working with more than 30 scholars on the New Testament translation, as well as serving on the Bible Translation Committee that oversaw the entire translation. The translation philosophy and methodology at work in this translation was dynamic equivalence, otherwise known as functional equivalence or thought-for-thought translation. This differs from a literal translation, which attempts to render the original word-for-word. Consequently, there will be significant differences in translations working according to two different philosophies and methodologies. Second, one of my key roles as the New Testament coordinating editor was to apprise the committee of significant textual variants in the New Testament Greek text—that is, variant readings in various manuscripts that have significant influence on how we translate a particular passage. Most modern English translations use the Greek text found in *Novum Testamentum Graece* (Nestle-Aland, 27th edition, abbreviated as NA^{27}), which has the same text as in the *Greek New Testament* (United Bible Societies,

4th ed., abbreviated as UBS[4]). But not one English translation follows this text slavishly. Rather, translators will often translate a variant reading (found in various manuscripts) that was rejected by the editors of NA[27] and UBS.[4] Responsible translators will use marginal notes to inform the reader about textual variants in other manuscripts for certain passages. I did this throughout the NLT. The reader of this book will see that I pay close attention to how translations differ based on textual variants in the manuscripts. Third, the NLT Bible Translation Committee (of which I was a member) made a conscious act of translating the Bible according to the standards of modern English writing, which calls for gender inclusiveness. Male dominated language is a thing of the past. Thus, we rendered *anthrōpos* not as "man" but as "human being" or "person" or the like (which happens to be the true meaning in the Greek). More will be said about this in specific texts analyzed below.

Translation Comparison

Passage 1. Exodus 2:5–6

[5] Soon Pharaoh's daughter came down to bathe in the river, and her attendants walked along the riverbank. When the princess saw the basket among the reeds, she sent her maid to get it for her. [6] When the princess opened it, she saw the <u>baby</u>. The little boy was crying, and she felt sorry for him. "This must be one of the Hebrew children," she said.

Aside from a few minor lexical differences, the four versions convey the same message. The only obvious difference is that the literal "babies" has become "boys" in HCSB and "children" in ESV and NLT—but with no real difference in meaning.

Passage 2. Psalm 1:1

Oh, the joys of <u>those</u> who do not <u>follow</u> the advice of the wicked, or <u>stand</u> around with sinners, or <u>join</u> in with mockers.

The concrete imagery of the verse is built on three verbs: "walk, stand, sit." They are rendered literally in ESV and NIV. The HCSB and NLT go a different direction. The verbs become "follow," "take the path," and "join" in HCSB, whereas NLT renders them as "follow," "stand," and "join." These verbs are good but not as "concrete" as in the literal renderings. The other issue pertains to gender inclusive language. Both the NLT and NIV are gender inclusive ("those" and "the one"), whereas HCSB and ESV are literal ("man").

Passage 3. Ezekiel 18:5–9,21–25

> [5] Suppose a certain man is righteous and does what is just and right. [6] He does not feast in the mountains before Israel's idols or <u>worship them</u>. He does not commit adultery or have intercourse with a woman during her menstrual period. [7] He is a merciful creditor, not keeping the items given as security by poor debtors. He does not rob the poor but instead gives food to the hungry and provides clothes for the needy. [8] He grants loans without interest, stays away from injustice, is honest and fair when judging others, [9] and faithfully obeys my decrees and regulations. Anyone who does these things is just and will surely live, says the Sovereign LORD. . . . [21] But if wicked <u>people</u> turn away from all their sins and begin to obey my decrees and do what is just and right, <u>they</u> will surely live and not die. [22] All <u>their</u> past sins will be forgotten, and <u>they</u> will live because of the righteous things <u>they</u> have done. [23] Do you think that I like to see wicked <u>people</u> die? says the <u>Sovereign LORD</u>. Of course not! I want <u>them</u> to turn from <u>their</u> wicked ways and live. [24] However, if righteous <u>people</u> turn from their righteous behavior and start doing sinful things and act like other sinners, should <u>they</u> be allowed to live? No, of course not! All <u>their</u> righteous acts will be forgotten, and <u>they</u> will die for <u>their</u> sins. [25] "Yet you say, 'The Lord isn't doing what's right!' Listen to me, O people of Israel. Am I the one not doing what's right, or is it you?"

The first passage in this section (18:5–9) is clearly addressing a male human ("man"); hence, all the translations reflect this. The second passage (18:21–24) appears to be addressed to all God's people (men and women). This is made gender inclusive in NLT and NIV, but HCSB and ESV use the masculine pronoun "he" as if the words from God were addressed only to men.

There are two other noteworthy differences in the translations. The first occurs in 18:5–6, which literally says that a man is righteous if a man does not eat on the mountains or lift up his eyes to idols. This is rendered word-for-word in the ESV, which leads readers to believe that eating in the mountains is a bad thing. So the other versions clarify that "the mountains" must have been "mountain shrines" (HCSB, NIV; this is also clarified in the NLT which says, "he does not feast in the mountains before Israel's idols"). The other noteworthy distinction between the translations occurs in 18:23 with reference to the divine name, which is literally "Adonai Yahweh" or "Adonai YHWH." The NLT and NIV render this combined divine title as "Sovereign LORD," in keeping with their practice of translating YHWH as "LORD." ("Adonai" would normally be translated as "Lord" but in this combination becomes "Sovereign.") The ESV and HCSB render the combined title as "Lord GOD," a tradition that goes back to the RSV and KJV. As such, "GOD" becomes a rendering for YHWH (Yahweh), a bit confusing for English readers who have become used to seeing "LORD" as the translation of YHWH (Yahweh).

Passage 4. Matthew 5:3

> God blesses those who are poor and realize their need for him,
> for the Kingdom of Heaven is theirs.

The ESV, HCSB, and NIV provide a literal translation of the first phrase in 5:3, "blessed are the poor in spirit" (see also NLT marginal note). The NLT translators understood the Greek for "blessed" (*makarioi*) to be a divine passive and therefore rendered it as "God blesses." The NLT translators also rendered "poor in spirit" dynamically, providing what they thought "poor in spirit" meant, which is to realize one's need for God.

Passage 5. Mark 1:41

> <u>Moved with compassion</u>, Jesus reached out and touched him. "I
> am willing," he said. "Be healed!"

The most notable difference between the translations occurs in Mark 1:41, where three translations (NLT, ESV, HCSB) indicate that Jesus was "moved with compassion/pity" (*splangchnistheis*) at the leper's request for healing. One translation (NLT) notes that some manuscripts read that Jesus was "moved with anger," and yet another translation (NIV) actually follows these manuscripts and reads that Jesus "was indignant" (*orgistheis*) at the leper's request for a healing. The two readings are very different! Was Jesus moved with compassion or was he indignant? First, let us look at the textual evidence. The number of manuscripts that support "was compassionate" is impressive (see fig. 6 below).

Figure 6: Manuscripts Supporting "Was Compassionate"

Manuscript	Date (AD)
ℵ (Codex Sinaiticus)	4th century
A (Codex Alexandrinus)	5th century
B (Codex Vaticanus)	4th century
C (Codex Ephraemi Rescriptus)	5th century
L (Codex Regius)	8th century
W (Codex Washington)	early 5th century
f^1	12th–14th centuries
f^{13}	11th–15th centuries
33	9th century
565	9th century
700	11th century
Syriac	2nd–6th centuries
Coptic	3rd–4th centuries
Diatessaron	160–175

The manuscript evidence for "was indignant"/"was moved with anger" is slim (see fig. 7 below).

Figure 7: Manuscripts Supporting "Was Indignant"

Manuscript	Date (AD)
D (Codex Bezae)	5th century
it^a (old Latin)	350
it^d (old Latin)	450

Most scholars believe this to be a significant textual dilemma because the variant is such an obviously difficult reading, while the text has such exceedingly strong documentation. The argument runs as thus: If "being compassionate" had originally been in the text, why would any scribe want to change it to "being indignant"? Thus, "being indignant" (or "being angry") must have been original, which was then changed to "being compassionate." But we must remember that the scribe who wrote "being indignant" was the scribe of D (who is often followed by it[a, d]). This scribe (or a predecessor) was a literary editor who had a propensity for making significant changes in the text. At this point he may have decided to make Jesus angry with the leper for wanting a miracle—in keeping with the tone of voice Jesus used in 1:43 when he sternly warned the leper. But this was not a warning about seeking a miracle; it was a warning about keeping the miracle a secret so as to protect Jesus' identity.

Therefore, it would have to be said that, though it is possible Mark wrote "was indignant," nearly all the documents line up against this. This is not to say that Jesus never got angry or exasperated with people; he did (see Mark 7:34; 9:19; John 11:33,38). It simply seems unwise to take the testimony of D in this instance when good arguments can be made against it, according to both external and internal criteria. As such, I think the translators of the NIV made a daring but wrong decision.

Passage 6. Ending of Mark's Gospel

The Gospel of Mark ends in five ways in various manuscripts. I have also noted what the four versions (NLT, HCSB, ESV, NIV) reflect:

1. The earliest manuscripts stop at verse 8: Codex Sinaiticus (4th century) and Codex Vaticanus (4th century). This is also evident in 304 (12th century), Syriac[s] (4th century), one Coptic Sahidic manuscript, Armenian manuscripts, Georgian manuscripts, Hesychius, Eusebius' Canons, manuscripts according to Eusebius, manuscripts according to Jerome, manuscripts according to Severus. (None of the four versions conclude with verse 8; it is noted in NLT, HCSB, ESV, NIV.)

2. One manuscript, Codex Bobiensis (it[k]), dated 400, supplies a shorter ending. (This is included in the text of NLT and noted in ESV and NIV.)

> And all that had been commanded them they told briefly to those with Peter. And afterward Jesus himself sent out through them, from the east and as far as the west, the holy and imperishable proclamation of eternal salvation. Amen.

3. Other manuscripts supply a longer ending: Codex Alexandrinus (5th century), Codex Ephraemi Rescriptus (5th century), Codex Bezae (5th century), Θ (9th century), f^{13} (11th–15th centuries), 33 (9th century), majority of manuscripts, manuscripts according to Eusebius, manuscripts according to Jerome, manuscripts according to Severus, Irenaeus, Apostolic Constitutions, Epiphanius, Severian, Nestorius, Ambrose, and Augustine. This is included in the text of NLT, HCSB, ESV, NIV (the last has it in italics):

> [9] Now after he rose early on the first day of the week, he appeared first to Mary Magdalene, from whom he had cast out seven demons. [10] She went out and told those who had been with him, while they were mourning and weeping. [11] But when they heard that he was alive and had been seen by her, they would not believe it. [12] After this he appeared in another form to two of them, as they were walking into the country. [13] And they went back and told the rest, but they did not believe them. [14] Later he appeared to the eleven themselves as they were sitting at the table; and he upbraided them for their lack of faith and stubbornness, because they had not believed those who saw him after he had risen. [15] And he said to them, "Go into all the world and proclaim the good news to the whole creation. [16] He who believes and is baptized will be saved; but the one who does not believe will be condemned. [17] And these signs will accompany those who believe: by using my Name they will cast out demons; they will speak in new tongues; [18] they will pick up snakes in their hands, and if they drink any deadly thing, it will not hurt them; they will lay their hands on the sick, and they will recover." [19] So then the Lord Jesus, after he had spoken to them, was taken up into heaven and sat down at the right hand of God. [20] And they went out and proclaimed the good news everywhere, while the Lord worked with them and confirmed the message by the signs that accompanied it.

4. Some manuscripts (Codex Washington [early 5th century], manuscripts according to Jerome) have this longer ending with an addition after 16:14. This is noted in NLT and reads as follows:

> And they excused themselves, saying, "This age of lawlessness and unbelief is under Satan, who does not allow the truth and power of God to prevail over the unclean things of the spirits. Therefore reveal your righteousness now"—thus they spoke to

Christ. And Christ replied to them, "The term of years of Satan's power has been fulfilled, but other terrible things draw near. And for those who have sinned I was handed over to death, that they may return to the truth and sin no more, that they may inherit the spiritual and imperishable glory of righteousness that is in heaven."

5. Some manuscripts have the shorter ending (listed as #2) and the longer ending (listed as #3). (In essence this is what the text of NLT reflects.) The ending to Mark's Gospel presents an intriguing dilemma for textual scholars and translators: Which of the five endings, as presented above, did Mark write? Or is it possible that the original ending to Mark's Gospel was lost forever and that none of the above endings is the way the book originally ended? But before we come to a conclusion, let us look at the evidence.

The textual evidence for the first reading (stopping at v. 8) is the best. This reading is attested to by Codex Sinaiticus and Codex Vaticanus (the two earliest extant manuscripts that preserve this portion of Mark) and some early versions (Syriac, Coptic, Armenian, Georgian). Of the church fathers, Clement, Origen, Cyprian, and Cyril of Jerusalem show no knowledge of any verses beyond 16:8. Eusebius, Jerome, and Severus knew manuscripts that concluded with 16:8. Eusebius said that the accurate copies of Mark ended with verse 8, adding that 16:9–20 were missing from almost all manuscripts.[1] Jerome affirmed the same by saying that almost all the Greek codices did not have 16:9–20.[2] Several later manuscripts that include 16:9–20 have marginal notes indicating that more ancient manuscripts do not include this section.

Other manuscripts mark off the longer reading with obeli (†) to indicate its questionable status. The textual evidence, therefore, shows that Mark's Gospel circulated in many ancient copies with an ending at verse 8. But this ending seemed to be too abrupt for many readers—both ancient and modern! As a result various endings were appended. One short ending was appended to round off verse 8 and to indicate that the women had followed the angels' orders in bringing the report to Peter and the disciples. But in order to make this addition, it is necessary to delete the words "and said nothing to no one" from verse 8—which is exactly what was done in one Old Latin manuscript.

---

[1] *Quaestiones ad Marinum* 1; MPG 22, 937.
[2] *Epistle* 120.3 *ad Hedibiam.*

The best-known ending is the longer, traditional ending of 16:9–20. The earliest witnesses to this ending come from Irenaeus (via a Latin translation). The other patristic witnesses cited above are no earlier than the fourth century (e.g., manuscripts according to Eusebius, Jerome, and Augustine). Thus we know that this ending was probably in circulation in the third century. It became the most popular of the endings after the fourth century and was copied again and again in many subsequent manuscripts. Eventually it was accepted as canonical by the Roman Catholic Council of Trent (1564).

But the longer ending is stylistically incongruous with 16:1–8. Any fair-minded reader can detect the non-Markan flavor of the style, tone, and vocabulary of 16:9–20. This is apparent in the first word in 16:9. The Greek verb *anastas* ("having risen") is an active aorist participle; it conveys the thought that Jesus himself rose from the dead. But almost everywhere else in the Gospels, the passive verb is used with respect to Jesus' resurrection. What is more, the additions are all transparently noncontinuous with the preceding narrative. This is especially apparent in the connection between verses 8 and 9. The subject of verse 8 is the women, whereas the presumed subject of verse 9 is Jesus. And Mary Magdalene is introduced as if she has not been mentioned before or was not among the women of 15:47–16:8.

This longer ending was made even longer in Codex Washington with an addition after 16:14. Prior to the discovery of this Codex, we had the record from Jerome that there was another similar ending:

> In certain exemplars and especially in the Greek manuscripts [of the Gospel] according to Mark, at the end of his Gospel, there is written, "Afterward, when the Eleven reclined at meal, Jesus appeared to them and upbraided them for their unbelief and hardness of heart because they had not believed those who had seen him after his resurrection. And they made excuse, saying, 'This age of iniquity and unbelief is under Satan who, through unclean spirits, does not permit the true power of God to be apprehended. Therefore, reveal your righteousness now.'"

The Codex Washington text is an expansion of what was known to Jerome inasmuch as Jesus gives a response to their excuse concerning unbelief. The disciples, blaming Satan for the unbelief, made an appeal to Jesus for his return, which brings the full revelation of his vindictive righteousness. In response, Jesus declares that Satan's time has already come to its end, but before he (Jesus) can reveal his righteous kingdom, there will come a time "of terrible things." This terrible time of apostasy and judgment would be the prelude to the second coming. Finally, some manuscripts include both the shorter reading and the traditional longer reading. The earliest evidence for these is in two eighth-century manuscripts. Some ancient versions also have both endings. This is clearly the result of scribal ambiguity.

What then do we make of the evidence? Scholarly consensus is that Mark did not write any of the endings (nos. 2–5 above); all are the work of other hands. Farmer's attempt to defend the view that Mark 16:9–20 was originally part of Mark's Gospel, which was later deleted by Alexandrian scribes, is not convincing.[3] Farmer argues that Alexandrian scribes were troubled by the references to picking up snakes and drinking poison and therefore deleted the passage. If they had been troubled by these references, they would have deleted only those verses, not the entire passage! No one else has made a good case for the originality of any of the various additions. The historical fact appears to be that various readers, concerned that Mark ended so abruptly, completed the Gospel with a variety of additions. According to Kurt Aland, the shorter and longer endings were composed independently in different geographical locations, and both were probably circulating in the second century.[4] Metzger says that the longer ending displays some vocabulary that "suggests that the composition of the ending is appropriately located at the end of the first century or in the middle of the second century."[5]

The reason the shorter ending was created has already been explained. The longer ending was composed afresh or taken verbatim from some other source so as to fill up what was perceived to be a gap in the text of Mark. This writer provided an extended conclusion derived from various sources, including the other Gospels and Acts, inserting his own theological peculiarities. The reason the longer ending has become so popular is that it is a collage of events found in the other Gospels and the book of Acts.

Jesus' appearance to Mary Magdalene (16:9) was adapted from John 20:11–17. Her report to the disciples (16:10) was taken from Luke 24:10

---

[3] William Farmer, *The Last Twelve Verses of Mark* (Cambridge: Cambridge University Press, 1974).

[4] Kurt Aland, "Bemerkungen zum Schluss des Markusevangeliums," in *Neotestamentica et Semitica*, ed. E. Earle Ellis and Max Wilcox (Edinburgh: T&T Clark, 1969), 157–80.

[5] Bruce M. Metzger, *The Text of the New Testament: Its Transmission, Corruption, and Restoration*, 3rd ed. (Oxford: Oxford University Press, 1992), 297.

and John 20:18. However, the writer of the longer ending has this report concerning Jesus' appearance, whereas Mary's report in John comes after she has seen the empty tomb. John's account is affirmed by the account in Luke 24:11. In both John and Luke, the disciples do not believe the report concerning the angelic appearance and the empty tomb; there was no mention yet of any appearance made by Jesus. The change of story in the longer ending to Mark was contrived because Mark 16:8 says the women said nothing to anybody after seeing the empty tomb and the angelic messenger. The writer could not controvert this blatantly (by saying that Mary and/ or any of the other women then went to the disciples and told them about the empty tomb), so the writer has Jesus appearing to Mary Magdalene, then Mary telling the disciples, who do not believe. Since this particular account contradicts the authentic Gospels, it should be dismissed.

After this the writer of the longer ending relates Jesus' appearance to two disciples as they were walking from Jerusalem into the country (16:12); this clearly was taken from Luke 24:13–35. The report of further unbelief (16:13) was the interpretation of the composer; Luke does not tell us that the report of the two disciples was disbelieved. Jesus' first resurrection appearance to the disciples (16:14) was borrowed from Luke 24:36–49—with an added emphasis on their unbelief (perhaps adapted from Matt 28:16–20). Jesus' Great Commission (16:15–16) is loosely based on Matt 28:19–20—with an emphasis on baptism as a prerequisite to salvation. The promise of signs accompanying the believers (16:17–18) comes from the record of what happened in Acts—including the speaking in tongues (2:4; 10:46) and protection against snakes (28:3–6). The ascension (16:19) is adapted from Luke 24:50–53, and the final verse (16:20) seems to be a summary of the book of Acts, which seems to be preemptively out of place for inclusion in a Gospel and is another indication of its spuriousness. (None of the other Gospels tell us anything about the disciples' work after Jesus' resurrection and ascension.)

Even though much of this longer ending was drawn from other Gospels and Acts, the composer had an unusual emphasis on the disciples' unbelief in the resurrection of Christ. In this regard the composer may have been following through on the Markan theme of identifying the unbelief and stubbornness of the disciples. Indeed, this Gospel, more than any other, focuses on the disciples' repeated failures to believe Jesus and follow him. The composer of the longer ending also had a preference for belief and baptism as a requisite for salvation, as well as an exalted view of signs. Christians need to be warned against using this text for Christian doctrine because it is not on the same par as verifiable New Testament Scripture. Nothing in it should be used to establish Christian doctrine or practice. Unfortunately, certain churches have used Mark 16:16 to affirm dogmatically that one must believe and be baptized in order to be saved, and other churches have used Mark 16:18 to promote the practice of snake-handling. (Some boxes that keep the rattlesnakes are even marked with "Mark 16:18" written on them.) Those who are bitten by rattlesnakes, they believe, will not be harmed if they are true followers of Christ. The writer of the longer ending also emphasized what we would call charismatic experiences—speaking in tongues, performing healings, or protection from snakes and poison. Although the book of Acts affirms these experiences for certain believers, they are not necessarily the norm for all.

The longer ending of Codex Washington (noted also by Jerome) was probably a marginal gloss written in the third century that found its way into the text of some manuscripts prior to the fourth century. This gloss was likely created by a scribe who wanted to provide a reason for the unbelief that is prevalent in the longer ending. Satan is blamed for the faithlessness, and an appeal is made for Jesus to reveal his righteousness immediately. But this revelation would be postponed until after a time of terrible things. This interpolation may have been drawn from several sources, including Acts (1:6–7; 3:19–21) and the Epistle of Barnabas (4:9; 15:7). In any case it is clear that Mark did not write it. The style is blatantly non-Markan.

Having concluded that Mark did not write any of the endings, we are still left with the question: did Mark originally conclude his Gospel with verse 8 or was an original extended ending lost? In defense of the view that Mark originally ended his Gospel at verse 8, four arguments can be posited. (1) As it is, the Gospel ends with an announcement of Christ's resurrection. Jesus does not need to actually appear in resurrection to validate the announcement. Our demand that the Gospel must record this appearance comes from our knowledge of the other Gospels. Mark did not have to end his Gospel the way the others did. (2) Mark, as a creative writer, may have purposely ended abruptly in order to force his readers to fill in the gap with their own imaginations. Perhaps Mark did not want to describe—or think himself capable of describing—the resurrection of Christ and/or the risen Christ; thus, he left it to the readers to imagine how the risen Christ appeared to Peter and the other disciples. (3) Throughout this Gospel, Mark presented a secrecy motif concerning Jesus being the Messiah (see Mark 8:26). The final verse is the culmination of this motif: the women "said nothing to anyone." Of course, the reader knows that this silence would not last; indeed, the opposite will happen—the word of Christ's resurrection will be announced to the disciples, and the disciples will proclaim this to the world. Thus, the ending was calculated by Mark to be the irony of ironies; perhaps he thought it would bring a smile to the face of the Christians reading or hearing this Gospel for the first time, for they knew how the word had gone out! (4) It ends on a note of failure—the women's failure to go to Peter and the other disciples—because this is consistent with another major theme in Mark's Gospel: discipleship failure. All these four reasons could account for Mark purposely concluding the Gospel at 16:8.

However, many readers are not satisfied with these reasons—primarily because they, having read the other Gospels, have a different horizon of expectation for the conclusion of Mark. Thus, many readers have questioned whether it was Mark's original design to conclude with verse 8. Why conclude with merely an announcement of Jesus' resurrection and a description of the women's fear and bewilderment? In the Gospel of Mark, a pattern is set in which every one of Jesus' predictions is actually fulfilled in narrative form. According to Gundry, the predictions were fulfilled as follows: God's kingdom having come with power at the transfiguration, the finding of a colt, the disciples' being met by a man carrying a jar of water, the showing of the upper room, the betrayal of Jesus by one of the Twelve, the scattering of the rest of the Twelve, the denials of Jesus by Peter, the passion, and the resurrection.[6] Thus, since Jesus announced that he would see his disciples in Galilee (14:28), the narrative should have depicted an actual appearance of the risen Christ to his disciples in Galilee.

Since there is no such record (even in the additions), some readers have thought an original extended ending got lost in the early transmission of Mark's Gospel—probably because it was written on the last leaf of a papyrus codex and was torn away from the rest of the manuscript. (Though Mark may have originally been written on a scroll, which would have preserved the last section rolled up inside, copies of Mark in codex form would have been in use as early as the end of the first century.)[7] This codex could have contained just the Gospel of Mark or all four Gospels set in the typical Western order: Matthew, John, Luke, Mark (which was likely the case for $\mathfrak{P}^{45}$ [c. AD 200]). In both scenarios, Mark 16 would have been

---

[6] Robert H. Gundry, *Mark: A Commentary on His Apology for the Cross* (Grand Rapids: Eerdmans, 1993), 1009.

[7] See Philip W. Comfort, *Encountering the Manuscripts: An Introduction to New Testament Paleography and Textual Criticism* (Nashville: B&H, 2005), 27–40.

the last sheet. However, it seems odd and most unusual that this ending would not have survived in some manuscript somewhere. The history of textual transmission is characterized by tenacity; once a reading enters the textual stream, it will usually be preserved in some manuscript and show up somewhere down the line. Thus, this imagined ending to Mark must have been lost soon after the composition of the Gospel, if there was such an ending.

It is possible that 16:7 was intended to be the concluding verse of the first paragraph of Mark's original last chapter (inasmuch as it concludes with the glorious angelic announcement of Christ's resurrection) and that 16:8 was the first sentence of the next paragraph. It seems that the last two words of 16:8, *ephobounto gar* ("for they were afraid"), could have been the first two words of a new sentence. Indeed, it is highly unusual for a sentence, let alone an entire Gospel, to end with the conjunctive *gar*; so it is likely that some word or words followed, such as *ephobounto gar lalein* ("for they were afraid to speak"). After this, Mark's narrative would have continued to relate, most likely, that Jesus appeared to the women (as in Matthew and John) and that the women, no longer afraid, then went and told the disciples what they saw. This would have probably been followed by Jesus' appearing to his disciples in Jerusalem and in Galilee. This is the basic pattern found in the other Gospels. And since Mark was probably used by the other Gospel writers, it stands to reason that their narrative pattern reflects Mark's original work.

Of the four English versions, only the NLT includes all five endings (two in the text and three notations in the margin). The other three versions vary in their presentation (see notes on each above). The NIV includes 16:9–20 in the text but sets it in italics to signal the secondary nature of the text; HCSB brackets 16:9–20. Given the external and internal evidence, the best solution would be to conclude Mark at 16:8 and then present the various endings in marginal notes.

Passage 7. Luke 17:3

So watch yourselves! "If <u>another believer sins</u>, rebuke <u>that person;</u> then if there is repentance, forgive.

There are two translation issues in this verse. The first pertains to how to render *adelphos*, and the second pertains to a textual variant ("sins" versus "sins against you"). When the text has the word *adelphos*, are we to understand it as literally "a brother," a male disciple or male Christian, or is it to be understood as referring to any disciple or Christian, whether male or female? Two translations (ESV, HCSB) render it literally, "brother," while two translations (NLT, NIV) render it gender inclusively. The NLT translates it "believer" (with a marginal note, "brother"), and the NIV renders it "brother or sister," with a marginal note: "The Greek word for brother or sister (*adelphos*) refers here to a fellow disciple, whether man or woman." Paul's epistles set a precedent for rendering it gender inclusively because he clearly used *adelphoi* (the plural form) to denote male and female believers. For example, in 1 Corinthians 8:11–13, Paul used *adelphos* and *adelphoi* in speaking of those for whom Christ died. Christ clearly died for all the believers, whether male or female. So, clearly, he was using *adelphoi* gender-inclusively.

The second issue pertains to the textual variant "sins" or "sins against you." This is easy to solve because "sins" has excellent textual support and "sins against you" is the result of scribal conformity to Matthew 18:15, a parallel passage with inferior textual documentation. The manuscripts that support "sins" are Codex Sinaiticus (4th century), Codex Alexandrinus (5th century), Codex Vaticanus (4th century), and others. The manuscript support for "sins against you" is inferior: Codex Bezae (5th century) and the Majority Text (Textus Receptus). All four translations (HCSB, ESV, NLT, NIV) follow the superior reading, and HCSB notes "other mss add 'against you!'"

Passage 8. John 1:3–4a,14,18

³ God created everything through him, and nothing was created except through him. ⁴ <u>The Word gave life to everything that was created</u>, and his life brought light to everyone. . . . ¹⁴ So the Word became human and made his home among us. He was full of unfailing love and faithfulness. And we have seen his glory, the glory of the Father's <u>one and only Son</u>. . . . ¹⁸ No one has ever seen God. But <u>the unique One, who is himself God</u>, is near to the Father's heart. He has revealed God to us.

Interpreters and translators have long been perplexed as to what to do with the Greek words *ho gegonen* (literally, "that which has come into being") that appear at the end of John 1:3. Do the words complete the thought of John 1:3, or do they begin the thought of John 1:4? The two Greek editions known as the Westcott and Hort *New Testament in the Original Greek* (WH) and the United Bible Societies' *Greek New Testament* (4th ed.; known as UBS[4]) punctuate the verses so as to have *ho gegonen* begin the thought of John 1:4. This translates literally as "All things came into being through him, and without him not one thing came into being. What has come into being in him was life." This arrangement has the manuscript support of $\mathfrak{P}^{75c}$ (late 2nd century), Codex Bezae (5th century), Codex Washington (early 5th century), and others. Of the four translations being analyzed, only the NLT follows this arrangement (it is noted in HCSB). The Textus Receptus punctuates the verses so as to have *ho gegonen* conclude John 1:3. This translates literally as "[3]All things came into being through him, and without him not one thing came into being that has come into being. [4] In him was life." This arrangement has the manuscript support of the corrector of Codex Sinaiticus and the Majority Text. Of the four translations being analyzed, it is followed by the HCSB, ESV, and NIV. It should be noted that the earliest manuscripts ($\mathfrak{P}^{66}$ [mid to late 2nd century], $\mathfrak{P}^{75*}$, Codex Sinaiticus* [original], Codex Alexandrinus, and Codex Vaticanus) do not have any punctuation in these verses. If John had read the passage out loud, the hearers would have known how he punctuated the text. Lacking his notations, all readers—from ancient to modern—have had to guess his intentions. Of course, it must also be said that since the prologue is poetic, it is possible that John intended ambiguity; thus, it is not a question of which reading is correct. The earliest scribes, by not adding punctuation, left the text ambiguous; ancient readers could read it both ways and still make sense of it.

The majority of the early church fathers interpreted John 1:3–4 according to the phrasing in the Westcott and Hort and UBS[4] texts. The passage was taken to mean that all created things were "life" by virtue of being in him. The statement affirms that the Word not only created the universe, he presently sustains it: "all that came into being has its life in him" (see Col 1:17; Heb 1:2–3). This idea is rendered well in the NLT: "The Word gave life to everything that was created." The next phrase in the prologue, "and the life was the light of men," was then interpreted by several early interpreters to mean that the Word enlightened people—even prior to his incarnation via the light of creation. This was the view of Justin Martyr and the Christian philosophers of Alexandria.

However, the expression "what has come into being in him was life" has been understood (or, should I say misunderstood) by some to mean that life had "come into being" in the Word (i.e., "that which came into being in him was life" or "life is that which came into being in him"). But that is not a legitimate translation because it would require a feminine pronoun (to coincide with zōē, "life"), whereas the pronoun is neuter. Nevertheless, certain fourth-century Arians, misunderstanding the grammar, took this to mean that the Son had undergone change and therefore was not truly equal with the Father.[8] Thereafter, many church fathers supported the reading as it is in the majority of manuscripts (so the Textus Receptus). This reading emphasizes the Word's impartation of life to men concurrent with the giving of light to men. In short, it speaks of Jesus' ministry on earth as the life-giver and light-giver. Some interpreters have followed this up to the present,[9] while other scholars support the arrangement in the Westcott and Hort and UBS[4] texts.[10] No matter which rendering a modern English version follows, it should note the alternative rendering. Thus, in future editions of the ESV and NIV, I would urge the translators to add a note.

With regard to John 1:18, the most significant difference between the translations pertains to a textual variant. Should the text read *monogenēs theos* ("one and only God") or *monogenēs huios* ("one and only Son")? In other words, is Jesus being called "God" or "Son"? Let's look at the textual evidence (see fig. 8 below).

Figure 8: Manuscripts Supporting Theos

Manuscript	Date
𝔓⁶⁶	mid to late 2nd century
𝔓⁷⁵	late 2nd century
ℵ (Codex Sinaiticus)	4th century
B (Codex Vaticanus)	4th century

Furthermore, the reading *theos* ("God") was known by many church fathers (Irenaeus, Clement, Origen, Eusebius, etc.). The reading *huios* ("Son") has inferior support (see fig. 9 below).

---

[8] Raymond E. Brown, *The Gospel According to St. John*, 2 vols., Anchor Bible 29–29A (Garden City, NY: Doubleday, 1996–70), 1:6.

[9] See the discussion in Rudolf Schnackenburg, *The Gospel According to St. John*, 3 vols. (New York: Crossroad, 1990), 1:239–40.

[10] E.g., B. F. Westcott, *The Gospel According to St. John* (Grand Rapids: Eerdmans, 1975), 28–31; Brown, *Gospel According to St. John*, 1.6–7; George R. Beasley-Murray, *John*, Word Biblical Commentary 36 (Waco, TX: Word, 1987), 2.

Figure 9: Manuscripts Supporting Huios

Manuscript	Date
A (Codex Alexandrinus)	5th century
W (Codex Washington)	early 5th century
Majority Text	5th century and later

The variant *huios* ("Son") was known by many church fathers (Irenaeus, Clement, Eusebius, etc.).

The two second-century papyri, $\mathfrak{P}^{66}$ and $\mathfrak{P}^{75}$, both of which read *theos* ("God"), strongly favor the originality of this reading. This was changed—as early as the beginning of the third century, if not—earlier, to the more ordinary reading, *huios* ("Son"). Even without the knowledge of the two papyri (which were discovered in the 1950s and 1960s), Hort argued extensively and convincingly for the reading *monogenes theos*.[11] He argued that Gnostics (such as Valentinus, the first known writer to have used this phrase) did not invent this phrase; rather, they simply quoted it. And he argued that this phrase is suitable for the closing verse of the prologue, in which Christ has been called "God" (*theos*, in 1:1) and "an only One" (*monogenēs*, in 1:14), and finally, "an only One, God" (*monogenēs theos*, which combines the two titles into one). This is a masterful way of concluding the prologue, for 1:18 then mirrors 1:1. Both verses have the following three corresponding phrases: (1) Christ as God's expression (the "Word" and "he has explained him"), (2) Christ as God ("the Word was God" and "an only One, God"), and (3) as the one close to God ("the Word was face-to-face with God" [Williams's translation] and "in the bosom of the Father").

After the discovery of the papyri, English translators started to adopt the reading "God." However, the entire phrase, *monogenēs theos*, is difficult to render because translators have not known whether to treat *monogenēs* as an adjective alone or as an adjective functioning as a substantive. Should this be rendered "an only-begotten God," "an only One, God," "unique God," or "the only God" (so ESV)? Since the term *monogenēs* more likely speaks of "uniqueness" than "only one born," it probably functions as a substantive indicating Jesus' unique identity as being both God and near to God. This is made clear in the NLT translation: "the unique One, who is himself God and is near the Father's heart." The NIV appears to offer

---

[11] Fenton Hort, *Two Dissertations* (Cambridge: Macmillan, 1876), 1–26.

a conflated reading, which has both "the one and only Son" and "God." Of course, the NIV translators were attempting to render *monogenēs* as "the one and only Son," but this rendering ends up becoming a translation of the inferior textual variant. Unfortunately, the HCSB follows the inferior reading, "the only Son," while noting the superior reading in the margin ("the only God"). In the final analysis, to reflect accurately what John wrote, an English translation could read, "No one has seen God at any time; a very unique One, who is God and who is in the bosom of the Father, has explained him."

What is important to note in this passage is that Jesus' deity is affirmed in the same manner as it is in John 1:1. He is unique in that he is God and with God, his Father. Jesus' deity is a major theme in John's Gospel, affirmed in 1:1; 5:17–18; 8:58; 10:30–36; 14:9–11; and 20:28. To these verses should be added 1:18, a profound conclusion to the prologue and a strong affirmation of Jesus' divine uniqueness. He alone who is God and near to God the Father is qualified to explain God to humanity.

Wildcard: John 1:34

I saw this happen to Jesus, so I testify that he is <u>the Chosen One of God</u>.

Footnote: Some manuscripts read *the Son of God*.

The translations differ in this verse based on a textual variant; some manuscripts read "Chosen One of God" and some read "Son of God." The NLT and NIV read "Chosen One of God/God's Chosen One" in their texts (with "Son of God" in the margin). The HCSB reads "Son of God" (with "Chosen One of God" in the margin); the ESV reads "Son of God" (with no alternative reading in the margin). The reading "Chosen One of God" has the textual support of $\mathfrak{P}^{5vid}$ (early 3rd century), $\mathfrak{P}^{106vid}$ (early 3rd century), Codex Sinaiticus (א*, original), and others. The reading "the Son of God" has the support of $\mathfrak{P}^{66}$, $\mathfrak{P}^{75}$, $\mathfrak{P}^{120}$ (3rd century), Codex Alexandrinus (A), Codex Vaticanus (B), Codex Bezae (D), and others. Though both $\mathfrak{P}^{5}$ and $\mathfrak{P}^{106}$ are listed as "vid" (i.e., evidently) in UBS[4] (not cited in NA[27]), it is fairly certain that both manuscripts read *eklektos* ("Chosen One"), not *huios* ("Son"; see the Oxyrhynchus volumes on $\mathfrak{P}^{5}$ and $\mathfrak{P}^{106}$).[12]

---

[12] See Philip W. Comfort and David Barrett, *The Text of the Earliest New Testament Greek Manuscripts* (Wheaton: Tyndale House, 2001), 75, 646.

Several scholars have argued that it is more likely that the reading *eklektos* ("chosen One") was changed to *huios* ("Son") than vice versa. For example, Fee thinks an orthodox scribe of the second century might have sensed "the possibility that the designation 'Chosen One' might be used to support adoptionism and so altered the text for orthodox reasons."[13] Or the change could have happened because scribes thought "Son" conformed with the Synoptic accounts of Jesus' baptism (where God calls Jesus "My Son") and/or suited John's Gospel better than "Chosen One." Indeed, "Son of God" frequently occurs in John's Gospel, but not all who recognized Jesus' deity called him "the Son of God." For example, Peter called him "the Holy One of God" (6:69). All these reasons strengthen the case for "Chosen One" being the original reading.

What is more, "Chosen One" adds one more messianic title to the chain of witnesses in John 1, while "Son" is repetitive (see 1:14; 1:49).[14] Christ as the Word is called "God" (1:1,18; cf. Isa 9:6), and Jesus is called "the Christ" or "Messiah" (1:17,41; cf. Ps 2:2; Dan 9:25), "the Son of God" (1:14,49, cf. Ps 2:7), "the Lamb of God" (1:29,36; cf. Isaiah 53), "the One predicted by Moses" (1:45; cf. Deut 18:16–18), "the King of Israel" (1:49; cf. Ps 2:6; Zeph 3:15), and "the Son of Man" (1:51; cf. Dan 7:13). If the title "the Chosen One of God" also were included, there is yet another messianic witness—this one referring to Isaiah 42:1 ("Behold, My Servant, whom I uphold; My chosen one *in whom* My soul delights" [NASB]).

A growing number of translators have decided to follow the reading "Chosen One." The recent publication of $\mathfrak{P}^{106}$ (early 3rd century) has strengthened the case for the translators of the NLT and NIV (2011) to choose this text, while noting "Son of God" in the margin. However, it must be admitted that both readings have early and diverse textual support, and therefore, either could be original. I would strongly suggest that whichever reading is selected for the text, the other be noted in the margin. The ESV should note that "the Chosen One of God" is found in other early manuscripts.

---

[13] Gordon D. Fee, "The Textual Criticism of the Greek New Testament," in vol. 1 of *The Expositor's Bible Commentary*, ed. Frank E. Gaebelein (Grand Rapids: Zondervan, 1978), 431–32.

[14] See James Williams, "Proposed Renderings for Some Johannine Passages," *The Bible Translator* 25 (1974): 351–53.

Passage 9. John 2:25–3:1

2:25 No one needed to tell him what <u>mankind</u> is really like. 3:1 There was <u>a man</u> named Nicodemus, a Jewish religious leader who was a Pharisee.

In the Greek text there is a clear lexical link between John 2:25 (the last verse of chap. 2) and 3:1. The link is supplied by the word *anthrōpos*, which appears twice in 2:25 and once in 3:1 and is literally translated as "man." In 2:25, John tells the reader that Jesus did not need any testimony about what is in "man" because he knew what was in "man." Then 3:1 immediately says that there was a "man" named Nicodemus, a Pharisee and leader of the Jews. The connection in the Greek is clear: Jesus did not need to be told about Nicodemus, and he knew Nicodemus because he knew what was in every man. In the two literal translations, the ESV and HCSB, the lexical link is immediately evident—that is, if the reader reads 3:1 immediately following 2:25. The link is not as clear in the NLT and NIV. The NLT uses "mankind" in 2:25 and "man" in 3:1. The NIV reads "person" in 2:25 and "man" in 3:1.

Passage 10. 1 Corinthians 2:1,13

1 When I first came to you, dear brothers and sisters, I didn't use lofty words and impressive wisdom to tell you God's <u>secret plan</u>. . . . 13 When we tell you these things, we do not use words that come from human wisdom. Instead, we speak words given to us by the Spirit, <u>using the Spirit's words to explain spiritual truths</u>.

The significant difference between the translations focuses on a textual variant. Does Paul say he proclaimed God's "mystery" (*mustērion*) or God's "testimony" (*marturion*)? Let us look at the textual evidence for each reading. The word *mustērion* (mystery) is found in 𝔓46vid (mid to late 2nd century), Codex Sinaiticus (א*, original hand), Codex Alexandrinus (A), and other manuscripts. UBS3 cites 𝔓46vid? in support of their text (which has *musterion*). The question mark follows "vid" (which means, "it appears to read") because the editors were not sure that 𝔓46 read the word *mustērion* ("mystery"). Having examined the actual papyrus, I can affirm that the reading is *mustērion* ("mystery"), not *marturion* ("testimony"), because the Greek letter *eta*, though partially broken, is visible before the final four letters—also visible (*rion*). The one letter makes all the difference in determining the reading. UBS[4] (as well as the Nestle-Aland text) now list this papyrus as 𝔓[46vid]. The manuscript evidence for *marturion* (testimony) is as follows: Codex Sinaiticus (ℵ[2], second corrector), Codex Vaticanus (B), the Majority Text, and a few other manuscripts.

The Nestle-Aland text has the clear support from the earliest extant document, 𝔓[46]. Several other witnesses, both early and diverse, also support the Nestle-Aland text. But the same can be said for the variant reading. So how then do we solve the problem? Competent textual critics such as Zuntz and Fee have argued that *musterion* is a scribal emendation influenced by 1 Corinthians 2:7.[15] Other scholars, such as Brown and Metzger, have argued that *marturion* is a scribal emendation influenced by 1 Corinthians 1:6.[16] Actually, one can draw upon the context of 1 Corinthians 1–2 to support either word because Paul's message in these chapters is that his mission was to testify only of Christ, who is the mystery of God. The immediate context seems to support "mystery" because chapter 2 focuses on the need for believers to receive revelation from the Spirit of God to truly understand all the hidden, secret riches of God that are in Christ Jesus (see 2:7ff.).

In summary, the internal and external evidence for this reading is divided, so it is not easy to make a decision of which variant is original. This indecision is reflected in the four translations, with the NLT following *mustērion* ("mystery"/"secret plan") in the text and noting the variant *marturion* ("testimony") in the margin. The other three versions (HCSB, ESV, NIV) do just the opposite, accepting *marturion* ("testimony") in the text and noting the variant *mustērion* ("mystery") in the margin.

The last expression of 1 Corinthians 2:13 (*pneumatikois pneumatika sugkrinontes*) has troubled many translators and exegetes. Does this phrase mean "matching spiritual truths with corresponding spiritual words" or "explaining spiritual truths to spiritual people"? The variety of translations is seen in the four translations (NLT, HCSB, ESV, NIV): "using the Spirit's words to explain spiritual truths," with two alternative renderings in the margin (NLT); "explaining spiritual things to spiritual people," with one alternative rendering (HCSB); "interpreting spiritual truths to those who

[15] Gunther Zuntz, *The Text of the Epistles* (London: Oxford University Press, 1953), 101; Gordon D. Fee, *The First Epistle to the Corinthians*, New International Commentary on the New Testament (Grand Rapids: Eerdmans, 1987), 88.

[16] Raymond E. Brown, *The Semitic Background of the Term "Mystery" in the New Testament* (Philadelphia: Fortress, 1968), 48–49; Bruce M. Metzger, *A Textual Commentary on the Greek New Testament*, 2nd ed. (New York: United Bible Societies, 1994), 480.

are spiritual," with two alternative renderings (ESV); "explaining spiritual realities with Spirit-taught words," with one alternative rendering (NIV).

The earliest interpreter of this passage was the scribe of $\mathfrak{P}^{46}$ (2nd century AD). He wrote *pneumatikois pneumatika sugkrinontes*. Had he wanted to indicate "spiritual people" he would have written *pneumatikois* as a *nomen sacrum* ("sacred word"), which is what he did for the same word in 1 Corinthians 2:15 and 3:1.[17] Because he wrote out the word *pneumatikois* in full in 2:13 rather than abbreviating it, we can be certain his interpretation was "matching/explaining spiritual truths with spiritual words," not "explaining spiritual truths to spiritual people." The scribe's interpretation of the last phrase of 2:13 completely accords with the previous part of the verse, which says, "When we tell you these things, we do not use words that come from human wisdom. Instead, we speak words given to us by the Spirit"—which is perfectly followed by "matching/explaining spiritual truths with spiritual words."

Passage 11. Galatians 5:2–6

> [2] Listen! I, Paul, tell you this: If you are counting on circumcision to make you right with God, then Christ will be of no benefit to you. [3] I'll say it again. If you are trying to find favor with God by being circumcised, you must obey every regulation in the whole law of Moses. [4] For if you are trying to make yourselves right with God by keeping the law, you have been cut off from Christ! You have fallen away from God's grace. [5] But we who live by the Spirit eagerly wait to receive by faith the righteousness God has promised to us. [6] For when we place our faith in Christ Jesus, there is no benefit in being circumcised or being uncircumcised. What is important is faith expressing itself in love.

Though the four translations offer some interesting variations in this passage, the message is essentially the same. In 5:4, three translations (ESV, HCSB, NIV) speak of those who are trying "would to be justified by the law." The NLT translators avoided what they considered to be a religious term ("justified"), known only by those who are churched, and spelled it out as "trying to make yourselves right with God by keeping the law." Paul says that two things will happen to such people: (1) they will be "severed from" (ESV)—otherwise rendered as "alienated from Christ" (HCBS,

---

[17] See Comfort and Barrett, *Text of the Earliest New Testament Greek Manuscripts*, 253.

NIV) or "cut off from Christ" (NLT); "they have fallen from grace" (all four versions; NLT adds "God's" before "grace"; ESV adds "away" before "from"). Instead of trying to be justified by the law, in 5:5 Paul says that Christians should "eagerly wait for the righteousness" (all four versions) that comes as the result of faith and hope (the essential wording of all four versions). Paul concludes this passage in 5:6 by saying that "in Christ Jesus neither circumcision nor uncircumcision accomplishes anything" (HCSB), but what matters is "faith working through love" (ESV, HCSB), otherwise rendered as "faith expressing itself in/through love" (NLT, NIV).

Passage 12. Colossians 2:8–15

> [8] Don't let anyone capture you with <u>empty philosophies and high-sounding nonsense</u> that come from human thinking and from the spiritual powers of this world, rather than from Christ. [9] For in Christ lives all the fullness of God in a human body. [10] So you also are complete through your union with Christ, who is the head over every ruler and authority. [11] When you came to Christ, you were "circumcised," but not by a physical procedure. <u>Christ performed a spiritual circumcision—the cutting away of your sinful nature.</u> [12] For you were buried with Christ when you were baptized. And with him you were raised to new life because you trusted the mighty power of God, who raised Christ from the dead. [13] You were dead because of your sins and because your sinful nature was not yet cut away. Then God made you alive with Christ, for he forgave all our sins. [14] He canceled the record of the charges against us and took it away by nailing it to the cross. [15] In this way, he disarmed the spiritual rulers and authorities. He shamed them publicly by his victory over them on the cross.

This passage offers a fascinating study of biblical interpretation as manifest in the four translations under scrutiny. Paul tells the Colossians in 2:8 not to be captivated by "philosophy and empty deceit" (HCSB, ESV), which is more colorfully rendered in the NLT as "empty philosophies and high-sounding nonsense." This "hollow and deceptive philosophy" is based on "human tradition" (HCSB, ESV, NIV) and on what the Greek calls "the *stocheia* of the world." The *stocheia* can be basic principles of any given philosophy or the elemental spirits of the world. Interestingly, all four versions reflect "the spiritual forces" interpretation, with three of them (ESV, NLT, NIV) representing the alternative interpretation in the margin. This choice is consistent with the greater context of Colossians, wherein Paul was trying to tell the Colossians that their appreciation (or even worship) of spirit beings and angels should be curtailed in light of the fact that Christ is premier over all such spiritual beings (see Col 1:16–17; 2:10,15,18). The next verse (2:9) tells us that Christ is superior to all the spiritual beings because "all the fullness of the deity dwells in him bodily." This awesome description of Christ's complete incarnate deity is rendered variously as "the entire fullness of God's nature dwells bodily in Christ" (HCSB), "the whole fullness of deity dwells bodily" (ESV), "in Christ lives all the fullness of God in a human body" (NLT), and "in Christ all the fullness of the Deity lives in bodily form" (NIV). As such, the Colossians need nothing more than Christ—they are filled in/by him and made complete in him (2:10).

Paul then uses two images, one drawn from Judaism and the other from early Christianity, to convey two spiritual realities the Colossians possessed. First, they had a spiritual circumcision in that they had cut off their sinful nature (see NLT)—literally, "the flesh," which the NIV margin tells us is "the sinful state of human beings" (2:11). Second, they have joined in Christ's death and resurrection via baptism, being made alive together with him (2:12–13). God gave spiritual life to all the believers by virtue of their union with the risen Christ.

In the final two verses (2:14–15), Paul reveals two acts that God in Christ accomplished on the cross. The first act is most simply expressed in the NLT: "He canceled the record of the charges against us and took it away by nailing it to the cross." This is more expansive in the other three versions, especially in the first part, which speak of "the certificate of debt, with its obligations" (HCSB), "the record of debt . . . with its legal demands" (ESV), and "the charge of our legal indebtedness" (NIV). The second act is that Christ is said to have "disarmed" (all four versions) or "stripped off" (NLT margin) the spiritual rulers and authorities—presumably while on the cross (though it could have been an act that happened right after the crucifixion). The Greek verb, *apekdusamenos,* is an aorist middle participle, which by grammatical definition means an act that Christ did to himself, not an action he directly did on another (which would require the accusative case). Hence, Christ "stripped himself" or "divested himself" (see NRSV margin) of these spiritual authorities, as if they had been cloaked around him. Grammatically speaking, Christ did not disarm (strip off) the spiritual rulers and authorities. As such, the four versions are misleading. What the Greek text tells us is that Christ divested himself of some spiritual powers (who were presumably trying to harm him) and then exposed them to public disgrace as he triumphed over them by his death on the cross. Although this is a difficult idea to grasp, translators should be faithful to the original text. In my opinion only the NLT marginal note presents the true reading.

Passage 13. 1 Thessalonians 1:3

> As we pray to our God and Father about you, we think of your faithful work, your loving deeds, and the enduring hope you have because of our Lord Jesus Christ.

All four versions essentially convey the same message, which indicates that Paul and Silvanus (with Timothy) recalled the Thessalonians' "work of faith," "labor of love," and "endurance of hope" (HCSB, so essentially ESV and NLT). This is expanded somewhat in the NIV: "work produced by faith," "labor prompted by love," and "endurance inspired by hope." Such expansions add a nice poetic touch.

Passage 14. 1 Timothy 2:12

> I do not let women teach men or have authority over them. Let them listen quietly.

Feminists are not happy with this statement of Paul's—nor am I happy with it, and I am not a feminist. But there it is. Paul said it. So we have to interpret it for what it says and means and then determine if the translations got it right. The first question is: was Paul issuing two prohibitions or one? Was he prohibiting women to teach and prohibiting women to exercise authority over men? Or was he prohibiting women to teach men because in doing so they would be usurping their authority? The Greek seems to favor two prohibitions, which is made evident in all four English versions. The only real significant difference between the versions is that the margin of the NIV suggests that Paul was speaking of the relationship between a wife and a husband, not just women and men. If this is what Paul was driving at, then we can limit the prohibition to a marital prohibition, not a prohibition for church meetings. Paul had female coworkers (Priscilla, Phoebe, Mary, Junia—see Rom 16:1–7); they obviously taught in church meetings.

Passage 15. Jude 4–5

> [4] I say this because some ungodly people have wormed their way into your churches, saying that God's marvelous grace allows us to live immoral lives. The condemnation of such people was recorded long ago, for they have denied <u>our only Master and Lord, Jesus Christ</u>. [5] So I want to remind you, though you already know these things, that Jesus first rescued the nation of Israel from Egypt, but later he destroyed those who did not remain faithful.

There are two textual variants in these verses. In Jude 4, the best manuscript evidence supports the reading "denying our only Master and Lord, Jesus Christ": $\mathfrak{P}^{78}$ (c. AD 300), Codex Sinaiticus (א), Codex Alexandinus (A), Codex Vaticanus (B), and others. All four versions (HCSB, ESV, NLT, NIV) follow this reading. Other manuscripts, including the Textus Receptus, read "denying the only Master God and our Lord Jesus Christ." $\mathfrak{P}^{72c}$ (AD 300) reads "denying our Master and our Lord Jesus Christ." The reading in the Textus Receptus, poorly attested, is probably an attempt to avoid "Jesus" being called *despotēn* ("Master"), when this title is usually ascribed to God (Luke 2:29; Acts 4:24; Rev 6:10). Hence, *theos* ("God") was appended to *despotēn*. However, 2 Peter 2:1, a parallel passage, identifies the Redeemer, Jesus Christ, as the *despotēn*. So here also, the preferred reading, which is extremely well documented, shows that Jude considered Jesus to be the absolute sovereign.

In Jude 5, there is a significant textual variant pertaining to who rescued the children of Israel out of Egypt. Some manuscripts say it was "the Lord": Codex Sinaiticus (א), Majority Text, and others. Other manuscripts say it was "Jesus": Codex Alexandrinus (A), Codex Vaticanus (B), and many church fathers (e.g., Origen, Cyril, and Jerome). One manuscript ($\mathfrak{P}^{72}$) reads: "Messiah God," and two manuscripts read "God." The most remarkable reading says that "Jesus delivered his people out of Egypt." It is supported by an impressive collection of witnesses. $\mathfrak{P}^{72}$ may possibly be an indirect witness to the reading with "Jesus" because it shows that the scribe had before him in his exemplar a messianic title—"Messiah" or "Christ." At any rate it is easier to argue (from a textual perspective) that the reading with "Jesus" is the one from which all the others deviated than to argue that the reading with "Lord" (or "God") was changed to "Jesus" because scribes were not known for fabricating difficult readings.

Some scholars, such as Wikgren, have argued that Jude may have written *Iesous* in Jude 5 intending to mean "Joshua" (e.g., see NEB margin), as in Hebrews 4:8.[18] But this is unlikely because Joshua led the Israelites into the good land of Canaan but not out of Egypt, and Joshua certainly did not destroy those who did not believe (Jude 5b). This was a divine activity. Thus, it is likely that Jesus is here being seen as Jesus Christ. In other words, from Jude's perspective he recognized that it was Jesus, the "I Am" (see John 8:58), who was present with the Israelites and operative in their deliverance from Egypt. Paul shared a similar view inasmuch as he proclaimed that "Christ" was the Rock that accompanied the Israelites in their desert journeys and that "Christ" was the one the Israelites constantly "tested" during these times (see 1 Cor 10:4,9). Thus, the reading "Jesus," though difficult, is not impossible. As such, it should be accepted as the original reading.[19] The first edition of the UBS *Greek New Testament* contained the reading "Jesus" in the text. But this was changed in the third edition, when a slim majority of the editors voted to put the reading with "Lord" in the text and the one with "Jesus" in the margin.[20]

As far as I know, the first English translation to adopt the wording "Jesus" was the NLT (2004). As the New Testament coordinator of the NLT who proposed this reading, I was glad to see the committee adopt it. (The NLT is the only version to list all the variants in the margin.) Three other recent versions have also adopted the reading with "Jesus": TNIV (a change from the original NIV), NET, and ESV. The latest edition of the NIV (2011) has followed the reading "the Lord" (noting "Jesus" in the margin). HCSB also reads "the Lord" and includes a marginal note.

Passage 16. Revelation 3:20

Look! I stand at the door and knock. If you hear my voice and open the door, I will come in, and <u>we will share a meal together as friends</u>.

---

[18] Allen Wikgren, "Some Problems in Jude 5," in *Studies in the History and Text of the New Testament in Honor of Kenneth Willis Clark*, ed. B. L. Daniels and M. J. Suggs, Studies and Documents 29 (Salt Lake City: University of Utah Press, 1967), 147–52.

[19] As did Eberhard Nestle, *Introduction to the Textual Criticism of the Greek New Testament*, trans. William Edie (London: Williams & Norgate, 1901), 328–29; and F. F. Bruce, *The Epistle to the Hebrews*, New International Commentary on the New Testament (Grand Rapids: Eerdmans, 1964), 63.

[20] Metzger and Wikgren voted against this decision and stated their reasons for doing so in *Textual Commentary on the Greek New Testament*, 657–58.

The only real translation issue here pertains to gender specificity or gender inclusiveness. Two groups of translators (those of the HCSB and ESV) rendered the passage literally and thereby have Christ speaking to a male believer: "I will come to him and eat with him, and he with me" (ESV; so essentially the HCSB which reads "have dinner" instead of "eat"). Two other groups of translators (those of the NLT and NIV) thought Christ was not speaking just to a man but to all believers, so they render the verse gender inclusively. The NLT renders it, "I will come in, and we will share a meal as friends," whereas the NIV says, "I will come in and eat with that person, and they with me." The NLT and NIV are following modern literary practice that urges gender inclusiveness in English writing.

Conclusion

So what do you think? If you're like us, reading the preceding chapters gave you a whole new appreciation for the complexity of the task of translating the Bible into proper contemporary English. A passage from the book of Proverbs comes to mind: "The first to speak in court sounds right—until the cross-examination begins" (Prov 18:17 NLT). The Bible is God's Word, and God's revelation is inspired, inerrant, and infallible. But, despite their best efforts, translators are not, and their choices at times are between several options, none of them completely satisfying. Nevertheless, as we've seen, each team of translators behind the four translations under review in this volume have wrestled earnestly with the many issues that confront anyone who tries to understand what God sought to convey in the original Greek and Hebrew.

Which Bible translation should you use? Well, at least for the purposes of this volume—we report, you decide. We hope to have put at your disposal some valuable background information, provided by insiders who have worked on the respective committees preparing these translations. Hopefully, this comparative data will make your choice a bit easier. In part, you will look and see how a given version handles some of the passages with which you are familiar and which you consider important. In part, you will want to look at the underlying translation philosophy to see which one resonates most closely with what you believe should guide responsible Bible translation.

When all is said and done, the most important thing is that you have a good English Bible and that you read it regularly and frequently because God's Word is your life, your light, and your spiritual food. As the prophet Jeremiah wrote, "Your words were found, and I ate them. Your words became a delight to me and the joy of my heart, for I am called by Your name, Yahweh God of Hosts" (Jer 15:16 HCSB). And the psalmist wrote, "Your word is a lamp to my feet and a light to my path" (Ps 119:105 ESV). "Oh, how I love your law! I meditate on it all day long" (Ps 119:97 NIV). As Peter confessed, "You alone have the words that give eternal life" (John 6:68 NLT). May this be your and my experience as we daily feast on the inestimable riches of God's Word.

Select Annotated Bibliography

Comfort, Philip W. "History of the English Bible." In *The Origen of the Bible*, ed. Philip Wesley Comfort, 273–309. Carol Stream, IL: Tyndale, 1992. Comfort was the New Testament coordinating editor from the NLT. His chapter covers Bible translations in English with short discussions on all major translations. This is a non-technical, good overview of Bible translations.

Fee, Gordon D., and Mark L. Strauss. *How to Choose a Translation for All Its Worth: A Guide to Understanding and Using Bible Versions*. Grand Rapids: Zondervan, 2007. 170 pages. The authors both worked on the recent TNIV and NIV (2011) translation committees. They have written a clear and concise book, and they fairly explain different translation theories. After explaining the necessity of Bible translation, they discuss the different approaches to translating the Bible. They include separate chapters on translating words, figurative language, and a particular Greek construction: the Greek genitive. Textual issues, gender translation issues, and a brief history of the Bible in translation are all included in this brief book.

France, Dick. "The Bible in English: An Overview." In *The Challenge of Bible Translation: Communicating God's Word to the World*, ed. Glen G. Scorgie, Mark L. Strauss, and Steven M. Voth, 177–97. Grand Rapids: Zondervan, 2003. France served on the NIV (1978;

1984) translation committee. This chapter swiftly covers the history of the English Bible in translation. France writes without many endnotes and without technical language. It is a great, quick overview of English translations.

Metzger, Bruce M. *The Bible in Translation: Ancient and English Versions*. Grand Rapids: Baker, 2001. 200 pages. Slightly more technical than others, no one is more qualified than Metzger at writing on Bible translations. His knowledge is unsurpassed as he has been on different translation committees himself. His discussions seem a little biased toward critiquing the translations he was not part of, but his illustrations of good and bad translations are part of what makes this helpful.

Rhodes, Ron. *The Complete Guide to Bible Translations*. Eugene, OR: Harvest House, 2009. 272 pages. After discussing theories of Bible translation and the gender neutral issue, Rhodes discusses virtually all the major Bible translations from the KJV to the TNIV. This book is easy to understand, leaving out technical language. Rhodes appears comfortable with a gender-neutral approach, and he advocates the use of Bibles that are translated with different philosophies in one's study of the Scripture.

Ryken, Leland. *The Word of God in English: Criteria for Excellence in Bible Translation*. Wheaton: Crossway, 2002. 336 pages. Ryken worked on the ESV translation committee. This book is a response to his concern over the proliferation of dynamic equivalence translations. Ryken breaks the 17 chapters into five parts. Part 1 argues that dynamic equivalence proponents argue for a translation technique that would never be accepted in translating classics in the English-language tradition. Part 2 discusses common mistakes in translation. For example, while all translating involves interpretation, not all translations are interpreted to the same extent. He also believes translators have too low an opinion about contemporary readers. Part 3 handles the topic of theological, ethical, and hermeneutical issues. Ryken believes that the stronger one's belief in verbal, plenary inspiration is, the more they will value formal equivalent translations. He believes some translation theories blur the lines between translation and hermeneutics. Part 4 analyzes modern translations. Ryken is concerned that the literary qualities of the original texts are compromised in a dynamic equivalent translation. He believes these translations also make it more difficult to remember the text. Part 5 provides the criteria of excellence in an English Bible. Ryken believes faithfulness to the original words and retaining the same ambiguity that was in the original texts is important, as well as several other issues. The author clearly favors the formal equivalence model and consistently argues for it throughout the book.

Thomas, Robert L. *How to Choose a Bible Version: An Introductory Guide to English Translations*. Revised. Fearn, Great Britain: Christian Focus Publications, 2005. 224 pages. This is a helpful, compact book that contains discussions on the history of Bible translation in English, the different Hebrew and Greek texts used in translation, techniques used, theological bias in translations, and different types of English used in Bible translation. The author is decidedly not in favor of dynamic (or, functional) equivalent translations.

Other Sources

Carson, D. A. *The Inclusive-Language Debate: A Plea for Realism.* Grand Rapids: Baker, 1998.

Comfort, Philip W. *The Essential Guide to Bible Versions*. Wheaton: Tyndale, 2000.

Dewey, David. *A User's Guide to Bible Translations: Making the Most of Different Versions*. Downers Grove: InterVarsity, 2004.

Poythress, Vern S., and Wayne A. Grudem. *The Gender-Neutral Bible Controversy: Muting the Masculinity of God's Words*. Nashville: B&H, 2000.

Strauss, Mark L. *Distorting Scripture? The Challenge of Bible Translation and Gender Accuracy*. Downers Grove: InterVarsity, 1998.

Online Resources

Blomberg, Craig L. "Review of *The Gender-Neutral Bible Controversy*." *Denver Journal* 4 (2001). http://www.denverseminary.edu/article/the-gender-neutral-bible-controversy.

_____. "Today's New International Version: The Untold Story of a Good Translation." *Denver Journal* (2002). http://www.denverseminary.edu/

article/todays-new-international-version-the-untold-story-of-a-good-translation.

Committee on Bible Translation. "A Brief Response from the Committee on Bible Translation to the Resolution Introduced on the Floor of the Southern Baptist Convention Regarding the Updated New International Version." (June 15, 2011). http://www.niv-cbt.org/wp-content/uploads/cbt-response-to-sbc.pdf.

_____. "A Brief Response from the Committee on Bible Translation to the Review of the Updated NIV by the Committee on Biblical Manhood and Womanhood." (June 9, 2011). http://www.niv-cbt.org/wp-content/uploads/cbt-response-to-cbmw-review.pdf.

_____. *Updating the New International Version of the Bible: Notes from the Committee on Bible Translation* (August 2010). http://www.niv-cbt.org/niv-2011-overview/translators-notes.

Council on Biblical Manhood and Womanhood."An Evaluation of Gender Language in the 2011 Edition of the NIV Bible." (June 6, 2011). http://www.cbmw.org/Resources/Articles/An-Evaluation-of-Gender-Language-in-the 2011-Edition-of-the-NIV-Bible.

Decker, Rodney J. "The English Standard Version: A Review Article." *Journal of Ministry and Theology* 9, no. 2 (2004): 5–56. http://ntresources.com/documents/ESV_Review.pdf.

_____. "An Evaluation of the 2011 Edition of the New International Version NT." Presented at the Bible Faculty Summit, Faith Baptist College and Seminary, Ankeny, IA (July 2011). http://ntresources.com/blog/wp-content/uploads/2011/07/NIV2011evaluationJust.pdf.

Hansen, Collin. "Perspectives in Translation: A Discussion on English Bible Versions—Five Most Intriguing Changes in the Updated NIV." A discussion hosted by The Gospel Coalition and BibleGateway.com (February 28, 2011). http://www.biblegateway.com/perspectives-in-translation.

Southern Baptist Convention resolution."On the Gender-Neutral 2011 New International Version." (June 15, 2011). http://www.sbc.net/resolutions/amResolution.asp?ID=1218.

Wallace, Daniel. "A Review of the New International Version 2011: Part 1." *Parchment and Pen* (July 21, 2011). http://www.reclaimingthemind.org/blog/2011/07/a-review-of-the-niv-2011-part-1-of-4.

_____. "A Review of the New International Version 2011: Part 2." *Parchment and Pen* (July 21, 2011). http://www.reclaimingthemind. org/blog/2011/07/a-review-of-the-niv-2011-part-2-of-4.

_____. "A Review of the New International Version 2011: Part 3." *Parchment and Pen* (July 25, 2011). http://www.reclaimingthemind. org/blog/2011/07/a-review-of-the-niv-2011-part-3-of-4.

_____. "A Review of the New International Version 2011: Part 4." *Parchment and Pen* (July 28, 2011). http://www.reclaimingthemind. org/blog/2011/07/a-review-of-the-new-international-version-2011-part-4-of-4.

Glossary

CALVINISTIC (IN REFERENCE TO THE GENEVA BIBLE)—a system of theology that emphasizes God's sovereignty and work in predestination

COMPLEMENTARIANS—those who believe that men and women have different but complementary roles; woman typically are seen to be limited in their leadership roles in the home and the church

DYNAMIC EQUIVALENCE—see functional equivalence

EGALITARIANS—those who believe that men and women have identical roles; women typically are seen as not limited in their leadership roles in the home and the church

ESSENTIALLY FORMAL (OR, ESSENTIALLY LITERAL)—a translation that leans toward a formal equivalence Bible translation philosophy; emphasis is placed on the meaning of every word in the original language; English word order and style are important as long as the original meaning is not distorted in translation

ESSENTIALLY FUNCTIONAL—a translation that leans toward the functional equivalence Bible translation philosophy

FORMAL EQUIVALENCE/EQUIVALENT—a translation philosophy that understands the relationship between the modern reader and the message of the text to be the same as that between the original reader and the message of the text; this philosophy emphasizes the importance of translating every word, using the same (or similar) grammatical structures as the original, preserving idioms, and consistency in translating the original language words

FUNCTIONAL EQUIVALENCE/EQUIVALENT (OR DYNAMIC EQUIVALENCE)—a translation philosophy that attempts to render the ancient text in a way so as to have the same impact on the contemporary reader that it had on the ancient reader; this philosophy emphasizes that the translation should have easy-to-read and contemporary-English-language grammar

GENDER-INCLUSIVE (OR INCLUSIVE LANGUAGE OR GENDER INCLUSIVENESS); GENDER NEUTRAL; GENDER SENSITIVE—all three terms are different ways in which translations approach the issue of the gender of certain words in Bible translation; there is a dialogue occurring over whether certain words or phrases in Hebrew and Greek were originally referring to a specific gender or if they were universal; for example, when Jesus said, "I will make you fishers of men" (Matt 4:19b ESV), did the word for "men" refer only to males or to both males and females

GENITIVE (PHRASE/CONSTRUCTION)—a genitive noun (or pronoun) is a type of noun that describes another noun; it can express possession ("the people **of God**," meaning "God's people"), origin ("the righteousness **of God**," meaning "the righteousness that comes from God"), content ("net **of fish**"), relationship ("Simon **of John**," meaning "Simon, son of John"), and many other concepts

INDEPENDENT TRANSLATION—a fresh translation of Scripture from the original languages that is not updating or revising an existing translation

INTERLINEAR—a reference book for Bible study that lists the original language word on one line and then an English translation below it

KING JAMES ONLY—the belief that the King James Version is the only translation of Scripture that should be used by Christians; there are many different manifestations of this belief; many adherents believe the Hebrew and Greek texts underlying the King James Version were superior

LITERAL TRANSLATION—another way to refer to a formal equivalence translation; see also word-for-word and woodenly literal

MANUSCRIPT—a handwritten copy of a portion of text

MARGINAL NOTES—alternate translations of a word, phrase, or verse placed in the margin of a Bible translation; they also contain other possible readings from different underlying original language texts

OPTIMAL EQUIVALENCE—a translation philosophy (adhered to by the HCSB) that attempts to balance the accuracy of the formal equivalence theory with the readability of the functional equivalence theory

PARAPHRASE—the goal of a paraphrase is not Bible translation as such but rewording the message of Scripture in the same language

PESHITTA—translation of the Bible into Syriac (an ancient Near Eastern language)

REVISED TRANSLATION—a translation of Scripture that is editing a previous translation of Scripture; contrast with *independent translation* (see above)

SEPTUAGINT (LXX)—the translation of the Old Testament from Hebrew into Greek; probably completed about 100 to 200 years before Jesus was born

TARGUM (PL. TARGUMIM)—Aramaic translations of the Hebrew Old Testament; they began to be written around the same time as the Septuagint

TRANSLATION PHILOSOPHY—the larger underlying principles and convictions that serve as the overall framework for a particular Bible translation; the spectrum ranges from literal, word-for-word translations (formal equivalence) to free, idiomatic thought-for-thought renderings (functional equivalence, also sometimes called dynamic equivalence)

TEXTUAL VARIANT—a version of a text that differs in wording from another text

TEXTUS RECEPTUS—Latin for "received text"; Robert Estienne (known as Stephanus) edited Desiderius Erasmus' third edition of the Greek New Testament (1522); his third edition (1550) became the standard Greek text for years and was used for the KJV

THOUGHT-FOR-THOUGHT—a phrase used to refer to a functional equivalence translation (or dynamic equivalence translation)

VULGATE—a translation of the Bible into Latin by Jerome in the late 4th century AD

WOODENLY LITERAL TRANSLATION—when attempting to translate a passage literally, the resulting text is in awkward English

WORD-FOR-WORD—a phrase used to refer to a formal equivalence translation; see also literal translation

Name Index

197

Subject Index

Scripture Index

Copyright page extension

Scripture quotations identified as CEV are taken from the Contemporary English Version Copyright © 1991, 1992, 1995 American Bible Society. Used by permission.

Scripture quotations marked NASB are from the New American Standard Bible . © The Lockman Foundation, 1960, 1962, 1963, 1968, 1971, 1972 , 1973, 1975, 1977. Used by permission.

Scripture quotations marked NET are from The NET Bible: The Translation That Explains Itself™ Copyright © 1996, 1997, 1998, 1999, 2000, 2001, 2001 by Biblical Studies Press, L.L.C. Used by permission.

Scripture quotations marked NKJV are from the New King James Version. Copyright © 1979, 1980, 1982, Thomas Nelson, Inc., Publishers.

Scripture quotations marked NRSV are from the New Revised Standard Version of the Bible, copyright © 1989 by the Division of Christian Education of the National Council of Churches of Christ in the United States of America. Used by permission. All rights reserved.

Scripture quotations marked RSV are from the Revised Standard Version of the Bible, copyrighted 1946, 1952, © 1971, 1973.

Scripture quotations identified as TEV are from the Today's English Version, Second Edition Copyright © 1966, 1971, 1976, 1992 American Bible Society. Used by permission.

Scripture taken from the HOLY BIBLE, TODAY'S NEW INTERNATIONAL VERSION ® TNIV ® Copyright © 2001, 2005 by Biblica www.biblica.com. All rights reserved worldwide.

The American Standard Version (ASV), King James Version (KJV), Tyndale, and Wycliffe translations are in the public domain.